Hadoop Beginner's Guide

Learn how to crunch big data to extract meaning from the data avalanche

Garry Turkington

[PACKT] open source ✻
PUBLISHING
community experience distilled

BIRMINGHAM - MUMBAI

Hadoop Beginner's Guide

First published: February 2013

Production Reference: 1150213

Published by Packt Publishing Ltd.
Livery Place
35 Livery Street
Birmingham B3 2PB, UK.

ISBN 978-1-84951-7-300

www.packtpub.com

Cover Image by Asher Wishkerman (a.wishkerman@mpic.de)

Credits

Author

Garry Turkington

Reviewers

David Gruzman

Muthusamy Manigandan

Vidyasagar N V

Acquisition Editor

Robin de Jongh

Lead Technical Editor

Azharuddin Sheikh

Technical Editors

Ankita Meshram

Varun Pius Rodrigues

Copy Editors

Brandt D'Mello

Aditya Nair

Laxmi Subramanian

Ruta Waghmare

Project Coordinator

Leena Purkait

Proofreader

Maria Gould

Indexer

Hemangini Bari

Production Coordinator

Nitesh Thakur

Cover Work

Nitesh Thakur

About the Author

Garry Turkington has 14 years of industry experience, most of which has been focused on the design and implementation of large-scale distributed systems. In his current roles as VP Data Engineering and Lead Architect at Improve Digital, he is primarily responsible for the realization of systems that store, process, and extract value from the company's large data volumes. Before joining Improve Digital, he spent time at Amazon.co.uk, where he led several software development teams building systems that process Amazon catalog data for every item worldwide. Prior to this, he spent a decade in various government positions in both the UK and USA.

He has BSc and PhD degrees in Computer Science from the Queens University of Belfast in Northern Ireland and an MEng in Systems Engineering from Stevens Institute of Technology in the USA.

I would like to thank my wife Lea for her support and encouragement—not to mention her patience—throughout the writing of this book and my daughter, Maya, whose spirit and curiosity is more of an inspiration than she could ever imagine.

About the Reviewers

David Gruzman is a Hadoop and big data architect with more than 18 years of hands-on experience, specializing in the design and implementation of scalable high-performance distributed systems. He has extensive expertise of OOA/OOD and (R)DBMS technology. He is an Agile methodology adept and strongly believes that a daily coding routine makes good software architects. He is interested in solving challenging problems related to real-time analytics and the application of machine learning algorithms to the big data sets.

He founded—and is working with—BigDataCraft.com, a boutique consulting firm in the area of big data. Visit their site at www.bigdatacraft.com. David can be contacted at david@bigdatacraft.com. More detailed information about his skills and experience can be found at http://www.linkedin.com/in/davidgruzman.

Muthusamy Manigandan is a systems architect for a startup. Prior to this, he was a Staff Engineer at VMWare and Principal Engineer with Oracle. Mani has been programming for the past 14 years on large-scale distributed-computing applications. His areas of interest are machine learning and algorithms.

Vidyasagar N V has been interested in computer science since an early age. Some of his serious work in computers and computer networks began during his high school days. Later, he went to the prestigious Institute Of Technology, Banaras Hindu University, for his B.Tech. He has been working as a software developer and data expert, developing and building scalable systems. He has worked with a variety of second, third, and fourth generation languages. He has worked with flat files, indexed files, hierarchical databases, network databases, relational databases, NoSQL databases, Hadoop, and related technologies. Currently, he is working as Senior Developer at Collective Inc., developing big data-based structured data extraction techniques from the Web and local information. He enjoys producing high-quality software and web-based solutions and designing secure and scalable data systems. He can be contacted at vidyasagar1729@gmail.com.

I would like to thank the Almighty, my parents, Mr. N Srinivasa Rao and Mrs. Latha Rao, and my family who supported and backed me throughout my life. I would also like to thank my friends for being good friends and all those people willing to donate their time, effort, and expertise by participating in open source software projects. Thank you, Packt Publishing for selecting me as one of the technical reviewers for this wonderful book. It is my honor to be a part of it.

www.PacktPub.com

Support files, eBooks, discount offers and more

You might want to visit www.PacktPub.com for support files and downloads related to your book.

Did you know that Packt offers eBook versions of every book published, with PDF and ePub files available? You can upgrade to the eBook version at www.PacktPub.com and as a print book customer, you are entitled to a discount on the eBook copy. Get in touch with us at service@packtpub.com for more details.

At www.PacktPub.com, you can also read a collection of free technical articles, sign up for a range of free newsletters and receive exclusive discounts and offers on Packt books and eBooks.

http://PacktLib.PacktPub.com

Do you need instant solutions to your IT questions? PacktLib is Packt's online digital book library. Here, you can access, read and search across Packt's entire library of books.

Why Subscribe?

- ◆ Fully searchable across every book published by Packt
- ◆ Copy and paste, print and bookmark content
- ◆ On demand and accessible via web browser

Free Access for Packt account holders

If you have an account with Packt at www.PacktPub.com, you can use this to access PacktLib today and view nine entirely free books. Simply use your login credentials for immediate access.

Table of Contents

Preface

This book is here to help you make sense of Hadoop and use it to solve your big data problems. It's a really exciting time to work with data processing technologies such as Hadoop. The ability to apply complex analytics to large data sets—once the monopoly of large corporations and government agencies—is now possible through free **open source software (OSS)**.

But because of the seeming complexity and pace of change in this area, getting a grip on the basics can be somewhat intimidating. That's where this book comes in, giving you an understanding of just what Hadoop is, how it works, and how you can use it to extract value from your data now.

In addition to an explanation of core Hadoop, we also spend several chapters exploring other technologies that either use Hadoop or integrate with it. Our goal is to give you an understanding not just of what Hadoop is but also how to use it as a part of your broader technical infrastructure.

A complementary technology is the use of cloud computing, and in particular, the offerings from Amazon Web Services. Throughout the book, we will show you how to use these services to host your Hadoop workloads, demonstrating that not only can you process large data volumes, but also you don't actually need to buy any physical hardware to do so.

What this book covers

This book comprises of three main parts: chapters 1 through 5, which cover the core of Hadoop and how it works, chapters 6 and 7, which cover the more operational aspects of Hadoop, and chapters 8 through 11, which look at the use of Hadoop alongside other products and technologies.

Chapter 1, What It's All About, gives an overview of the trends that have made Hadoop and cloud computing such important technologies today.

Chapter 2, Getting Hadoop Up and Running, walks you through the initial setup of a local Hadoop cluster and the running of some demo jobs. For comparison, the same work is also executed on the hosted Hadoop Amazon service.

Chapter 3, Understanding MapReduce, goes inside the workings of Hadoop to show how MapReduce jobs are executed and shows how to write applications using the Java API.

Chapter 4, Developing MapReduce Programs, takes a case study of a moderately sized data set to demonstrate techniques to help when deciding how to approach the processing and analysis of a new data source.

Chapter 5, Advanced MapReduce Techniques, looks at a few more sophisticated ways of applying MapReduce to problems that don't necessarily seem immediately applicable to the Hadoop processing model.

Chapter 6, When Things Break, examines Hadoop's much-vaunted high availability and fault tolerance in some detail and sees just how good it is by intentionally causing havoc through killing processes and intentionally using corrupt data.

Chapter 7, Keeping Things Running, takes a more operational view of Hadoop and will be of most use for those who need to administer a Hadoop cluster. Along with demonstrating some best practice, it describes how to prepare for the worst operational disasters so you can sleep at night.

Chapter 8, A Relational View On Data With Hive, introduces Apache Hive, which allows Hadoop data to be queried with a SQL-like syntax.

Chapter 9, Working With Relational Databases, explores how Hadoop can be integrated with existing databases, and in particular, how to move data from one to the other.

Chapter 10, Data Collection with Flume, shows how Apache Flume can be used to gather data from multiple sources and deliver it to destinations such as Hadoop.

Chapter 11, Where To Go Next, wraps up the book with an overview of the broader Hadoop ecosystem, highlighting other products and technologies of potential interest. In addition, it gives some ideas on how to get involved with the Hadoop community and to get help.

What you need for this book

As we discuss the various Hadoop-related software packages used in this book, we will describe the particular requirements for each chapter. However, you will generally need somewhere to run your Hadoop cluster.

In the simplest case, a single Linux-based machine will give you a platform to explore almost all the exercises in this book. We assume you have a recent distribution of Ubuntu, but as long as you have command-line Linux familiarity any modern distribution will suffice.

Some of the examples in later chapters really need multiple machines to see things working, so you will require access to at least four such hosts. Virtual machines are completely acceptable; they're not ideal for production but are fine for learning and exploration.

Since we also explore Amazon Web Services in this book, you can run all the examples on EC2 instances, and we will look at some other more Hadoop-specific uses of AWS throughout the book. AWS services are usable by anyone, but you will need a credit card to sign up!

Who this book is for

We assume you are reading this book because you want to know more about Hadoop at a hands-on level; the key audience is those with software development experience but no prior exposure to Hadoop or similar big data technologies.

For developers who want to know how to write MapReduce applications, we assume you are comfortable writing Java programs and are familiar with the Unix command-line interface. We will also show you a few programs in Ruby, but these are usually only to demonstrate language independence, and you don't need to be a Ruby expert.

For architects and system administrators, the book also provides significant value in explaining how Hadoop works, its place in the broader architecture, and how it can be managed operationally. Some of the more involved techniques in *Chapter 4, Developing MapReduce Programs*, and *Chapter 5, Advanced MapReduce Techniques*, are probably of less direct interest to this audience.

Conventions

In this book, you will find several headings appearing frequently.

To give clear instructions of how to complete a procedure or task, we use:

Time for action – heading

1. Action 1
2. Action 2
3. Action 3

Instructions often need some extra explanation so that they make sense, so they are followed with:

What just happened?

This heading explains the working of tasks or instructions that you have just completed.

You will also find some other learning aids in the book, including:

Pop quiz – heading

These are short multiple-choice questions intended to help you test your own understanding.

Have a go hero – heading

These set practical challenges and give you ideas for experimenting with what you have learned.

You will also find a number of styles of text that distinguish between different kinds of information. Here are some examples of these styles, and an explanation of their meaning.

Code words in text are shown as follows: "You may notice that we used the Unix command rm to remove the Drush directory rather than the DOS del command."

A block of code is set as follows:

```
# * Fine Tuning
#
key_buffer = 16M
key_buffer_size = 32M
max_allowed_packet = 16M
thread_stack = 512K
thread_cache_size = 8
max_connections = 300
```

When we wish to draw your attention to a particular part of a code block, the relevant lines or items are set in bold:

```
# * Fine Tuning
#
key_buffer = 16M
key_buffer_size = 32M
max_allowed_packet = 16M
thread_stack = 512K
thread_cache_size = 8
max_connections = 300
```

Any command-line input or output is written as follows:

```
cd /ProgramData/Propeople
rm -r Drush
git clone --branch master http://git.drupal.org/project/drush.git
```

Newterms and **important words** are shown in bold. Words that you see on the screen, in menus or dialog boxes for example, appear in the text like this: "On the **Select Destination Location** screen, click on **Next** to accept the default destination."

Warnings or important notes appear in a box like this.

Tips and tricks appear like this.

Reader feedback

Feedback from our readers is always welcome. Let us know what you think about this book—what you liked or may have disliked. Reader feedback is important for us to develop titles that you really get the most out of.

To send us general feedback, simply send an e-mail to feedback@packtpub.com, and mention the book title through the subject of your message.

If there is a topic that you have expertise in and you are interested in either writing or contributing to a book, see our author guide on www.packtpub.com/authors.

Customer support

Now that you are the proud owner of a Packt book, we have a number of things to help you to get the most from your purchase.

Downloading the example code

You can download the example code files for all Packt books you have purchased from your account at http://www.packtpub.com. If you purchased this book elsewhere, you can visit http://www.packtpub.com/support and register to have the files e-mailed directly to you.

Errata

Although we have taken every care to ensure the accuracy of our content, mistakes do happen. If you find a mistake in one of our books—maybe a mistake in the text or the code—we would be grateful if you would report this to us. By doing so, you can save other readers from frustration and help us improve subsequent versions of this book. If you find any errata, please report them by visiting http://www.packtpub.com/submit-errata, selecting your book, clicking on the **errata submission form** link, and entering the details of your errata. Once your errata are verified, your submission will be accepted and the errata will be uploaded to our website, or added to any list of existing errata, under the Errata section of that title.

Piracy

Piracy of copyright material on the Internet is an ongoing problem across all media. At Packt, we take the protection of our copyright and licenses very seriously. If you come across any illegal copies of our works, in any form, on the Internet, please provide us with the location address or website name immediately so that we can pursue a remedy.

Please contact us at copyright@packtpub.com with a link to the suspected pirated material.

We appreciate your help in protecting our authors, and our ability to bring you valuable content.

Questions

You can contact us at questions@packtpub.com if you are having a problem with any aspect of the book, and we will do our best to address it.

1
What It's All About

This book is about Hadoop, an open source framework for large-scale data processing. Before we get into the details of the technology and its use in later chapters, it is important to spend a little time exploring the trends that led to Hadoop's creation and its enormous success.

Hadoop was not created in a vacuum; instead, it exists due to the explosion in the amount of data being created and consumed and a shift that sees this data deluge arrive at small startups and not just huge multinationals. At the same time, other trends have changed how software and systems are deployed, using cloud resources alongside or even in preference to more traditional infrastructures.

This chapter will explore some of these trends and explain in detail the specific problems Hadoop seeks to solve and the drivers that shaped its design.

In the rest of this chapter we shall:

- ◆ Learn about the big data revolution
- ◆ Understand what Hadoop is and how it can extract value from data
- ◆ Look into cloud computing and understand what Amazon Web Services provides
- ◆ See how powerful the combination of big data processing and cloud computing can be
- ◆ Get an overview of the topics covered in the rest of this book

So let's get on with it!

Big data processing

Look around at the technology we have today, and it's easy to come to the conclusion that it's all about data. As consumers, we have an increasing appetite for rich media, both in terms of the movies we watch and the pictures and videos we create and upload. We also, often without thinking, leave a trail of data across the Web as we perform the actions of our daily lives.

Not only is the amount of data being generated increasing, but the rate of increase is also accelerating. From emails to Facebook posts, from purchase histories to web links, there are large data sets growing everywhere. The challenge is in extracting from this data the most valuable aspects; sometimes this means particular data elements, and at other times, the focus is instead on identifying trends and relationships between pieces of data.

There's a subtle change occurring behind the scenes that is all about using data in more and more meaningful ways. Large companies have realized the value in data for some time and have been using it to improve the services they provide to their customers, that is, us. Consider how Google displays advertisements relevant to our web surfing, or how Amazon or Netflix recommend new products or titles that often match well to our tastes and interests.

The value of data

These corporations wouldn't invest in large-scale data processing if it didn't provide a meaningful return on the investment or a competitive advantage. There are several main aspects to big data that should be appreciated:

◆ Some questions only give value when asked of sufficiently large data sets. Recommending a movie based on the preferences of another person is, in the absence of other factors, unlikely to be very accurate. Increase the number of people to a hundred and the chances increase slightly. Use the viewing history of ten million other people and the chances of detecting patterns that can be used to give relevant recommendations improve dramatically.

◆ Big data tools often enable the processing of data on a larger scale and at a lower cost than previous solutions. As a consequence, it is often possible to perform data processing tasks that were previously prohibitively expensive.

◆ The cost of large-scale data processing isn't just about financial expense; latency is also a critical factor. A system may be able to process as much data as is thrown at it, but if the average processing time is measured in weeks, it is likely not useful. Big data tools allow data volumes to be increased while keeping processing time under control, usually by matching the increased data volume with additional hardware.

- ◆ Previous assumptions of what a database should look like or how its data should be structured may need to be revisited to meet the needs of the biggest data problems.
- ◆ In combination with the preceding points, sufficiently large data sets and flexible tools allow previously unimagined questions to be answered.

Historically for the few and not the many

The examples discussed in the previous section have generally been seen in the form of innovations of large search engines and online companies. This is a continuation of a much older trend wherein processing large data sets was an expensive and complex undertaking, out of the reach of small- or medium-sized organizations.

Similarly, the broader approach of data mining has been around for a very long time but has never really been a practical tool outside the largest corporations and government agencies.

This situation may have been regrettable but most smaller organizations were not at a disadvantage as they rarely had access to the volume of data requiring such an investment.

The increase in data is not limited to the big players anymore, however; many small and medium companies—not to mention some individuals—find themselves gathering larger and larger amounts of data that they suspect may have some value they want to unlock.

Before understanding how this can be achieved, it is important to appreciate some of these broader historical trends that have laid the foundations for systems such as Hadoop today.

Classic data processing systems

The fundamental reason that big data mining systems were rare and expensive is that scaling a system to process large data sets is very difficult; as we will see, it has traditionally been limited to the processing power that can be built into a single computer.

There are however two broad approaches to scaling a system as the size of the data increases, generally referred to as scale-up and scale-out.

Scale-up

In most enterprises, data processing has typically been performed on impressively large computers with impressively larger price tags. As the size of the data grows, the approach is to move to a bigger server or storage array. Through an effective architecture—even today, as we'll describe later in this chapter—the cost of such hardware could easily be measured in hundreds of thousands or in millions of dollars.

The advantage of simple scale-up is that the architecture does not significantly change through the growth. Though larger components are used, the basic relationship (for example, database server and storage array) stays the same. For applications such as commercial database engines, the software handles the complexities of utilizing the available hardware, but in theory, increased scale is achieved by migrating the same software onto larger and larger servers. Note though that the difficulty of moving software onto more and more processors is never trivial; in addition, there are practical limits on just how big a single host can be, so at some point, scale-up cannot be extended any further.

The promise of a single architecture at any scale is also unrealistic. Designing a scale-up system to handle data sets of sizes such as 1 terabyte, 100 terabyte, and 1 petabyte may conceptually apply larger versions of the same components, but the complexity of their connectivity may vary from cheap commodity through custom hardware as the scale increases.

Early approaches to scale-out

Instead of growing a system onto larger and larger hardware, the scale-out approach spreads the processing onto more and more machines. If the data set doubles, simply use two servers instead of a single double-sized one. If it doubles again, move to four hosts.

The obvious benefit of this approach is that purchase costs remain much lower than for scale-up. Server hardware costs tend to increase sharply when one seeks to purchase larger machines, and though a single host may cost $5,000, one with ten times the processing power may cost a hundred times as much. The downside is that we need to develop strategies for splitting our data processing across a fleet of servers and the tools historically used for this purpose have proven to be complex.

As a consequence, deploying a scale-out solution has required significant engineering effort; the system developer often needs to handcraft the mechanisms for data partitioning and reassembly, not to mention the logic to schedule the work across the cluster and handle individual machine failures.

Limiting factors

These traditional approaches to scale-up and scale-out have not been widely adopted outside large enterprises, government, and academia. The purchase costs are often high, as is the effort to develop and manage the systems. These factors alone put them out of the reach of many smaller businesses. In addition, the approaches themselves have had several weaknesses that have become apparent over time:

- As scale-out systems get large, or as scale-up systems deal with multiple CPUs, the difficulties caused by the complexity of the concurrency in the systems have become significant. Effectively utilizing multiple hosts or CPUs is a very difficult task, and implementing the necessary strategy to maintain efficiency throughout execution of the desired workloads can entail enormous effort.

◆ Hardware advances—often couched in terms of Moore's law—have begun to highlight discrepancies in system capability. CPU power has grown much faster than network or disk speeds have; once CPU cycles were the most valuable resource in the system, but today, that no longer holds. Whereas a modern CPU may be able to execute millions of times as many operations as a CPU 20 years ago would, memory and hard disk speeds have only increased by factors of thousands or even hundreds. It is quite easy to build a modern system with so much CPU power that the storage system simply cannot feed it data fast enough to keep the CPUs busy.

A different approach

From the preceding scenarios there are a number of techniques that have been used successfully to ease the pain in scaling data processing systems to the large scales required by big data.

All roads lead to scale-out

As just hinted, taking a scale-up approach to scaling is not an open-ended tactic. There is a limit to the size of individual servers that can be purchased from mainstream hardware suppliers, and even more niche players can't offer an arbitrarily large server. At some point, the workload will increase beyond the capacity of the single, monolithic scale-up server, so then what? The unfortunate answer is that the best approach is to have two large servers instead of one. Then, later, three, four, and so on. Or, in other words, the natural tendency of scale-up architecture is—in extreme cases—to add a scale-out strategy to the mix. Though this gives some of the benefits of both approaches, it also compounds the costs and weaknesses; instead of very expensive hardware or the need to manually develop the cross-cluster logic, this hybrid architecture requires both.

As a consequence of this end-game tendency and the general cost profile of scale-up architectures, they are rarely used in the big data processing field and scale-out architectures are the de facto standard.

[If your problem space involves data workloads with strong internal cross-references and a need for transactional integrity, big iron scale-up relational databases are still likely to be a great option.]

Share nothing

Anyone with children will have spent considerable time teaching the little ones that it's good to share. This principle does not extend into data processing systems, and this idea applies to both data and hardware.

The conceptual view of a scale-out architecture in particular shows individual hosts, each processing a subset of the overall data set to produce its portion of the final result. Reality is rarely so straightforward. Instead, hosts may need to communicate between each other, or some pieces of data may be required by multiple hosts. These additional dependencies create opportunities for the system to be negatively affected in two ways: bottlenecks and increased risk of failure.

If a piece of data or individual server is required by every calculation in the system, there is a likelihood of contention and delays as the competing clients access the common data or host. If, for example, in a system with 25 hosts there is a single host that must be accessed by all the rest, the overall system performance will be bounded by the capabilities of this key host.

Worse still, if this "hot" server or storage system holding the key data fails, the entire workload will collapse in a heap. Earlier cluster solutions often demonstrated this risk; even though the workload was processed across a farm of servers, they often used a shared storage system to hold all the data.

Instead of sharing resources, the individual components of a system should be as independent as possible, allowing each to proceed regardless of whether others are tied up in complex work or are experiencing failures.

Expect failure

Implicit in the preceding tenets is that more hardware will be thrown at the problem with as much independence as possible. This is only achievable if the system is built with an expectation that individual components will fail, often regularly and with inconvenient timing.

> You'll often hear terms such as "five nines" (referring to 99.999 percent uptime or availability). Though this is absolute best-in-class availability, it is important to realize that the overall reliability of a system comprised of many such devices can vary greatly depending on whether the system can tolerate individual component failures.
>
> Assume a server with 99 percent reliability and a system that requires five such hosts to function. The system availability is 0.99*0.99*0.99*0.99*0.99 which equates to 95 percent availability. But if the individual servers are only rated at 95 percent, the system reliability drops to a mere 76 percent.

Instead, if you build a system that only needs one of the five hosts to be functional at any given time, the system availability is well into five nines territory. Thinking about system uptime in relation to the criticality of each component can help focus on just what the system availability is likely to be.

If figures such as 99 percent availability seem a little abstract to you, consider it in terms of how much downtime that would mean in a given time period. For example, 99 percent availability equates to a downtime of just over 3.5 days a year or 7 hours a month. Still sound as good as 99 percent?

This approach of embracing failure is often one of the most difficult aspects of big data systems for newcomers to fully appreciate. This is also where the approach diverges most strongly from scale-up architectures. One of the main reasons for the high cost of large scale-up servers is the amount of effort that goes into mitigating the impact of component failures. Even low-end servers may have redundant power supplies, but in a big iron box, you will see CPUs mounted on cards that connect across multiple backplanes to banks of memory and storage systems. Big iron vendors have often gone to extremes to show how resilient their systems are by doing everything from pulling out parts of the server while it's running to actually shooting a gun at it. But if the system is built in such a way that instead of treating every failure as a crisis to be mitigated it is reduced to irrelevance, a very different architecture emerges.

Smart software, dumb hardware

If we wish to see a cluster of hardware used in as flexible a way as possible, providing hosting to multiple parallel workflows, the answer is to push the smarts into the software and away from the hardware.

In this model, the hardware is treated as a set of resources, and the responsibility for allocating hardware to a particular workload is given to the software layer. This allows hardware to be generic and hence both easier and less expensive to acquire, and the functionality to efficiently use the hardware moves to the software, where the knowledge about effectively performing this task resides.

Move processing, not data

Imagine you have a very large data set, say, 1000 terabytes (that is, 1 petabyte), and you need to perform a set of four operations on every piece of data in the data set. Let's look at different ways of implementing a system to solve this problem.

A traditional big iron scale-up solution would see a massive server attached to an equally impressive storage system, almost certainly using technologies such as fibre channel to maximize storage bandwidth. The system will perform the task but will become I/O-bound; even high-end storage switches have a limit on how fast data can be delivered to the host.

Alternatively, the processing approach of previous cluster technologies would perhaps see a cluster of 1,000 machines, each with 1 terabyte of data divided into four quadrants, with each responsible for performing one of the operations. The cluster management software would then coordinate the movement of the data around the cluster to ensure each piece receives all four processing steps. As each piece of data can have one step performed on the host on which it resides, it will need to stream the data to the other three quadrants, so we are in effect consuming 3 petabytes of network bandwidth to perform the processing.

Remembering that processing power has increased faster than networking or disk technologies, so are these really the best ways to address the problem? Recent experience suggests the answer is no and that an alternative approach is to avoid moving the data and instead move the processing. Use a cluster as just mentioned, but don't segment it into quadrants; instead, have each of the thousand nodes perform all four processing stages on the locally held data. If you're lucky, you'll only have to stream the data from the disk once and the only things travelling across the network will be program binaries and status reports, both of which are dwarfed by the actual data set in question.

If a 1,000-node cluster sounds ridiculously large, think of some modern server form factors being utilized for big data solutions. These see single hosts with as many as twelve 1- or 2-terabyte disks in each. Because modern processors have multiple cores it is possible to build a 50-node cluster with a petabyte of storage and still have a CPU core dedicated to process the data stream coming off each individual disk.

Build applications, not infrastructure

When thinking of the scenario in the previous section, many people will focus on the questions of data movement and processing. But, anyone who has ever built such a system will know that less obvious elements such as job scheduling, error handling, and coordination are where much of the magic truly lies.

If we had to implement the mechanisms for determining where to execute processing, performing the processing, and combining all the subresults into the overall result, we wouldn't have gained much from the older model. There, we needed to explicitly manage data partitioning; we'd just be exchanging one difficult problem with another.

This touches on the most recent trend, which we'll highlight here: a system that handles most of the cluster mechanics transparently and allows the developer to think in terms of the business problem. Frameworks that provide well-defined interfaces that abstract all this complexity—smart software—upon which business domain-specific applications can be built give the best combination of developer and system efficiency.

Hadoop

The thoughtful (or perhaps suspicious) reader will not be surprised to learn that the preceding approaches are all key aspects of Hadoop. But we still haven't actually answered the question about exactly what Hadoop is.

Thanks, Google

It all started with Google, which in 2003 and 2004 released two academic papers describing Google technology: the **Google File System (GFS)** (http://research.google.com/archive/gfs.html) and MapReduce (http://research.google.com/archive/mapreduce.html). The two together provided a platform for processing data on a very large scale in a highly efficient manner.

Thanks, Doug

At the same time, Doug Cutting was working on the Nutch open source web search engine. He had been working on elements within the system that resonated strongly once the Google GFS and MapReduce papers were published. Doug started work on the implementations of these Google systems, and Hadoop was soon born, firstly as a subproject of Lucene and soon was its own top-level project within the Apache open source foundation. At its core, therefore, Hadoop is an open source platform that provides implementations of both the MapReduce and GFS technologies and allows the processing of very large data sets across clusters of low-cost commodity hardware.

Thanks, Yahoo

Yahoo hired Doug Cutting in 2006 and quickly became one of the most prominent supporters of the Hadoop project. In addition to often publicizing some of the largest Hadoop deployments in the world, Yahoo has allowed Doug and other engineers to contribute to Hadoop while still under its employ; it has contributed some of its own internally developed Hadoop improvements and extensions. Though Doug has now moved on to Cloudera (another prominent startup supporting the Hadoop community) and much of the Yahoo's Hadoop team has been spun off into a startup called Hortonworks, Yahoo remains a major Hadoop contributor.

Parts of Hadoop

The top-level Hadoop project has many component subprojects, several of which we'll discuss in this book, but the two main ones are **Hadoop Distributed File System (HDFS)** and MapReduce. These are direct implementations of Google's own GFS and MapReduce. We'll discuss both in much greater detail, but for now, it's best to think of HDFS and MapReduce as a pair of complementary yet distinct technologies.

HDFS is a filesystem that can store very large data sets by scaling out across a cluster of hosts. It has specific design and performance characteristics; in particular, it is optimized for throughput instead of latency, and it achieves high availability through replication instead of redundancy.

MapReduce is a data processing paradigm that takes a specification of how the data will be input and output from its two stages (called map and reduce) and then applies this across arbitrarily large data sets. MapReduce integrates tightly with HDFS, ensuring that wherever possible, MapReduce tasks run directly on the HDFS nodes that hold the required data.

Common building blocks

Both HDFS and MapReduce exhibit several of the architectural principles described in the previous section. In particular:

- Both are designed to run on clusters of commodity (that is, low-to-medium specification) servers

- Both scale their capacity by adding more servers (scale-out)

- Both have mechanisms for identifying and working around failures

- Both provide many of their services transparently, allowing the user to concentrate on the problem at hand

- Both have an architecture where a software cluster sits on the physical servers and controls all aspects of system execution

HDFS

HDFS is a filesystem unlike most you may have encountered before. It is not a POSIX-compliant filesystem, which basically means it does not provide the same guarantees as a regular filesystem. It is also a distributed filesystem, meaning that it spreads storage across multiple nodes; lack of such an efficient distributed filesystem was a limiting factor in some historical technologies. The key features are:

- HDFS stores files in blocks typically at least 64 MB in size, much larger than the 4-32 KB seen in most filesystems.

- HDFS is optimized for throughput over latency; it is very efficient at streaming read requests for large files but poor at seek requests for many small ones.

- HDFS is optimized for workloads that are generally of the write-once and read-many type.

- Each storage node runs a process called a DataNode that manages the blocks on that host, and these are coordinated by a master NameNode process running on a separate host.

♦ Instead of handling disk failures by having physical redundancies in disk arrays or similar strategies, HDFS uses replication. Each of the blocks comprising a file is stored on multiple nodes within the cluster, and the HDFS NameNode constantly monitors reports sent by each DataNode to ensure that failures have not dropped any block below the desired replication factor. If this does happen, it schedules the addition of another copy within the cluster.

MapReduce

Though MapReduce as a technology is relatively new, it builds upon much of the fundamental work from both mathematics and computer science, particularly approaches that look to express operations that would then be applied to each element in a set of data. Indeed the individual concepts of functions called map and reduce come straight from functional programming languages where they were applied to lists of input data.

Another key underlying concept is that of "divide and conquer", where a single problem is broken into multiple individual subtasks. This approach becomes even more powerful when the subtasks are executed in parallel; in a perfect case, a task that takes 1000 minutes could be processed in 1 minute by 1,000 parallel subtasks.

MapReduce is a processing paradigm that builds upon these principles; it provides a series of transformations from a source to a result data set. In the simplest case, the input data is fed to the map function and the resultant temporary data to a reduce function. The developer only defines the data transformations; Hadoop's MapReduce job manages the process of how to apply these transformations to the data across the cluster in parallel. Though the underlying ideas may not be novel, a major strength of Hadoop is in how it has brought these principles together into an accessible and well-engineered platform.

Unlike traditional relational databases that require structured data with well-defined schemas, MapReduce and Hadoop work best on semi-structured or unstructured data. Instead of data conforming to rigid schemas, the requirement is instead that the data be provided to the map function as a series of key value pairs. The output of the map function is a set of other key value pairs, and the reduce function performs aggregation to collect the final set of results.

Hadoop provides a standard specification (that is, interface) for the map and reduce functions, and implementations of these are often referred to as **mappers** and **reducers**. A typical MapReduce job will comprise of a number of mappers and reducers, and it is not unusual for several of these to be extremely simple. The developer focuses on expressing the transformation between source and result data sets, and the Hadoop framework manages all aspects of job execution, parallelization, and coordination.

This last point is possibly the most important aspect of Hadoop. The platform takes responsibility for every aspect of executing the processing across the data. After the user defines the key criteria for the job, everything else becomes the responsibility of the system. Critically, from the perspective of the size of data, the same MapReduce job can be applied to data sets of any size hosted on clusters of any size. If the data is 1 gigabyte in size and on a single host, Hadoop will schedule the processing accordingly. Even if the data is 1 petabyte in size and hosted across one thousand machines, it still does likewise, determining how best to utilize all the hosts to perform the work most efficiently. From the user's perspective, the actual size of the data and cluster are transparent, and apart from affecting the time taken to process the job, they do not change how the user interacts with Hadoop.

Better together

It is possible to appreciate the individual merits of HDFS and MapReduce, but they are even more powerful when combined. HDFS can be used without MapReduce, as it is intrinsically a large-scale data storage platform. Though MapReduce can read data from non-HDFS sources, the nature of its processing aligns so well with HDFS that using the two together is by far the most common use case.

When a MapReduce job is executed, Hadoop needs to decide where to execute the code most efficiently to process the data set. If the MapReduce-cluster hosts all pull their data from a single storage host or an array, it largely doesn't matter as the storage system is a shared resource that will cause contention. But if the storage system is HDFS, it allows MapReduce to execute data processing on the node holding the data of interest, building on the principle of it being less expensive to move data processing than the data itself.

The most common deployment model for Hadoop sees the HDFS and MapReduce clusters deployed on the same set of servers. Each host that contains data and the HDFS component to manage it also hosts a MapReduce component that can schedule and execute data processing. When a job is submitted to Hadoop, it can use an optimization process as much as possible to schedule data on the hosts where the data resides, minimizing network traffic and maximizing performance.

Think back to our earlier example of how to process a four-step task on 1 petabyte of data spread across one thousand servers. The MapReduce model would (in a somewhat simplified and idealized way) perform the processing in a `map` function on each piece of data on a host where the data resides in HDFS and then reuse the cluster in the `reduce` function to collect the individual results into the final result set.

A part of the challenge with Hadoop is in breaking down the overall problem into the best combination of `map` and `reduce` functions. The preceding approach would only work if the four-stage processing chain could be applied independently to each data element in turn. As we'll see in later chapters, the answer is sometimes to use multiple MapReduce jobs where the output of one is the input to the next.

Common architecture

Both HDFS and MapReduce are, as mentioned, software clusters that display common characteristics:

- ◆ Each follows an architecture where a cluster of worker nodes is managed by a special master/coordinator node
- ◆ The master in each case (NameNode for HDFS and JobTracker for MapReduce) monitors the health of the cluster and handle failures, either by moving data blocks around or by rescheduling failed work
- ◆ Processes on each server (DataNode for HDFS and TaskTracker for MapReduce) are responsible for performing work on the physical host, receiving instructions from the NameNode or JobTracker, and reporting health/progress status back to it

As a minor terminology point, we will generally use the terms **host** or **server** to refer to the physical hardware hosting Hadoop's various components. The term **node** will refer to the software component comprising a part of the cluster.

What it is and isn't good for

As with any tool, it's important to understand when Hadoop is a good fit for the problem in question. Much of this book will highlight its strengths, based on the previous broad overview on processing large data volumes, but it's important to also start appreciating at an early stage where it isn't the best choice.

The architecture choices made within Hadoop enable it to be the flexible and scalable data processing platform it is today. But, as with most architecture or design choices, there are consequences that must be understood. Primary amongst these is the fact that Hadoop is a batch processing system. When you execute a job across a large data set, the framework will churn away until the final results are ready. With a large cluster, answers across even huge data sets can be generated relatively quickly, but the fact remains that the answers are not generated fast enough to service impatient users. Consequently, Hadoop alone is not well suited to low-latency queries such as those received on a website, a real-time system, or a similar problem domain.

When Hadoop is running jobs on large data sets, the overhead of setting up the job, determining which tasks are run on each node, and all the other housekeeping activities that are required is a trivial part of the overall execution time. But, for jobs on small data sets, there is an execution overhead that means even simple MapReduce jobs may take a minimum of 10 seconds.

Another member of the broader Hadoop family is **HBase**, an open-source implementation of another Google technology. This provides a (non-relational) database atop Hadoop that uses various means to allow it to serve low-latency queries.

But haven't Google and Yahoo both been among the strongest proponents of this method of computation, and aren't they all about such websites where response time is critical? The answer is yes, and it highlights an important aspect of how to incorporate Hadoop into any organization or activity or use it in conjunction with other technologies in a way that exploits the strengths of each. In a paper (`http://research.google.com/archive/googlecluster.html`), Google sketches how they utilized MapReduce at the time; after a web crawler retrieved updated webpage data, MapReduce processed the huge data set, and from this, produced the web index that a fleet of MySQL servers used to service end-user search requests.

Cloud computing with Amazon Web Services

The other technology area we'll explore in this book is cloud computing, in the form of several offerings from Amazon Web Services. But first, we need to cut through some hype and buzzwords that surround this thing called cloud computing.

Too many clouds

Cloud computing has become an overused term, arguably to the point that its overuse risks it being rendered meaningless. In this book, therefore, let's be clear what we mean—and care about—when using the term. There are two main aspects to this: a new architecture option and a different approach to cost.

A third way

We've talked about scale-up and scale-out as the options for scaling data processing systems. But our discussion thus far has taken for granted that the physical hardware that makes either option a reality will be purchased, owned, hosted, and managed by the organization doing the system development. The cloud computing we care about adds a third approach; put your application into the cloud and let the provider deal with the scaling problem.

It's not always that simple, of course. But for many cloud services, the model truly is this revolutionary. You develop the software according to some published guidelines or interface and then deploy it onto the cloud platform and allow it to scale the service based on the demand, for a cost of course. But given the costs usually involved in making scaling systems, this is often a compelling proposition.

Different types of costs

This approach to cloud computing also changes how system hardware is paid for. By offloading infrastructure costs, all users benefit from the economies of scale achieved by the cloud provider by building their platforms up to a size capable of hosting thousands or millions of clients. As a user, not only do you get someone else to worry about difficult engineering problems, such as scaling, but you pay for capacity as it's needed and you don't have to size the system based on the largest possible workloads. Instead, you gain the benefit of elasticity and use more or fewer resources as your workload demands.

An example helps illustrate this. Many companies' financial groups run end-of-month workloads to generate tax and payroll data, and often, much larger data crunching occurs at year end. If you were tasked with designing such a system, how much hardware would you buy? If you only buy enough to handle the day-to-day workload, the system may struggle at month end and may likely be in real trouble when the end-of-year processing rolls around. If you scale for the end-of-month workloads, the system will have idle capacity for most of the year and possibly still be in trouble performing the end-of-year processing. If you size for the end-of-year workload, the system will have significant capacity sitting idle for the rest of the year. And considering the purchase cost of hardware in addition to the hosting and running costs—a server's electricity usage may account for a large majority of its lifetime costs—you are basically wasting huge amounts of money.

The service-on-demand aspects of cloud computing allow you to start your application on a small hardware footprint and then scale it up and down as the year progresses. With a pay-for-use model, your costs follow your utilization and you have the capacity to process your workloads without having to buy enough hardware to handle the peaks.

A more subtle aspect of this model is that this greatly reduces the costs of entry for an organization to launch an online service. We all know that a new hot service that fails to meet demand and suffers performance problems will find it hard to recover momentum and user interest. For example, say in the year 2000, an organization wanting to have a successful launch needed to put in place, on launch day, enough capacity to meet the massive surge of user traffic they hoped for but did n't know for sure to expect. When taking costs of physical location into consideration, it would have been easy to spend millions on a product launch.

Today, with cloud computing, the initial infrastructure cost could literally be as low as a few tens or hundreds of dollars a month and that would only increase when—and if—the traffic demanded.

AWS – infrastructure on demand from Amazon

Amazon Web Services (AWS) is a set of such cloud computing services offered by Amazon. We will be using several of these services in this book.

Elastic Compute Cloud (EC2)

Amazon's **Elastic Compute Cloud (EC2)**, found at `http://aws.amazon.com/ec2/`, is basically a server on demand. After registering with AWS and EC2, credit card details are all that's required to gain access to a dedicated virtual machine, it's easy to run a variety of operating systems including Windows and many variants of Linux on our server.

Need more servers? Start more. Need more powerful servers? Change to one of the higher specification (and cost) types offered. Along with this, EC2 offers a suite of complimentary services, including load balancers, static IP addresses, high-performance additional virtual disk drives, and many more.

Simple Storage Service (S3)

Amazon's **Simple Storage Service (S3)**, found at `http://aws.amazon.com/s3/`, is a storage service that provides a simple key/value storage model. Using web, command-line, or programmatic interfaces to create objects, which can be everything from text files to images to MP3s, you can store and retrieve your data based on a hierarchical model. You create buckets in this model that contain objects. Each bucket has a unique identifier, and within each bucket, every object is uniquely named. This simple strategy enables an extremely powerful service for which Amazon takes complete responsibility (for service scaling, in addition to reliability and availability of data).

Elastic MapReduce (EMR)

Amazon's **Elastic MapReduce (EMR)**, found at `http://aws.amazon.com/elasticmapreduce/`, is basically Hadoop in the cloud and builds atop both EC2 and S3. Once again, using any of the multiple interfaces (web console, CLI, or API), a Hadoop workflow is defined with attributes such as the number of Hadoop hosts required and the location of the source data. The Hadoop code implementing the MapReduce jobs is provided and the virtual go button is pressed.

In its most impressive mode, EMR can pull source data from S3, process it on a Hadoop cluster it creates on EC2, push the results back into S3, and terminate the Hadoop cluster and the EC2 virtual machines hosting it. Naturally, each of these services has a cost (usually on per GB stored and server time usage basis), but the ability to access such powerful data processing capabilities with no need for dedicated hardware is a powerful one.

What this book covers

In this book we will be learning how to write MapReduce programs to do some serious data crunching and how to run them on both locally managed and AWS-hosted Hadoop clusters.

Not only will we be looking at Hadoop as an engine for performing MapReduce processing, but we'll also explore how a Hadoop capability can fit into the rest of an organization's infrastructure and systems. We'll look at some of the common points of integration, such as getting data between Hadoop and a relational database and also how to make Hadoop look more like such a relational database.

A dual approach

In this book we will not be limiting our discussion to EMR or Hadoop hosted on Amazon EC2; we will be discussing both the building and the management of local Hadoop clusters (on Ubuntu Linux) in addition to showing how to push the processing into the cloud via EMR.

The reason for this is twofold: firstly, though EMR makes Hadoop much more accessible, there are aspects of the technology that only become apparent when manually administering the cluster. Though it is also possible to use EMR in a more manual mode, we'll generally use a local cluster for such explorations. Secondly, though it isn't necessarily an either/or decision, many organizations use a mixture of in-house and cloud-hosted capacities, sometimes due to a concern of over reliance on a single external provider, but practically speaking, it's often convenient to do development and small-scale tests on local capacity then deploy at production scale into the cloud.

In some of the latter chapters, where we discuss additional products that integrate with Hadoop, we'll only give examples of local clusters as there is no difference in how the products work regardless of where they are deployed.

Summary

We learned a lot in this chapter about big data, Hadoop, and cloud computing.

Specifically, we covered the emergence of big data and how changes in the approach to data processing and system architecture bring within the reach of almost any organization techniques that were previously prohibitively expensive.

We also looked at the history of Hadoop and how it builds upon many of these trends to provide a flexible and powerful data processing platform that can scale to massive volumes. We also looked at how cloud computing provides another system architecture approach, one which exchanges large up-front costs and direct physical responsibility for a pay-as-you-go model and a reliance on the cloud provider for hardware provision, management and scaling. We also saw what Amazon Web Services is and how its Elastic MapReduce service utilizes other AWS services to provide Hadoop in the cloud.

We also discussed the aim of this book and its approach to exploration on both locally-managed and AWS-hosted Hadoop clusters.

Now that we've covered the basics and know where this technology is coming from and what its benefits are, we need to get our hands dirty and get things running, which is what we'll do in *Chapter 2, Getting Hadoop Up and Running*.

2
Getting Hadoop Up and Running

Now that we have explored the opportunities and challenges presented by large-scale data processing and why Hadoop is a compelling choice, it's time to get things set up and running.

In this chapter, we will do the following:

- Learn how to install and run Hadoop on a local Ubuntu host
- Run some example Hadoop programs and get familiar with the system
- Set up the accounts required to use Amazon Web Services products such as EMR
- Create an on-demand Hadoop cluster on Elastic MapReduce
- Explore the key differences between a local and hosted Hadoop cluster

Hadoop on a local Ubuntu host

For our exploration of Hadoop outside the cloud, we shall give examples using one or more Ubuntu hosts. A single machine (be it a physical computer or a virtual machine) will be sufficient to run all the parts of Hadoop and explore MapReduce. However, production clusters will most likely involve many more machines, so having even a development Hadoop cluster deployed on multiple hosts will be good experience. However, for getting started, a single host will suffice.

Nothing we discuss will be unique to Ubuntu, and Hadoop should run on any Linux distribution. Obviously, you may have to alter how the environment is configured if you use a distribution other than Ubuntu, but the differences should be slight.

Other operating systems

Hadoop does run well on other platforms. Windows and Mac OS X are popular choices for developers. Windows is supported only as a development platform and Mac OS X is not formally supported at all.

If you choose to use such a platform, the general situation will be similar to other Linux distributions; all aspects of how to work with Hadoop will be the same on both platforms but you will need use the operating system-specific mechanisms for setting up environment variables and similar tasks. The Hadoop FAQs contain some information on alternative platforms and should be your first port of call if you are considering such an approach. The Hadoop FAQs can be found at `http://wiki.apache.org/hadoop/FAQ`.

Time for action – checking the prerequisites

Hadoop is written in Java, so you will need a recent **Java Development Kit (JDK)** installed on the Ubuntu host. Perform the following steps to check the prerequisites:

1. First, check what's already available by opening up a terminal and typing the following:

    ```
    $ javac
    $ java -version
    ```

2. If either of these commands gives a `no such file or directory` or similar error, or if the latter mentions "Open JDK", it's likely you need to download the full JDK. Grab this from the Oracle download page at `http://www.oracle.com/technetwork/java/javase/downloads/index.html`; you should get the latest release.

3. Once Java is installed, add the `JDK/bin` directory to your path and set the `JAVA_HOME` environment variable with commands such as the following, modified for your specific Java version:

    ```
    $ export JAVA_HOME=/opt/jdk1.6.0_24
    $ export PATH=$JAVA_HOME/bin:${PATH}
    ```

What just happened?

These steps ensure the right version of Java is installed and available from the command line without having to use lengthy pathnames to refer to the install location.

Remember that the preceding commands only affect the currently running shell and the settings will be lost after you log out, close the shell, or reboot. To ensure the same setup is always available, you can add these to the startup files for your shell of choice, within the `.bash_profile` file for the BASH shell or the `.cshrc` file for TCSH, for example.

An alternative favored by me is to put all required configuration settings into a standalone file and then explicitly call this from the command line; for example:

```
$ source Hadoop_config.sh
```

This technique allows you to keep multiple setup files in the same account without making the shell startup overly complex; not to mention, the required configurations for several applications may actually be incompatible. Just remember to begin by loading the file at the start of each session!

Setting up Hadoop

One of the most confusing aspects of Hadoop to a newcomer is its various components, projects, sub-projects, and their interrelationships. The fact that these have evolved over time hasn't made the task of understanding it all any easier. For now, though, go to `http://hadoop.apache.org` and you'll see that there are three prominent projects mentioned:

◆ Common
◆ HDFS
◆ MapReduce

The last two of these should be familiar from the explanation in *Chapter 1, What It's All About*, and common projects comprise a set of libraries and tools that help the Hadoop product work in the real world. For now, the important thing is that the standard Hadoop distribution bundles the latest versions all of three of these projects and the combination is what you need to get going.

A note on versions

Hadoop underwent a major change in the transition from the 0.19 to the 0.20 versions, most notably with a migration to a set of new APIs used to develop MapReduce applications. We will be primarily using the new APIs in this book, though we do include a few examples of the older API in later chapters as not of all the existing features have been ported to the new API.

Hadoop versioning also became complicated when the 0.20 branch was renamed to 1.0. The 0.22 and 0.23 branches remained, and in fact included features not included in the 1.0 branch. At the time of this writing, things were becoming clearer with 1.1 and 2.0 branches being used for future development releases. As most existing systems and third-party tools are built against the 0.20 branch, we will use Hadoop 1.0 for the examples in this book.

Time for action – downloading Hadoop

Carry out the following steps to download Hadoop:

1. Go to the Hadoop download page at `http://hadoop.apache.org/common/ releases.html` and retrieve the latest stable version of the 1.0.x branch; at the time of this writing, it was 1.0.4.

2. You'll be asked to select a local mirror; after that you need to download the file with a name such as `hadoop-1.0.4-bin.tar.gz`.

3. Copy this file to the directory where you want Hadoop to be installed (for example, `/usr/local`), using the following command:

   ```
   $ cp Hadoop-1.0.4.bin.tar.gz /usr/local
   ```

4. Decompress the file by using the following command:

   ```
   $ tar -xf hadoop-1.0.4-bin.tar.gz
   ```

5. Add a convenient symlink to the Hadoop installation directory.

   ```
   $ ln -s /usr/local/hadoop-1.0.4 /opt/hadoop
   ```

6. Now you need to add the Hadoop binary directory to your path and set the HADOOP_HOME environment variable, just as we did earlier with Java.

   ```
   $ export HADOOP_HOME=/usr/local/Hadoop
   $ export PATH=$HADOOP_HOME/bin:$PATH
   ```

7. Go into the `conf` directory within the Hadoop installation and edit the `Hadoop-env.sh` file. Search for JAVA_HOME and uncomment the line, modifying the location to point to your JDK installation, as mentioned earlier.

What just happened?

These steps ensure that Hadoop is installed and available from the command line. By setting the path and configuration variables, we can use the Hadoop command-line tool. The modification to the Hadoop configuration file is the only required change to the setup needed to integrate with your host settings.

As mentioned earlier, you should put the export commands in your shell startup file or a standalone-configuration script that you specify at the start of the session.

Don't worry about some of the details here; we'll cover Hadoop setup and use later.

Time for action – setting up SSH

Carry out the following steps to set up SSH:

1. Create a new OpenSSL key pair with the following commands:

```
$ ssh-keygen
Generating public/private rsa key pair.
Enter file in which to save the key (/home/hadoop/.ssh/id_rsa):
Created directory '/home/hadoop/.ssh'.
Enter passphrase (empty for no passphrase):
Enter same passphrase again:
Your identification has been saved in /home/hadoop/.ssh/id_rsa.
Your public key has been saved in /home/hadoop/.ssh/id_rsa.pub.
...
```

2. Copy the new public key to the list of authorized keys by using the following command:

```
$ cp .ssh/id _rsa.pub  .ssh/authorized_keys
```

3. Connect to the local host.

```
$ ssh localhost
The authenticity of host 'localhost (127.0.0.1)' can't be
established.
RSA key fingerprint is b6:0c:bd:57:32:b6:66:7c:33:7b:62:92:61:fd:c
a:2a.
Are you sure you want to continue connecting (yes/no)? yes
Warning: Permanently added 'localhost' (RSA) to the list of known
hosts.
```

4. Confirm that the password-less SSH is working.

```
$ ssh localhost
$ ssh localhost
```

What just happened?

Because Hadoop requires communication between multiple processes on one or more machines, we need to ensure that the user we are using for Hadoop can connect to each required host without needing a password. We do this by creating a **Secure Shell (SSH)** key pair that has an empty passphrase. We use the `ssh-keygen` command to start this process and accept the offered defaults.

Once we create the key pair, we need to add the new public key to the stored list of trusted keys; this means that when trying to connect to this machine, the public key will be trusted. After doing so, we use the `ssh` command to connect to the local machine and should expect to get a warning about trusting the host certificate as just shown. After confirming this, we should then be able to connect without further passwords or prompts.

 Note that when we move later to use a fully distributed cluster, we will need to ensure that the Hadoop user account has the same key set up on every host in the cluster.

Configuring and running Hadoop

So far this has all been pretty straightforward, just downloading and system administration. Now we can deal with Hadoop directly. Finally! We'll run a quick example to show Hadoop in action. There is additional configuration and set up to be performed, but this next step will help give confidence that things are installed and configured correctly so far.

Time for action – using Hadoop to calculate Pi

We will now use a sample Hadoop program to calculate the value of Pi. Right now, this is primarily to validate the installation and to show how quickly you can get a MapReduce job to execute. Assuming the HADOOP_HOME/bin directory is in your path, type the following commands:

```
$ Hadoop jar hadoop/hadoop-examples-1.0.4.jar  pi 4 1000
Number of Maps  = 4
Samples per Map = 1000
Wrote input for Map #0
Wrote input for Map #1
Wrote input for Map #2
Wrote input for Map #3
Starting Job
12/10/26 22:56:11 INFO jvm.JvmMetrics: Initializing JVM Metrics
with processName=JobTracker, sessionId=
12/10/26 22:56:11 INFO mapred.FileInputFormat: Total input paths
to process : 4
12/10/26 22:56:12 INFO mapred.JobClient: Running job: job_
local_0001
```

```
12/10/26 22:56:12 INFO mapred.FileInputFormat: Total input paths
to process : 4
12/10/26 22:56:12 INFO mapred.MapTask: numReduceTasks: 1


...

12/10/26 22:56:14 INFO mapred.JobClient:  map 100% reduce 100%
12/10/26 22:56:14 INFO mapred.JobClient: Job complete: job_
local_0001
12/10/26 22:56:14 INFO mapred.JobClient: Counters: 13
12/10/26 22:56:14 INFO mapred.JobClient:    FileSystemCounters

...

Job Finished in 2.904 seconds
Estimated value of Pi is 3.14000000000000000000
$
```

What just happened?

There's a lot of information here; even more so when you get the full output on your screen. For now, let's unpack the fundamentals and not worry about much of Hadoop's status output until later in the book. The first thing to clarify is some terminology; each Hadoop program runs as a job that creates multiple tasks to do its work.

Looking at the output, we see it is broadly split into three sections:

◆ The start up of the job
◆ The status as the job executes
◆ The output of the job

In our case, we can see the job creates four tasks to calculate Pi, and the overall job result will be the combination of these subresults. This pattern should sound familiar to the one we came across in *Chapter 1, What It's All About*; the model is used to split a larger job into smaller pieces and then bring together the results.

The majority of the output will appear as the job is being executed and provide status messages showing progress. On successful completion, the job will print out a number of counters and other statistics. The preceding example is actually unusual in that it is rare to see the result of a MapReduce job displayed on the console. This is not a limitation of Hadoop, but rather a consequence of the fact that jobs that process large data sets usually produce a significant amount of output data that isn't well suited to a simple echoing on the screen.

Congratulations on your first successful MapReduce job!

Three modes

In our desire to get something running on Hadoop, we sidestepped an important issue: in which mode should we run Hadoop? There are three possibilities that alter where the various Hadoop components execute. Recall that HDFS comprises a single NameNode that acts as the cluster coordinator and is the master for one or more DataNodes that store the data. For MapReduce, the JobTracker is the cluster master and it coordinates the work executed by one or more TaskTracker processes. The Hadoop modes deploy these components as follows:

- **Local standalone mode**: This is the default mode if, as in the preceding Pi example, you don't configure anything else. In this mode, all the components of Hadoop, such as NameNode, DataNode, JobTracker, and TaskTracker, run in a single Java process.

- **Pseudo-distributed mode**: In this mode, a separate JVM is spawned for each of the Hadoop components and they communicate across network sockets, effectively giving a fully functioning minicluster on a single host.

- **Fully distributed mode**: In this mode, Hadoop is spread across multiple machines, some of which will be general-purpose workers and others will be dedicated hosts for components, such as NameNode and JobTracker.

Each mode has its benefits and drawbacks. Fully distributed mode is obviously the only one that can scale Hadoop across a cluster of machines, but it requires more configuration work, not to mention the cluster of machines. Local, or standalone, mode is the easiest to set up, but you interact with it in a different manner than you would with the fully distributed mode. In this book, we shall generally prefer the pseudo-distributed mode even when using examples on a single host, as everything done in the pseudo-distributed mode is almost identical to how it works on a much larger cluster.

Time for action – configuring the pseudo-distributed mode

Take a look in the `conf` directory within the Hadoop distribution. There are many configuration files, but the ones we need to modify are `core-site.xml`, `hdfs-site.xml` and `mapred-site.xml`.

1. Modify `core-site.xml` to look like the following code:

```
<?xml version="1.0"?>
<?xml-stylesheet type="text/xsl" href="configuration.xsl"?>

<!-- Put site-specific property overrides in this file. -->

<configuration>
<property>
<name>fs.default.name</name>
```

```
<value>hdfs://localhost:9000</value>
</property>
</configuration>
```

2. Modify `hdfs-site.xml` to look like the following code:

```
<?xml version="1.0"?>
<?xml-stylesheet type="text/xsl" href="configuration.xsl"?>

<!-- Put site-specific property overrides in this file. -->

<configuration>
<property>
<name>dfs.replication</name>
<value>1</value>
</property>
</configuration>
```

3. Modify `mapred-site.xml` to look like the following code:

```
<?xml version="1.0"?>
<?xml-stylesheet type="text/xsl" href="configuration.xsl"?>

<!-- Put site-specific property overrides in this file. -->

<configuration>
<property>
<name>mapred.job.tracker</name>
<value>localhost:9001</value>
</property>
</configuration>
```

What just happened?

The first thing to note is the general format of these configuration files. They are obviously XML and contain multiple property specifications within a single configuration element.

The property specifications always contain name and value elements with the possibility for optional comments not shown in the preceding code.

We set three configuration variables here:

◆ The `dfs.default.name` variable holds the location of the NameNode and is required by both HDFS and MapReduce components, which explains why it's in `core-site.xml` and not `hdfs-site.xml`.

- The `dfs.replication` variable specifies how many times each HDFS block should be replicated. Recall from *Chapter 1, What It's All About*, that HDFS handles failures by ensuring each block of filesystem data is replicated to a number of different hosts, usually 3. As we only have a single host and one DataNode in the pseudo-distributed mode, we change this value to 1.

- The `mapred.job.tracker` variable holds the location of the JobTracker just like `dfs.default.name` holds the location of the NameNode. Because only MapReduce components need know this location, it is in `mapred-site.xml`.

You are free, of course, to change the port numbers used, though 9000 and 9001 are common conventions in Hadoop.

The network addresses for the NameNode and the JobTracker specify the ports on which the actual system requests should be directed. These are not user-facing locations, so don't bother pointing your web browser at them. There are web interfaces that we will look at shortly.

Configuring the base directory and formatting the filesystem

If the pseudo-distributed or fully distributed mode is chosen, there are two steps that need to be performed before we start our first Hadoop cluster.

1. Set the base directory where Hadoop files will be stored.

2. Format the HDFS filesystem.

To be precise, we don't need to change the default directory; but, as seen later, it's a good thing to think about it now.

Time for action – changing the base HDFS directory

Let's first set the base directory that specifies the location on the local filesystem under which Hadoop will keep all its data. Carry out the following steps:

1. Create a directory into which Hadoop will store its data:

```
$ mkdir /var/lib/hadoop
```

2. Ensure the directory is writeable by any user:

```
$ chmod 777 /var/lib/hadoop
```

3. Modify `core-site.xml` once again to add the following property:

```
<property>
<name>hadoop.tmp.dir</name>
<value>/var/lib/hadoop</value>
</property>
```

What just happened?

As we will be storing data in Hadoop and all the various components are running on our local host, this data will need to be stored on our local filesystem somewhere. Regardless of the mode, Hadoop by default uses the `hadoop.tmp.dir` property as the base directory under which all files and data are written.

MapReduce, for example, uses a `/mapred` directory under this base directory; HDFS uses `/dfs`. The danger is that the default value of `hadoop.tmp.dir` is `/tmp` and some Linux distributions delete the contents of `/tmp` on each reboot. So it's safer to explicitly state where the data is to be held.

Time for action – formatting the NameNode

Before starting Hadoop in either pseudo-distributed or fully distributed mode for the first time, we need to format the HDFS filesystem that it will use. Type the following:

```
$   hadoop namenode -format
```

The output of this should look like the following:

```
$ hadoop namenode -format
12/10/26 22:45:25 INFO namenode.NameNode: STARTUP_MSG:
/************************************************************
STARTUP_MSG: Starting NameNode
STARTUP_MSG:    host = vm193/10.0.0.193
STARTUP_MSG:    args = [-format]
...
12/10/26 22:45:25 INFO namenode.FSNamesystem: fsOwner=hadoop,hadoop
12/10/26 22:45:25 INFO namenode.FSNamesystem: supergroup=supergroup
12/10/26 22:45:25 INFO namenode.FSNamesystem: isPermissionEnabled=true
12/10/26 22:45:25 INFO common.Storage: Image file of size 96 saved in 0
seconds.
```

```
12/10/26 22:45:25 INFO common.Storage: Storage directory /var/lib/hadoop-
hadoop/dfs/name has been successfully formatted.
12/10/26 22:45:26 INFO namenode.NameNode: SHUTDOWN_MSG:
/************************************************************
SHUTDOWN_MSG: Shutting down NameNode at vm193/10.0.0.193
$
```

What just happened?

This is not a very exciting output because the step is only an enabler for our future use of HDFS. However, it does help us think of HDFS as a filesystem; just like any new storage device on any operating system, we need to format the device before we can use it. The same is true for HDFS; initially there is a default location for the filesystem data but no actual data for the equivalents of filesystem indexes.

> Do this every time!
>
> If your experience with Hadoop has been similar to the one I have had, there will be a series of simple mistakes that are frequently made when setting up new installations. It is very easy to forget about the formatting of the NameNode and then get a cascade of failure messages when the first Hadoop activity is tried.
>
> But do it only once!
>
> The command to format the NameNode can be executed multiple times, but in doing so all existing filesystem data will be destroyed. It can only be executed when the Hadoop cluster is shut down and sometimes you will want to do it but in most other cases it is a quick way to irrevocably delete every piece of data on HDFS; it does take much longer on large clusters. So be careful!

Starting and using Hadoop

After all that configuration and setup, let's now start our cluster and actually do something with it.

Time for action – starting Hadoop

Unlike the local mode of Hadoop, where all the components run only for the lifetime of the submitted job, with the pseudo-distributed or fully distributed mode of Hadoop, the cluster components exist as long-running processes. Before we use HDFS or MapReduce, we need to start up the needed components. Type the following commands; the output should look as shown next, where the commands are included on the lines prefixed by $:

1. Type in the first command:

```
$ start-dfs.sh
```

starting namenode, logging to /home/hadoop/hadoop/bin/../logs/
hadoop-hadoop-namenode-vm193.out

localhost: starting datanode, logging to /home/hadoop/hadoop/
bin/../logs/hadoop-hadoop-datanode-vm193.out

localhost: starting secondarynamenode, logging to /home/hadoop/
hadoop/bin/../logs/hadoop-hadoop-secondarynamenode-vm193.out

2. Type in the second command:

```
$ jps
9550 DataNode
9687 Jps
9638 SecondaryNameNode
9471 NameNode
```

3. Type in the third command:

```
$ hadoop dfs -ls /
Found 2 items
drwxr-xr-x    - hadoop supergroup          0 2012-10-26 23:03 /tmp
drwxr-xr-x    - hadoop supergroup          0 2012-10-26 23:06 /user
```

4. Type in the fourth command:

```
$ start-mapred.sh
```

starting jobtracker, logging to /home/hadoop/hadoop/bin/../logs/
hadoop-hadoop-jobtracker-vm193.out

localhost: starting tasktracker, logging to /home/hadoop/hadoop/
bin/../logs/hadoop-hadoop-tasktracker-vm193.out

5. Type in the fifth command:

```
$ jps
9550 DataNode
9877 TaskTracker
9638 SecondaryNameNode
9471 NameNode
9798 JobTracker
9913 Jps
```

What just happened?

The `start-dfs.sh` command, as the name suggests, starts the components necessary for HDFS. This is the NameNode to manage the filesystem and a single DataNode to hold data. The SecondaryNameNode is an availability aid that we'll discuss in a later chapter.

After starting these components, we use the JDK's `jps` utility to see which Java processes are running, and, as the output looks good, we then use Hadoop's `dfs` utility to list the root of the HDFS filesystem.

After this, we use `start-mapred.sh` to start the MapReduce components—this time the JobTracker and a single TaskTracker—and then use `jps` again to verify the result.

There is also a combined `start-all.sh` file that we'll use at a later stage, but in the early days it's useful to do a two-stage start up to more easily verify the cluster configuration.

Time for action – using HDFS

As the preceding example shows, there is a familiar-looking interface to HDFS that allows us to use commands similar to those in Unix to manipulate files and directories on the filesystem. Let's try it out by typing the following commands:

Type in the following commands:

```
$ hadoop -mkdir /user
$ hadoop -mkdir /user/hadoop
$ hadoop fs -ls /user
Found 1 items
drwxr-xr-x   - hadoop supergroup          0 2012-10-26 23:09 /user/Hadoop
$ echo "This is a test." >> test.txt
$ cat test.txt
This is a test.
$ hadoop dfs -copyFromLocal test.txt   .
$ hadoop dfs -ls
Found 1 items
-rw-r--r--   1 hadoop supergroup         16 2012-10-26 23:19/user/hadoop/
test.txt
$ hadoop dfs -cat test.txt
This is a test.
$ rm test.txt
$ hadoop dfs -cat test.txt
```

```
This is a test.
$ hadoop fs -copyToLocal test.txt
$ cat test.txt
This is a test.
```

What just happened?

This example shows the use of the `fs` subcommand to the Hadoop utility. Note that both `dfs` and `fs` commands are equivalent). Like most filesystems, Hadoop has the concept of a home directory for each user. These home directories are stored under the `/user` directory on HDFS and, before we go further, we create our home directory if it does not already exist.

We then create a simple text file on the local filesystem and copy it to HDFS by using the `copyFromLocal` command and then check its existence and contents by using the `-ls` and `-cat` utilities. As can be seen, the user home directory is aliased to . because, in Unix, `-ls` commands with no path specified are assumed to refer to that location and relative paths (not starting with /) will start there.

We then deleted the file from the local filesystem, copied it back from HDFS by using the `-copyToLocal` command, and checked its contents using the local `cat` utility.

 Mixing HDFS and local filesystem commands, as in the preceding example, is a powerful combination, and it's very easy to execute on HDFS commands that were intended for the local filesystem and vice versa. So be careful, especially when deleting.

There are other HDFS manipulation commands; try `Hadoop fs -help` for a detailed list.

Time for action – WordCount, the Hello World of MapReduce

Many applications, over time, acquire a canonical example that no beginner's guide should be without. For Hadoop, this is WordCount – an example bundled with Hadoop that counts the frequency of words in an input text file.

1. First execute the following commands:

```
$ hadoop dfs -mkdir data
$ hadoop dfs -cp test.txt data
$ hadoop dfs -ls data
Found 1 items
-rw-r--r--   1 hadoop supergroup        16 2012-10-26 23:20 /
user/hadoop/data/test.txt
```

2. Now execute these commands:

```
$ Hadoop Hadoop/hadoop-examples-1.0.4.jar  wordcount data out
12/10/26 23:22:49 INFO input.FileInputFormat: Total input paths to
process : 1
12/10/26 23:22:50 INFO mapred.JobClient: Running job:
job_201210262315_0002
12/10/26 23:22:51 INFO mapred.JobClient:  map 0% reduce 0%
12/10/26 23:23:03 INFO mapred.JobClient:  map 100% reduce 0%
12/10/26 23:23:15 INFO mapred.JobClient:  map 100% reduce 100%
12/10/26 23:23:17 INFO mapred.JobClient: Job complete:
job_201210262315_0002
12/10/26 23:23:17 INFO mapred.JobClient: Counters: 17
12/10/26 23:23:17 INFO mapred.JobClient:     Job Counters
12/10/26 23:23:17 INFO mapred.JobClient:       Launched reduce
tasks=1
12/10/26 23:23:17 INFO mapred.JobClient:       Launched map tasks=1
12/10/26 23:23:17 INFO mapred.JobClient:       Data-local map
tasks=1
12/10/26 23:23:17 INFO mapred.JobClient:     FileSystemCounters
12/10/26 23:23:17 INFO mapred.JobClient:       FILE_BYTES_READ=46
12/10/26 23:23:17 INFO mapred.JobClient:       HDFS_BYTES_READ=16
12/10/26 23:23:17 INFO mapred.JobClient:       FILE_BYTES_
WRITTEN=124
12/10/26 23:23:17 INFO mapred.JobClient:       HDFS_BYTES_WRITTEN=24
12/10/26 23:23:17 INFO mapred.JobClient:     Map-Reduce Framework
12/10/26 23:23:17 INFO mapred.JobClient:       Reduce input groups=4
12/10/26 23:23:17 INFO mapred.JobClient:       Combine output
records=4
12/10/26 23:23:17 INFO mapred.JobClient:       Map input records=1
12/10/26 23:23:17 INFO mapred.JobClient:       Reduce shuffle
bytes=46
12/10/26 23:23:17 INFO mapred.JobClient:       Reduce output
records=4
12/10/26 23:23:17 INFO mapred.JobClient:       Spilled Records=8
12/10/26 23:23:17 INFO mapred.JobClient:       Map output bytes=32
12/10/26 23:23:17 INFO mapred.JobClient:       Combine input
records=4
12/10/26 23:23:17 INFO mapred.JobClient:       Map output records=4
12/10/26 23:23:17 INFO mapred.JobClient:       Reduce input
records=4
```

3. Execute the following command:

```
$ hadoop fs -ls out
Found 2 items
drwxr-xr-x   - hadoop supergroup          0 2012-10-26 23:22 /
user/hadoop/out/_logs
-rw-r--r--   1 hadoop supergroup         24 2012-10-26 23:23 /
user/hadoop/out/part-r-00000
```

4. Now execute this command:

```
$ hadoop fs -cat out/part-0-00000
This   1
a   1
is   1
test.   1
```

What just happened?

We did three things here, as follows:

- ◆ Moved the previously created text file into a new directory on HDFS
- ◆ Ran the example WordCount job specifying this new directory and a non-existent output directory as arguments
- ◆ Used the `fs` utility to examine the output of the MapReduce job

As we said earlier, the pseudo-distributed mode has more Java processes, so it may seem curious that the job output is significantly shorter than for the standalone Pi. The reason is that the local standalone mode prints information about each individual task execution to the screen, whereas in the other modes this information is written only to logfiles on the running hosts.

The output directory is created by Hadoop itself and the actual result files follow the part-*nnnnn* convention illustrated here; though given our setup, there is only one result file. We use the `fs -cat` command to examine the file, and the results are as expected.

> If you specify an existing directory as the output source for a Hadoop job, it will fail to run and will throw an exception complaining of an already existing directory. If you want Hadoop to store the output to a directory, it must not exist. Treat this as a safety mechanism that stops Hadoop from writing over previous valuable job runs and something you will forget to ascertain frequently. If you are confident, you can override this behavior, as we will see later.

The Pi and WordCount programs are only some of the examples that ship with Hadoop. Here is how to get a list of them all. See if you can figure some of them out.

```
$ hadoop jar hadoop/hadoop-examples-1.0.4.jar
```

Have a go hero – WordCount on a larger body of text

Running a complex framework like Hadoop utilizing five discrete Java processes to count the words in a single-line text file is not terribly impressive. The power comes from the fact that we can use exactly the same program to run WordCount on a larger file, or even a massive corpus of text spread across a multinode Hadoop cluster. If we had such a setup, we would execute exactly the same commands as we just did by running the program and simply specifying the location of the directories for the source and output data.

Find a large online text file—Project Gutenberg at http://www.gutenberg.org is a good starting point—and run WordCount on it by copying it onto the HDFS and executing the WordCount example. The output may not be as you expect because, in a large body of text, issues of dirty data, punctuation, and formatting will need to be addressed. Think about how WordCount could be improved; we'll study how to expand it into a more complex processing chain in the next chapter.

Monitoring Hadoop from the browser

So far, we have been relying on command-line tools and direct command output to see what our system is doing. Hadoop provides two web interfaces that you should become familiar with, one for HDFS and the other for MapReduce. Both are useful in pseudo-distributed mode and are critical tools when you have a fully distributed setup.

The HDFS web UI

Point your web browser to port 50030 on the host running Hadoop. By default, the web interface should be available from both the local host and any other machine that has network access. Here is an example screenshot:

NameNode 'vm193:9000'

Started: Wed Oct 26 23:35:45 BST 2011
Version: 0.20.2, r911707
Compiled: Fri Feb 19 08:07:34 UTC 2010 by chrisdo
Upgrades: There are no upgrades in progress.

Browse the filesystem
Namenode Logs

Cluster Summary

Safe mode is ON. *The ratio of reported blocks 0.0000 has not reached the threshold 0.9990. Safe mode will be turned off automatically.*
19 files and directories, 7 blocks = 26 total. Heap Size is 15.31 MB / 966.69 MB (1%)

Configured Capacity	:	0 KB
DFS Used	:	0 KB
Non DFS Used	:	0 KB
DFS Remaining	:	0 KB
DFS Used%	:	100 %
DFS Remaining%	:	0 %
Live Nodes	:	0
Dead Nodes	:	0

There are no datanodes in the cluster

There is a lot going on here, but the immediately critical data tells us the number of nodes in the cluster, the filesystem size, used space, and links to drill down for more info and even browse the filesystem.

Spend a little time playing with this interface; it needs to become familiar. With a multinode cluster, the information about live and dead nodes plus the detailed information on their status history will be critical to debugging cluster problems.

The MapReduce web UI

The JobTracker UI is available on port 50070 by default, and the same access rules stated earlier apply. Here is an example screenshot:

This is more complex than the HDFS interface! Along with a similar count of the number of live/dead nodes, there is a history of the number of jobs executed since startup and a breakdown of their individual task counts.

The list of executing and historical jobs is a doorway to much more information; for every job, we can access the history of every task attempt on every node and access logs for detailed information. We now expose one of the most painful parts of working with any distributed system: debugging. It can be really hard.

Imagine you have a cluster of 100 machines trying to process a massive data set where the full job requires each host to execute hundreds of map and reduce tasks. If the job starts running very slowly or explicitly fails, it is not always obvious where the problem lies. Looking at the MapReduce web UI will likely be the first port of call because it provides such a rich starting point to investigate the health of running and historical jobs.

Using Elastic MapReduce

We will now turn to Hadoop in the cloud, the Elastic MapReduce service offered by Amazon Web Services. There are multiple ways to access EMR, but for now we will focus on the provided web console to contrast a full point-and-click approach to Hadoop with the previous command-line-driven examples.

Setting up an account in Amazon Web Services

Before using Elastic MapReduce, we need to set up an Amazon Web Services account and register it with the necessary services.

Creating an AWS account

Amazon has integrated their general accounts with AWS, meaning that if you already have an account for any of the Amazon retail websites, this is the only account you will need to use AWS services.

Note that AWS services have a cost; you will need an active credit card associated with the account to which charges can be made.

If you require a new Amazon account, go to http://aws.amazon.com, select **create a new AWS account**, and follow the prompts. Amazon has added a free tier for some services, so you may find that in the early days of testing and exploration you are keeping many of your activities within the non-charged tier. The scope of the free tier has been expanding, so make sure you know for what you will and won't be charged.

Signing up for the necessary services

Once you have an Amazon account, you will need to register it for use with the required AWS services, that is, **Simple Storage Service (S3)**, **Elastic Compute Cloud (EC2)**, and **Elastic MapReduce (EMR)**. There is no cost for simply signing up to any AWS service; the process just makes the service available to your account.

Go to the S3, EC2, and EMR pages linked from http://aws.amazon.com and click on the **Sign up** button on each page; then follow the prompts.

Caution! This costs real money!

Before going any further, it is critical to understand that use of AWS services will incur charges that will appear on the credit card associated with your Amazon account. Most of the charges are quite small and increase with the amount of infrastructure consumed; storing 10 GB of data in S3 costs 10 times more than for 1 GB, and running 20 EC2 instances costs 20 times as much as a single one. There are tiered cost models, so the actual costs tend to have smaller marginal increases at higher levels. But you should read carefully through the pricing sections for each service before using any of them. Note also that currently data transfer out of AWS services, such as EC2 and S3, is chargeable but data transfer between services is not. This means it is often most cost-effective to carefully design your use of AWS to keep data within AWS through as much of the data processing as possible.

Time for action – WordCount on EMR using the management console

Let's jump straight into an example on EMR using some provided example code. Carry out the following steps:

1. Browse to `http://aws.amazon.com`, go to **Developers | AWS Management Console**, and then click on the **Sign in to the AWS Console** button. The default view should look like the following screenshot. If it does not, click on **Amazon S3** from within the console.

2. As shown in the preceding screenshot, click on the **Create bucket** button and enter a name for the new bucket. Bucket names must be globally unique across all AWS users, so do not expect obvious bucket names such as `mybucket` or `s3test` to be available.

3. Click on the **Region** drop-down menu and select the geographic area nearest to you.

Create a Bucket - Select a Bucket Name and Region   Cancel ☒

A bucket is a container for objects stored in Amazon S3. When creating a bucket, you can choose a Region to optimize for latency, minimize costs, or address regulatory requirements. For more information regarding bucket naming conventions, please visit the Amazon S3 documentation.

Bucket Name: garryt1use
Region: US Standard ▾

Set Up Logging >   Create   Cancel

4. Click on the **Elastic MapReduce** link and click on the **Create a new Job Flow** button. You should see a screen like the following screenshot:

Create a New Job Flow   Cancel ☒

DEFINE JOB FLOW   SPECIFY PARAMETERS   CONFIGURE EC2 INSTANCES   ADVANCED OPTIONS   BOOTSTRAP ACTIONS   REVIEW

Creating a job flow to process your data using Amazon Elastic MapReduce is simple and quick. Let's begin by giving your job flow a name and selecting its type. If you don't already have an application you'd like to run on Amazon Elastic MapReduce, samples are available to help you get started.

Job Flow Name*: My Job Flow

Job Flow Name doesn't need to be unique. We suggest you give it a descriptive name.

Create a Job Flow*: ⊙ Run your own application

○ Run a sample application

Choose a Job Type ▾

Run your own application: specify your own parameters for your applications using Hive Program, Custom JAR, Streaming or Pig Program

Run a sample application: by selecting a sample application, parameters will be filled with the necessary data to create a sample Job Flow.

Continue ▷   * Required field

5. You should now see a screen like the preceding screenshot. Select the **Run a sample application** radio button and the **Word Count (Streaming)** menu item from the sample application drop-down box and click on the **Continue** button.

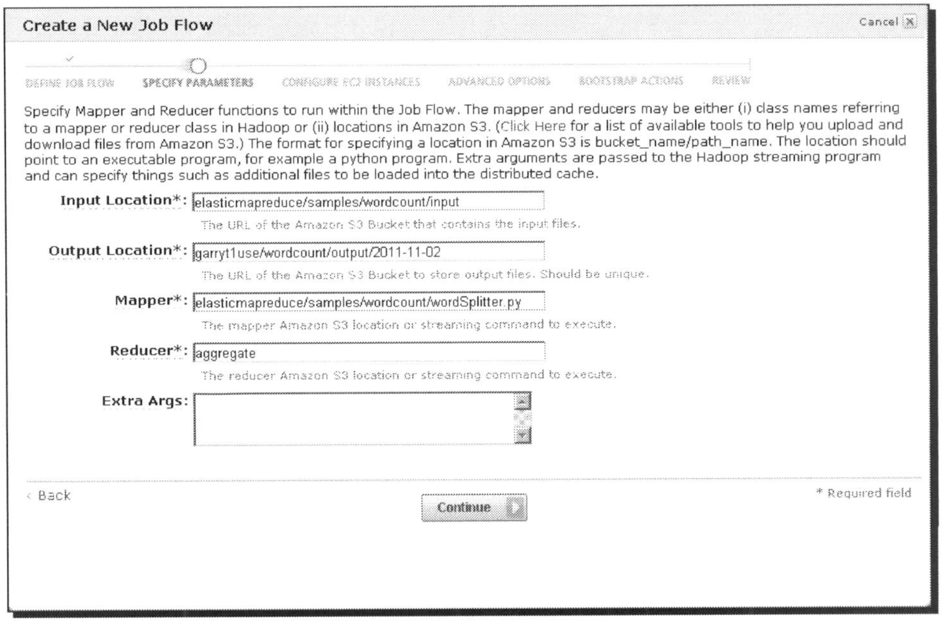

6. The next screen, shown in the preceding screenshot, allows us to specify the location of the output produced by running the job. In the edit box for the output location, enter the name of the bucket created in step 1 (`garryt1use` is the bucket we are using here); then click on the **Continue** button.

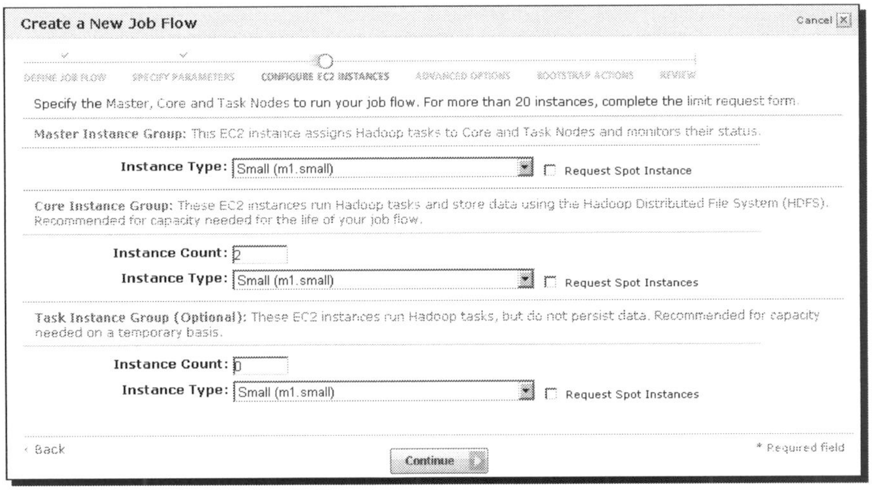

7. The next screenshot shows the page where we can modify the number and size of the virtual hosts utilized by our job. Confirm that the instance type for each combo box is **Small (m1.small)**, and the number of nodes for the Core group is **2** and for the Task group it is **0**. Then click on the **Continue** button.

8. This next screenshot involves options we will not be using in this example. For the **Amazon EC2 key pair** field, select the **Proceed without key pair** menu item and click on the **No** radio button for the **Enable Debugging** field. Ensure that the **Keep Alive** radio button is set to **No** and click on the **Continue** button.

9. The next screen, shown in the preceding screenshot, is one we will not be doing much with right now. Confirm that the **Proceed with no Bootstrap Actions** radio button is selected and click on the **Continue** button.

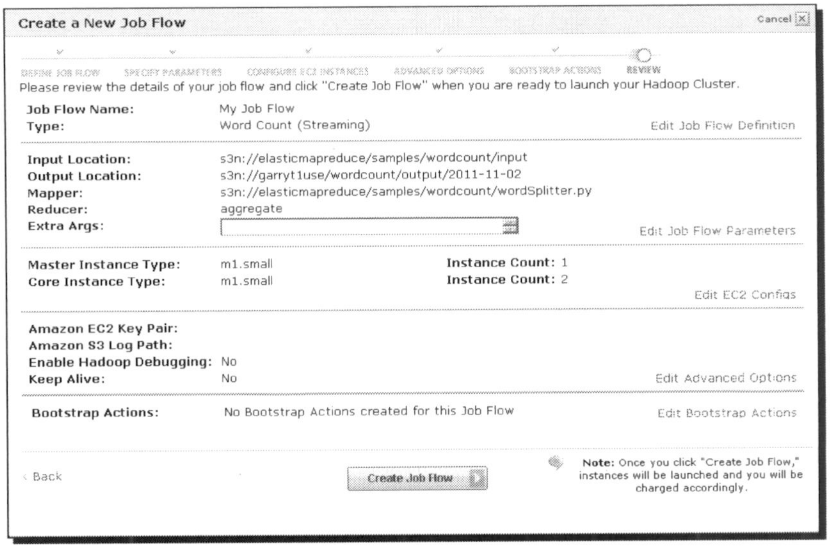

10. Confirm the job flow specifications are as expected and click on the **Create Job Flow** button. Then click on the **View my Job Flows** and **check status** buttons. This will give a list of your job flows; you can filter to show only running or completed jobs. The default is to show all, as in the example shown in the following screenshot:

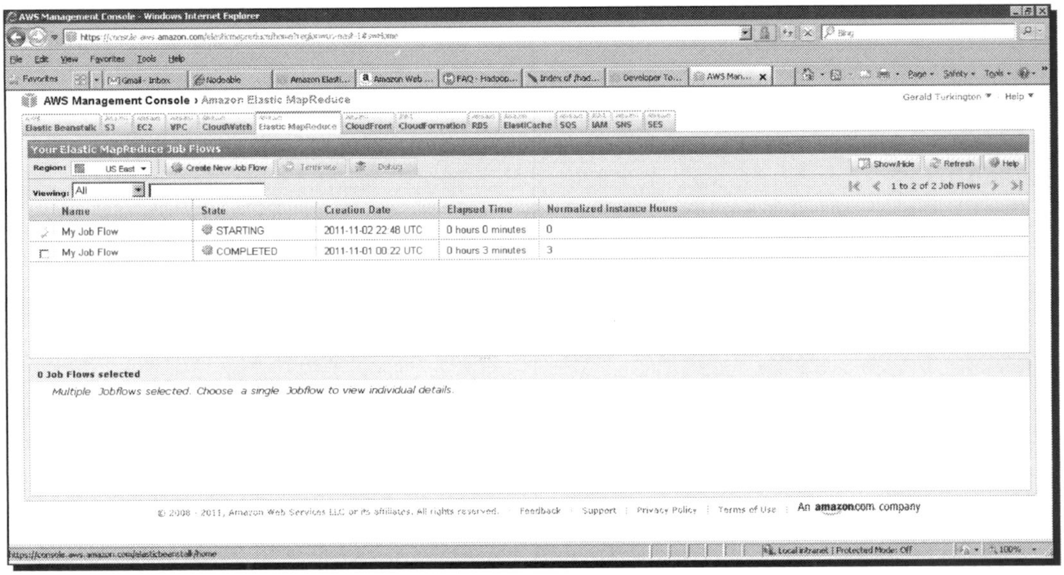

11. Occasionally hit the **Refresh** button until the status of the listed job, **Running** or **Starting**, changes to **Complete**; then click its checkbox to see details of the job flow, as shown in the following screenshot:

12. Click the **S3** tab and select the bucket you created for the output location. You will see it has a single entry called **wordcount**, which is a directory. Right-click on that and select **Open**. Then do the same until you see a list of actual files following the familiar Hadoop part-*nnnnn* naming scheme, as shown in the following screenshot:

Right click on **part-00000** and open it. It should look something like this:

```
a              14716
aa             52
aakar          3
aargau         3
abad           3
abandoned      46
abandonment    6
abate          9
abauj          3
abbassid       4
abbes          3
abbl           3
...
```

Does this type of output look familiar?

What just happened?

The first step deals with S3, and not EMR. S3 is a scalable storage service that allows you to store files (called objects) within containers called buckets, and to access objects by their bucket and object key (that is, name). The model is analogous to the usage of a filesystem, and though there are underlying differences, they are unlikely to be important within this book.

S3 is where you will place the MapReduce programs and source data you want to process in EMR, and where the output and logs of EMR Hadoop jobs will be stored. There is a plethora of third-party tools to access S3, but here we are using the AWS management console, a browser interface to most AWS services.

Though we suggested you choose the nearest geographic region for S3, this is not required; non-US locations will typically give better latency for customers located nearer to them, but they also tend to have a slightly higher cost. The decision of where to host your data and applications is one you need to make after considering all these factors.

After creating the S3 bucket, we moved to the EMR console and created a new job flow. This term is used within EMR to refer to a data processing task. As we will see, this can be a one-time deal where the underlying Hadoop cluster is created and destroyed on demand or it can be a long-running cluster on which multiple jobs are executed.

We left the default job flow name and then selected the use of an example application, in this case, the Python implementation of WordCount. The term Hadoop Streaming refers to a mechanism allowing scripting languages to be used to write map and reduce tasks, but the functionality is the same as the Java WordCount we used earlier.

The form to specify the job flow requires a location for the source data, program, map and reduce classes, and a desired location for the output data. For the example we just saw, most of the fields were prepopulated; and, as can be seen, there are clear similarities to what was required when running local Hadoop from the command line.

By not selecting the **Keep Alive** option, we chose a Hadoop cluster that would be created specifically to execute this job, and destroyed afterwards. Such a cluster will have a longer startup time but will minimize costs. If you choose to keep the job flow alive, you will see additional jobs executed more quickly as you don't have to wait for the cluster to start up. But you will be charged for the underlying EC2 resources until you explicitly terminate the job flow.

After confirming, we do not need to add any additional bootstrap options; we selected the number and types of hosts we wanted to deploy into our Hadoop cluster. EMR distinguishes between three different groups of hosts:

- **Master group**: This is a controlling node hosting the NameNode and the JobTracker. There is only 1 of these.

- **Core group**: These are nodes running both HDFS DataNodes and MapReduce TaskTrackers. The number of hosts is configurable.

- **Task group**: These hosts don't hold HDFS data but do run TaskTrackers and can provide more processing horsepower. The number of hosts is configurable.

The type of host refers to different classes of hardware capability, the details of which can be found on the EC2 page. Larger hosts are more powerful but have a higher cost. Currently, by default, the total number of hosts in a job flow must be 20 or less, though Amazon has a simple form to request higher limits.

After confirming, all is as expected—we launch the job flow and monitor it on the console until the status changes to **COMPLETED**. At this point, we go back to S3, look inside the bucket we specified as the output destination, and examine the output of our WordCount job, which should look very similar to the output of a local Hadoop WordCount.

An obvious question is where did the source data come from? This was one of the prepopulated fields in the job flow specification we saw during the creation process. For nonpersistent job flows, the most common model is for the source data to be read from a specified S3 source location and the resulting data written to the specified result S3 bucket.

That is it! The AWS management console allows fine-grained control of services such as S3 and EMR from the browser. Armed with nothing more than a browser and a credit card, we can launch Hadoop jobs to crunch data without ever having to worry about any of the mechanics around installing, running, or managing Hadoop.

Have a go hero – other EMR sample applications

EMR provides several other sample applications. Why not try some of them as well?

Other ways of using EMR

Although a powerful and impressive tool, the AWS management console is not always how we want to access S3 and run EMR jobs. As with all AWS services, there are both programmatic and command-line tools to use the services.

AWS credentials

Before using either programmatic or command-line tools, however, we need to look at how an account holder authenticates for AWS to make such requests. As these are chargeable services, we really do not want anyone else to make requests on our behalf. Note that as we logged directly into the AWS management console with our AWS account in the preceding example, we did not have to worry about this.

Each AWS account has several identifiers that are used when accessing the various services:

- **Account ID**: Each AWS account has a numeric ID.
- **Access key**: Each account has an associated access key that is used to identify the account making the request.
- **Secret access key**: The partner to the access key is the secret access key. The access key is not a secret and could be exposed in service requests, but the secret access key is what you use to validate yourself as the account owner.
- **Key pairs**: These are the key pairs used to log in to EC2 hosts. It is possible to either generate public/private key pairs within EC2 or to import externally generated keys into the system.

If this sounds confusing, it's because it is. At least at first. When using a tool to access an AWS service, however, there's usually a single up-front step of adding the right credentials to a configured file, and then everything just works. However, if you do decide to explore programmatic or command-line tools, it will be worth a little time investment to read the documentation for each service to understand how its security works.

The EMR command-line tools

In this book, we will not do anything with S3 and EMR that cannot be done from the AWS management console. However, when working with operational workloads, looking to integrate into other workflows, or automating service access, a browser-based tool is not appropriate, regardless of how powerful it is. Using the direct programmatic interfaces to a service provides the most granular control but requires the most effort.

Amazon provides for many services a group of command-line tools that provide a useful way of automating access to AWS services that minimizes the amount of required development. The Elastic MapReduce command-line tools, linked from the main EMR page, are worth a look if you want a more CLI-based interface to EMR but don't want to write custom code just yet.

The AWS ecosystem

Each AWS service also has a plethora of third-party tools, services, and libraries that can provide different ways of accessing the service, provide additional functionality, or offer new utility programs. Check out the developer tools hub at http://aws.amazon.com/developertools, as a starting point.

Comparison of local versus EMR Hadoop

After our first experience of both a local Hadoop cluster and its equivalent in EMR, this is a good point at which we can consider the differences of the two approaches.

As may be apparent, the key differences are not really about capability; if all we want is an environment to run MapReduce jobs, either approach is completely suited. Instead, the distinguishing characteristics revolve around a topic we touched on in *Chapter 1, What It's All About*, that being whether you prefer a cost model that involves upfront infrastructure costs and ongoing maintenance effort over one with a pay-as-you-go model with a lower maintenance burden along with rapid and conceptually infinite scalability. Other than the cost decisions, there are a few things to keep in mind:

   ◆ EMR supports specific versions of Hadoop and has a policy of upgrading over time. If you have a need for a specific version, in particular if you need the latest and greatest versions immediately after release, then the lag before these are live on EMR may be unacceptable.

   ◆ You can start up a persistent EMR job flow and treat it much as you would a local Hadoop cluster, logging into the hosting nodes and tweaking their configuration. If you find yourself doing this, its worth asking if that level of control is really needed and, if so, is it stopping you getting all the cost model benefits of a move to EMR?

   ◆ If it does come down to a cost consideration, remember to factor in all the hidden costs of a local cluster that are often forgotten. Think about the costs of power, space, cooling, and facilities. Not to mention the administration overhead, which can be nontrivial if things start breaking in the early hours of the morning.

Summary

We covered a lot of ground in this chapter, in regards to getting a Hadoop cluster up and running and executing MapReduce programs on it.

Specifically, we covered the prerequisites for running Hadoop on local Ubuntu hosts. We also saw how to install and configure a local Hadoop cluster in either standalone or pseudo-distributed modes. Then, we looked at how to access the HDFS filesystem and submit MapReduce jobs. We then moved on and learned what accounts are needed to access Elastic MapReduce and other AWS services.

We saw how to browse and create S3 buckets and objects using the AWS management console, and also how to create a job flow and use it to execute a MapReduce job on an EMR-hosted Hadoop cluster. We also discussed other ways of accessing AWS services and studied the differences between local and EMR-hosted Hadoop.

Now that we have learned about running Hadoop locally or on EMR, we are ready to start writing our own MapReduce programs, which is the topic of the next chapter.

3
Understanding MapReduce

The previous two chapters have discussed the problems that Hadoop allows us to solve, and gave some hands-on experience of running example MapReduce jobs. With this foundation, we will now go a little deeper.

In this chapter we will be:

- Understanding how key/value pairs are the basis of Hadoop tasks
- Learning the various stages of a MapReduce job
- Examining the workings of the map, reduce, and optional combined stages in detail
- Looking at the Java API for Hadoop and use it to develop some simple MapReduce jobs
- Learning about Hadoop input and output

Key/value pairs

Since *Chapter 1*, *What It's All About*, we have been talking about operations that process and provide the output in terms of key/value pairs without explaining why. It is time to address that.

What it mean

Firstly, we will clarify just what we mean by key/value pairs by highlighting similar concepts in the Java standard library. The `java.util.Map` interface is the parent of commonly used classes such as `HashMap` and (through some library backward reengineering) even the original `Hashtable`.

For any Java `Map` object, its contents are a set of mappings from a given key of a specified type to a related value of a potentially different type. A `HashMap` object could, for example, contain mappings from a person's name (`String`) to his or her birthday (`Date`).

In the context of Hadoop, we are referring to data that also comprises keys that relate to associated values. This data is stored in such a way that the various values in the data set can be sorted and rearranged across a set of keys. If we are using key/value data, it will make sense to ask questions such as the following:

- Does a given key have a mapping in the data set?
- What are the values associated with a given key?
- What is the complete set of keys?

Think back to WordCount from the previous chapter. We will go into it in more detail shortly, but the output of the program is clearly a set of key/value relationships; for each word (the key), there is a count (the value) of its number of occurrences. Think about this simple example and some important features of key/value data will become apparent, as follows:

- Keys must be unique but values need not be
- Each value must be associated with a key, but a key could have no values (though not in this particular example)
- Careful definition of the key is important; deciding on whether or not the counts are applied with case sensitivity will give different results

> Note that we need to define carefully what we mean by keys being unique here. This does not mean the key occurs only once; in our data set we may see a key occur numerous times and, as we shall see, the MapReduce model has a stage where all values associated with each key are collected together. The uniqueness of keys guarantees that if we collect together every value seen for any given key, the result will be an association from a single instance of the key to every value mapped in such a way, and none will be omitted.

Why key/value data?

Using key/value data as the foundation of MapReduce operations allows for a powerful programming model that is surprisingly widely applicable, as can be seen by the adoption of Hadoop and MapReduce across a wide variety of industries and problem scenarios. Much data is either intrinsically key/value in nature or can be represented in such a way. It is a simple model with broad applicability and semantics straightforward enough that programs defined in terms of it can be applied by a framework like Hadoop.

Of course, the data model itself is not the only thing that makes Hadoop useful; its real power lies in how it uses the techniques of parallel execution, and divide and conquer discussed in *Chapter 1, What It's All About*. We can have a large number of hosts on which we can store and execute data and even use a framework that manages the division of the larger task into smaller chunks, and the combination of partial results into the overall answer. But we need this framework to provide us with a way of expressing our problems that doesn't require us to be an expert in the execution mechanics; we want to express the transformations required on our data and then let the framework do the rest. MapReduce, with its key/value interface, provides such a level of abstraction, whereby the programmer only has to specify these transformations and Hadoop handles the complex process of applying this to arbitrarily large data sets.

Some real-world examples

To become less abstract, let's think of some real-world data that is key/value pair:

- An address book relates a name (key) to contact information (value)
- A bank account uses an account number (key) to associate with the account details (value)
- The index of a book relates a word (key) to the pages on which it occurs (value)
- On a computer filesystem, filenames (keys) allow access to any sort of data, such as text, images, and sound (values)

These examples are intentionally broad in scope, to help and encourage you to think that key/value data is not some very constrained model used only in high-end data mining but a very common model that is all around us.

We would not be having this discussion if this was not important to Hadoop. The bottom line is that if the data can be expressed as key/value pairs, it can be processed by MapReduce.

MapReduce as a series of key/value transformations

You may have come across MapReduce described in terms of key/value transformations, in particular the intimidating one looking like this:

```
{K1,V1} -> {K2, List<V2>} -> {K3,V3}
```

We are now in a position to understand what this means:

- The input to the map method of a MapReduce job is a series of key/value pairs that we'll call K1 and V1.

- The output of the `map` method (and hence input to the `reduce` method) is a series of keys and an associated list of values that are called K2 and V2. Note that each mapper simply outputs a series of individual key/value outputs; these are combined into a key and list of values in the `shuffle` method.

- The final output of the MapReduce job is another series of key/value pairs, called K3 and V3.

These sets of key/value pairs don't have to be different; it would be quite possible to input, say, names and contact details and output the same, with perhaps some intermediary format used in collating the information. Keep this three-stage model in mind as we explore the Java API for MapReduce next. We will first walk through the main parts of the API you will need and then do a systematic examination of the execution of a MapReduce job.

Pop quiz – key/value pairs

Q1. The concept of key/value pairs is...

1. Something created by and specific to Hadoop.

2. A way of expressing relationships we often see but don't think of as such.

3. An academic concept from computer science.

Q2. Are username/password combinations an example of key/value data?

1. Yes, it's a clear case of one value being associated to the other.

2. No, the password is more of an attribute of the username, there's no index-type relationship.

3. We'd not usually think of them as such, but Hadoop could still process a series of username/password combinations as key/value pairs.

The Hadoop Java API for MapReduce

Hadoop underwent a major API change in its 0.20 release, which is the primary interface in the 1.0 version we use in this book. Though the prior API was certainly functional, the community felt it was unwieldy and unnecessarily complex in some regards.

The new API, sometimes generally referred to as context objects, for reasons we'll see later, is the future of Java's MapReduce development; and as such we will use it wherever possible in this book. Note that caveat: there are parts of the pre-0.20 MapReduce libraries that have not been ported to the new API, so we will use the old interfaces when we need to examine any of these.

The 0.20 MapReduce Java API

The 0.20 and above versions of MapReduce API have most of the key classes and interfaces either in the `org.apache.hadoop.mapreduce` package or its subpackages.

In most cases, the implementation of a MapReduce job will provide job-specific subclasses of the `Mapper` and `Reducer` base classes found in this package.

> We'll stick to the commonly used K1 / K2 / K3 / and so on terminology, though more recently the Hadoop API has, in places, used terms such as KEYIN/VALUEIN and KEYOUT/VALUEOUT instead. For now, we will stick with K1 / K2 / K3 as it helps understand the end-to-end data flow.

The Mapper class

This is a cut-down view of the base `Mapper` class provided by Hadoop. For our own mapper implementations, we will subclass this base class and override the specified method as follows:

```
class Mapper<K1, V1, K2, V2>
{
        void map(K1 key, V1 value Mapper.Context context)
                throws IOException, InterruptedException
{..}
}
```

Although the use of Java generics can make this look a little opaque at first, there is actually not that much going on. The class is defined in terms of the key/value input and output types, and then the `map` method takes an input key/value pair in its parameters. The other parameter is an instance of the `Context` class that provides various mechanisms to communicate with the Hadoop framework, one of which is to output the results of a `map` or `reduce` method.

> Notice that the `map` method only refers to a single instance of K1 and V1 key/value pairs. This is a critical aspect of the MapReduce paradigm in which you write classes that process single records and the framework is responsible for all the work required to turn an enormous data set into a stream of key/value pairs. You will never have to write `map` or `reduce` classes that try to deal with the full data set. Hadoop also provides mechanisms through its `InputFormat` and `OutputFormat` classes that provide implementations of common file formats and likewise remove the need of having to write file parsers for any but custom file types.

There are three additional methods that sometimes may be required to be overridden.

```
protected void setup( Mapper.Context context)
      throws IOException, Interrupted Exception
```

This method is called once before any key/value pairs are presented to the map method. The default implementation does nothing.

```
protected void cleanup( Mapper.Context context)
      throws IOException, Interrupted Exception
```

This method is called once after all key/value pairs have been presented to the map method. The default implementation does nothing.

```
protected void run( Mapper.Context context)
      throws IOException, Interrupted Exception
```

This method controls the overall flow of task processing within a JVM. The default implementation calls the setup method once before repeatedly calling the map method for each key/value pair in the split, and then finally calls the cleanup method.

Downloading the example code

You can download the example code files for all Packt books you have purchased from your account at http://www.packtpub.com. If you purchased this book elsewhere, you can visit http://www.packtpub.com/support and register to have the files e-mailed directly to you.

The Reducer class

The Reducer base class works very similarly to the Mapper class, and usually requires only subclasses to override a single reduce method. Here is the cut-down class definition:

```
public class Reducer<K2, V2, K3, V3>
{
void reduce(K1 key, Iterable<V2> values,
      Reducer.Context context)
         throws IOException, InterruptedException
{..}
}
```

Again, notice the class definition in terms of the broader data flow (the reduce method accepts K2/V2 as input and provides K3/V3 as output) while the actual reduce method takes only a single key and its associated list of values. The Context object is again the mechanism to output the result of the method.

This class also has the setup, run, and cleanup methods with similar default implementations as with the Mapper class that can optionally be overridden:

```
protected void setup( Reduce.Context context)
throws IOException, InterruptedException
```

This method is called once before any key/lists of values are presented to the reduce method. The default implementation does nothing.

```
protected void cleanup( Reducer.Context context)
throws IOException, InterruptedException
```

This method is called once after all key/lists of values have been presented to the reduce method. The default implementation does nothing.

```
protected void run( Reducer.Context context)
throws IOException, InterruptedException
```

This method controls the overall flow of processing the task within JVM. The default implementation calls the setup method before repeatedly calling the reduce method for as many key/values provided to the Reducer class, and then finally calls the cleanup method.

The Driver class

Although our mapper and reducer implementations are all we need to perform the MapReduce job, there is one more piece of code required: the driver that communicates with the Hadoop framework and specifies the configuration elements needed to run a MapReduce job. This involves aspects such as telling Hadoop which Mapper and Reducer classes to use, where to find the input data and in what format, and where to place the output data and how to format it. There is an additional variety of other configuration options that can be set and which we will see throughout this book.

There is no default parent Driver class as a subclass; the driver logic usually exists in the main method of the class written to encapsulate a MapReduce job. Take a look at the following code snippet as an example driver. Don't worry about how each line works, though you should be able to work out generally what each is doing:

```
public class ExampleDriver
{
...
public static void main(String[] args) throws Exception
{
// Create a Configuration object that is used to set other options
    Configuration conf = new Configuration() ;
// Create the object representing the job
Job job = new Job(conf, "ExampleJob") ;
// Set the name of the main class in the job jarfile
    job.setJarByClass(ExampleDriver.class) ;
// Set the mapper class
    job.setMapperClass(ExampleMapper.class) ;
```

```
// Set the reducer class
    job.setReducerClass(ExampleReducer.class) ;
// Set the types for the final output key and value
    job.setOutputKeyClass(Text.class) ;
    job.setOutputValueClass(IntWritable.class) ;
// Set input and output file paths
FileInputFormat.addInputPath(job, new Path(args[0])) ;
FileOutputFormat.setOutputPath(job, new Path(args[1]))
// Execute the job and wait for it to complete
 System.exit(job.waitForCompletion(true) ? 0 : 1);
}
}}
```

Given our previous talk of jobs, it is not surprising that much of the setup involves operations on a `Job` object. This includes setting the job name and specifying which classes are to be used for the mapper and reducer implementations.

Certain input/output configurations are set and, finally, the arguments passed to the main method are used to specify the input and output locations for the job. This is a very common model that you will see often.

There are a number of default values for configuration options, and we are implicitly using some of them in the preceding class. Most notably, we don't say anything about the file format of the input files or how the output files are to be written. These are defined through the `InputFormat` and `OutputFormat` classes mentioned earlier; we will explore them in detail later. The default input and output formats are text files that suit our WordCount example. There are multiple ways of expressing the format within text files in addition to particularly optimized binary formats.

A common model for less complex MapReduce jobs is to have the `Mapper` and `Reducer` classes as inner classes within the driver. This allows everything to be kept in a single file, which simplifies the code distribution.

Writing MapReduce programs

We have been using and talking about WordCount for quite some time now; let's actually write an implementation, compile, and run it, and then explore some modifications.

Time for action – setting up the classpath

To compile any Hadoop-related code, we will need to refer to the standard Hadoop-bundled classes.

Add the `Hadoop-1.0.4.core.jar` file from the distribution to the Java classpath as follows:

```
$ export CLASSPATH=.:${HADOOP_HOME}/Hadoop-1.0.4.core.jar:${CLASSPATH}
```

What just happened?

This adds the `Hadoop-1.0.4.core.jar` file explicitly to the classpath alongside the current directory and the previous contents of the CLASSPATH environment variable.

Once again, it would be good to put this in your shell startup file or a standalone file to be sourced.

 We will later need to also have many of the supplied third-party libraries that come with Hadoop on our classpath, and there is a shortcut to do this. For now, the explicit addition of the core JAR file will suffice.

Time for action – implementing WordCount

We have seen the use of the WordCount example program in *Chapter 2, Getting Hadoop Up and Running*. Now we will explore our own Java implementation by performing the following steps:

1. Enter the following code into the `WordCount1.java` file:

```
Import java.io.* ;
import org.apache.hadoop.conf.Configuration ;
import org.apache.hadoop.fs.Path;
import org.apache.hadoop.io.IntWritable;
import org.apache.hadoop.io.Text;
import org.apache.hadoop.mapreduce.Job;
import org.apache.hadoop.mapreduce.Mapper;
import org.apache.hadoop.mapreduce.Reducer;
import org.apache.hadoop.mapreduce.lib.input.FileInputFormat;
import org.apache.hadoop.mapreduce.lib.output.FileOutputFormat;
```

```
public class WordCount1
{


    public static class WordCountMapper
    extends Mapper<Object, Text, Text, IntWritable>
{

        private final static IntWritable one = new IntWritable(1);
        private Text word = new Text();

        public void map(Object key, Text value, Context context
        ) throws IOException, InterruptedException {
            String[] words = value.toString().split(" ") ;

            for (String str: words)
            {
                word.set(str);
                context.write(word, one);
            }
        }
    }

    public static class WordCountReducer
    extends Reducer<Text,IntWritable,Text,IntWritable> {
        public void reduce(Text key, Iterable<IntWritable> values,
            Context context
            ) throws IOException, InterruptedException {
                int total = 0;
            for (IntWritable val : values) {
                total++ ;
            }
            context.write(key, new IntWritable(total));
        }
    }

    public static void main(String[] args) throws Exception {
        Configuration conf = new Configuration();
        Job job = new Job(conf, "word count");
        job.setJarByClass(WordCount1.class);
```

```
job.setMapperClass(WordCountMapper.class);
job.setReducerClass(WordCountReducer.class);
job.setOutputKeyClass(Text.class);
job.setOutputValueClass(IntWritable.class);
FileInputFormat.addInputPath(job, new Path(args[0]));
FileOutputFormat.setOutputPath(job, new Path(args[1]));
System.exit(job.waitForCompletion(true) ? 0 : 1);
    }
}
```

2. Now compile it by executing the following command:

```
$ javac WordCount1.java
```

What just happened?

This is our first complete MapReduce job. Look at the structure and you should recognize the elements we have previously discussed: the overall Job class with the driver configuration in its main method and the Mapper and Reducer implementations defined as inner classes.

We'll do a more detailed walkthrough of the mechanics of MapReduce in the next section, but for now let's look at the preceding code and think of how it realizes the key/value transformations we talked about earlier.

The input to the Mapper class is arguably the hardest to understand, as the key is not actually used. The job specifies TextInputFormat as the format of the input data and, by default, this delivers to the mapper data where the key is the line number in the file and the value is the text of that line. In reality, you may never actually see a mapper that uses that line number key, but it is provided.

The mapper is executed once for each line of text in the input source and every time it takes the line and breaks it into words. It then uses the Context object to output (more commonly known as emitting) each new key/value of the form <word, 1>. These are our K2/V2 values.

We said before that the input to the reducer is a key and a corresponding list of values, and there is some magic that happens between the map and reduce methods to collect together the values for each key that facilitates this, which we'll not describe right now. Hadoop executes the reducer once for each key and the preceding reducer implementation simply counts the numbers in the Iterable object and gives output for each word in the form of <word, count>. This is our K3/V3 values.

Take a look at the signatures of our `mapper` and `reducer` classes: the `WordCountMapper` class gives `IntWritable` and `Text` as input and gives `Text` and `IntWritable` as output. The `WordCountReducer` class gives `Text` and `IntWritable` both as input and output. This is again quite a common pattern, where the `map` method performs an inversion on the key and values, and instead emits a series of data pairs on which the reducer performs aggregation.

The driver is more meaningful here, as we have real values for the parameters. We use arguments passed to the class to specify the input and output locations.

Time for action – building a JAR file

Before we run our job in Hadoop, we must collect the required class files into a single JAR file that we will submit to the system.

Create a JAR file from the generated class files.

```
$ jar cvf wc1.jar WordCount1*class
```

What just happened?

We must always package our class files into a JAR file before submitting to Hadoop, be it local or on Elastic MapReduce.

 Be careful with the JAR command and file paths. If you include in a JAR file class the files from a subdirectory, the class may not be stored with the path you expect. This is especially common when using a catch-all classes directory where all source data gets compiled. It may be useful to write a script to change into the directory, convert the required files into JAR files, and move the JAR files to the required location.

Time for action – running WordCount on a local Hadoop cluster

Now we have generated the class files and collected them into a JAR file, we can run the application by performing the following steps:

1. Submit the new JAR file to Hadoop for execution.

   ```
   $ hadoop jar wc1.jar WordCount1 test.txt output
   ```

2. If successful, you should see the output being very similar to the one we obtained when we ran the Hadoop-provided sample WordCount in the previous chapter. Check the output file; it should be as follows:

```
$ Hadoop fs -cat output/part-r-00000
This 1
yes 1
a 1
is 2
test 1
this 1
```

What just happened?

This is the first time we have used the Hadoop JAR command with our own code. There are four arguments:

1. The name of the JAR file.

2. The name of the driver class within the JAR file.

3. The location, on HDFS, of the input file (a relative reference to the /user/Hadoop home folder, in this case).

4. The desired location of the output folder (again, a relative path).

> The name of the driver class is only required if a main class has not (as in this case) been specified within the JAR file manifest.

Time for action – running WordCount on EMR

We will now show you how to run this same JAR file on EMR. Remember, as always, that this costs money!

1. Go to the AWS console at http://aws.amazon.com/console, sign in, and select **S3**.

2. You'll need two buckets: one to hold the JAR file and another for the job output. You can use existing buckets or create new ones.

3. Open the bucket where you will store the job file, click on **Upload**, and add the wc1. jar file created earlier.

4. Return to the main console home page, and then go to the EMR portion of the console by selecting **Elastic MapReduce**.

5. Click on the **Create a New Job Flow** button and you'll see a familiar screen as shown in the following screenshot:

6. Previously, we used a sample application; to run our code, we need to perform different steps. Firstly, select the **Run your own application** radio button.

7. In the **Select a Job Type** combobox, select **Custom JAR**.

8. Click on the **Continue** button and you'll see a new form, as shown in the following screenshot:

We now specify the arguments to the job. Within our uploaded JAR file, our code—particularly the driver class—specifies aspects such as the `Mapper` and `Reducer` classes.

What we need to provide is the path to the JAR file and the input and output paths for the job. In the **JAR Location** field, put the location where you uploaded the JAR file. If the JAR file is called `wc1.jar` and you uploaded it into a bucket called `mybucket`, the path would be `mybucket/wc1.jar`.

In the **JAR Arguments** field, you need to enter the name of the main class and the input and output locations for the job. For files on **S3**, we can use URLs of the form `s3://bucketname/objectname`. Click on **Continue** and the familiar screen to specify the virtual machines for the job flow appears, as shown in the following screenshot:

Now continue through the job flow setup and execution as we did in *Chapter 2, Getting Hadoop Up and Running*.

What just happened?

The important lesson here is that we can reuse the code written on and for a local Hadoop cluster in EMR. Also, besides these first few steps, the majority of the EMR console is the same regardless of the source of the job code to be executed.

Through the remainder of this chapter, we will not explicitly show code being executed on EMR and will instead focus more on the local cluster, because running a JAR file on EMR is very easy.

The pre-0.20 Java MapReduce API

Our preference in this book is for the 0.20 and above versions of MapReduce Java API, but we'll need to take a quick look at the older APIs for two reasons:

1. Many online examples and other reference materials are written for the older APIs.

2. Several areas within the MapReduce framework are not yet ported to the new API, and we will need to use the older APIs to explore them.

The older API's classes are found primarily in the `org.apache.hadoop.mapred` package.

The new API classes use concrete `Mapper` and `Reducer` classes, while the older API had this responsibility split across abstract classes and interfaces.

An implementation of a `Mapper` class will subclass the abstract `MapReduceBase` class and implement the `Mapper` interface, while a custom `Reducer` class will subclass the same `MapReduceBase` abstract class but implement the `Reducer` interface.

We'll not explore `MapReduceBase` in much detail as its functionality deals with job setup and configuration, which aren't really core to understanding the `MapReduce` model. But the interfaces of pre-0.20 `Mapper` and `Reducer` are worth showing:

```
public interface Mapper<K1, V1, K2, V2>
{
void map( K1 key, V1 value, OutputCollector< K2, V2> output, Reporter
reporter) throws IOException ;
}

public interface Reducer<K2, V2, K3, V3>
{
void reduce( K2 key, Iterator<V2> values,
OutputCollector<K3, V3> output, Reporter reporter)
throws IOException ;
}
```

There are a few points to understand here:

◆ The generic parameters to the `OutputCollector` class show more explicitly how the result of the methods is presented as output.

◆ The old API used the `OutputCollector` class for this purpose, and the `Reporter` class to write status and metrics information to the Hadoop framework. The 0.20 API combines these responsibilities in the `Context` class.

- The Reducer interface uses an Iterator object instead of an Iterable object; this was changed as the latter works with the Java for each syntax and makes for cleaner code.

- Neither the map nor the reduce method could throw InterruptedException in the old API.

As you can see, the changes between the APIs alter how MapReduce programs are written but don't change the purpose or responsibilities of mappers or reducers. Don't feel obliged to become an expert in both APIs unless you need to; familiarity with either should allow you to follow the rest of this book.

Hadoop-provided mapper and reducer implementations

We don't always have to write our own Mapper and Reducer classes from scratch. Hadoop provides several common Mapper and Reducer implementations that can be used in our jobs. If we don't override any of the methods in the Mapper and Reducer classes in the new API, the default implementations are the identity Mapper and Reducer classes, which simply output the input unchanged.

Note that more such prewritten Mapper and Reducer implementations may be added over time, and currently the new API does not have as many as the older one.

The mappers are found at org.apache.hadoop.mapreduce.lib.mapper, and include the following:

- InverseMapper: This outputs (value, key)
- TokenCounterMapper: This counts the number of discrete tokens in each line of input

The reducers are found at org.apache.hadoop.mapreduce.lib.reduce, and currently include the following:

- IntSumReducer: This outputs the sum of the list of integer values per key
- ·LongSumReducer: This outputs the sum of the list of long values per key

Time for action – WordCount the easy way

Let's revisit WordCount, but this time use some of these predefined map and reduce implementations:

1. Create a new WordCountPredefined.java file containing the following code:
   ```
   import org.apache.hadoop.conf.Configuration ;
   import org.apache.hadoop.fs.Path;
   ```

```java
import org.apache.hadoop.io.IntWritable;
import org.apache.hadoop.io.Text;
import org.apache.hadoop.mapreduce.Job;
import org.apache.hadoop.mapreduce.lib.input.FileInputFormat;
import org.apache.hadoop.mapreduce.lib.output.FileOutputFormat;
import org.apache.hadoop.mapreduce.lib.map.TokenCounterMapper ;
import org.apache.hadoop.mapreduce.lib.reduce.IntSumReducer ;

public class WordCountPredefined
{
    public static void main(String[] args) throws Exception
    {
        Configuration conf = new Configuration();
        Job job = new Job(conf, "word count1");
        job.setJarByClass(WordCountPredefined.class);
        job.setMapperClass(TokenCounterMapper.class);
        job.setReducerClass(IntSumReducer.class);
        job.setOutputKeyClass(Text.class);
        job.setOutputValueClass(IntWritable.class);
        FileInputFormat.addInputPath(job, new Path(args[0]));
        FileOutputFormat.setOutputPath(job, new Path(args[1]));
        System.exit(job.waitForCompletion(true) ? 0 : 1);
    }
}
```

2. Now compile, create the JAR file, and run it as before.

3. Don't forget to delete the output directory before running the job, if you want to use the same location. Use the `hadoop fs -rmr` output, for example.

What just happened?

Given the ubiquity of WordCount as an example in the MapReduce world, it's perhaps not entirely surprising that there are predefined `Mapper` and `Reducer` implementations that together realize the entire WordCount solution. The `TokenCounterMapper` class simply breaks each input line into a series of (`token, 1`) pairs and the `IntSumReducer` class provides a final count by summing the number of values for each key.

There are two important things to appreciate here:

◆ Though WordCount was doubtless an inspiration for these implementations, they are in no way specific to it and can be widely applicable

◆ This model of having reusable mapper and reducer implementations is one thing to remember, especially in combination with the fact that often the best starting point for a new MapReduce job implementation is an existing one

Walking through a run of WordCount

To explore the relationship between mapper and reducer in more detail, and to expose some of Hadoop's inner working, we'll now go through just how WordCount (or indeed any MapReduce job) is executed.

Startup

The call to `Job.waitForCompletion()` in the driver is where all the action starts. The driver is the only piece of code that runs on our local machine, and this call starts the communication with the JobTracker. Remember that the JobTracker is responsible for all aspects of job scheduling and execution, so it becomes our primary interface when performing any task related to job management. The JobTracker communicates with the NameNode on our behalf and manages all interactions relating to the data stored on HDFS.

Splitting the input

The first of these interactions happens when the JobTracker looks at the input data and determines how to assign it to map tasks. Recall that HDFS files are usually split into blocks of at least 64 MB and the JobTracker will assign each block to one map task.

Our WordCount example, of course, used a trivial amount of data that was well within a single block. Picture a much larger input file measured in terabytes, and the split model makes more sense. Each segment of the file—or **split**, in MapReduce terminology—is processed uniquely by one map task.

Once it has computed the splits, the JobTracker places them and the JAR file containing the `Mapper` and `Reducer` classes into a job-specific directory on HDFS, whose path will be passed to each task as it starts.

Task assignment

Once the JobTracker has determined how many map tasks will be needed, it looks at the number of hosts in the cluster, how many TaskTrackers are working, and how many map tasks each can concurrently execute (a user-definable configuration variable). The JobTracker also looks to see where the various input data blocks are located across the cluster and attempts to define an execution plan that maximizes the cases when a TaskTracker processes a split/block located on the same physical host, or, failing that, it processes at least one in the same hardware rack.

This data locality optimization is a huge reason behind Hadoop's ability to efficiently process such large datasets. Recall also that, by default, each block is replicated across three different hosts, so the likelihood of producing a task/host plan that sees most blocks processed locally is higher than it may seem at first.

Task startup

Each TaskTracker then starts up a separate Java virtual machine to execute the tasks. This does add a startup time penalty, but it isolates the TaskTracker from problems caused by misbehaving map or reduce tasks, and it can be configured to be shared between subsequently executed tasks.

If the cluster has enough capacity to execute all the map tasks at once, they will all be started and given a reference to the split they are to process and the job JAR file. Each TaskTracker then copies the split to the local filesystem.

If there are more tasks than the cluster capacity, the JobTracker will keep a queue of pending tasks and assign them to nodes as they complete their initially assigned map tasks.

We are now ready to see the executed data of map tasks. If this all sounds like a lot of work, it is; and it explains why when running any MapReduce job, there is always a non-trivial amount of time taken as the system gets started and performs all these steps.

Ongoing JobTracker monitoring

The JobTracker doesn't just stop work now and wait for the TaskTrackers to execute all the mappers and reducers. It is constantly exchanging heartbeat and status messages with the TaskTrackers, looking for evidence of progress or problems. It also collects metrics from the tasks throughout the job execution, some provided by Hadoop and others specified by the developer of the map and reduce tasks, though we don't use any in this example.

Mapper input

In *Chapter 2*, *Getting Hadoop Up and Running*, our WordCount input was a simple one-line text file. For the rest of this walkthrough, let's assume it was a not-much-less trivial two-line text file:

```
This is a test
Yes this is
```

The driver class specifies the format and structure of the input file by using TextInputFormat, and from this Hadoop knows to treat this as text with the line number as the key and line contents as the value. The two invocations of the mapper will therefore be given the following input:

```
1 This is a test
2 Yes it is.
```

Mapper execution

The key/value pairs received by the mapper are the offset in the file of the line and the line contents respectively because of how the job is configured. Our implementation of the map method in WordCountMapper discards the key as we do not care where each line occurred in the file and splits the provided value into words using the split method on the standard Java String class. Note that better tokenization could be provided by use of regular expressions or the StringTokenizer class, but for our purposes this simple approach will suffice.

For each individual word, the mapper then emits a key comprised of the actual word itself, and a value of 1.

> We add a few optimizations that we'll mention here, but don't worry too much about them at this point. You will see that we don't create the IntWritable object containing the value 1 each time, instead we create it as a static variable and re-use it in each invocation. Similarly, we use a single Text object and reset its contents for each execution of the method. The reason for this is that though it doesn't help much for our tiny input file, the processing of a huge data set would see the mapper potentially called thousands or millions of times. If each invocation potentially created a new object for both the key and value output, this would become a resource issue and likely cause much more frequent pauses due to garbage collection. We use this single value and know the Context.write method will not alter it.

Mapper output and reduce input

The output of the mapper is a series of pairs of the form (word, 1); in our example these will be:

```
(This,1), (is, 1), (a, 1), (test., 1), (Yes, 1), (it, 1), (is, 1)
```

These output pairs from the mapper are not passed directly to the reducer. Between mapping and reducing is the shuffle stage where much of the magic of MapReduce occurs.

Partitioning

One of the implicit guarantees of the Reduce interface is that a single reducer will be given all the values associated with a given key. With multiple reduce tasks running across a cluster, each mapper output must therefore be partitioned into the separate outputs destined for each reducer. These partitioned files are stored on the local node filesystem.

The number of reduce tasks across the cluster is not as dynamic as that of mappers, and indeed we can specify the value as part of our job submission. Each TaskTracker therefore knows how many reducers are in the cluster and from this how many partitions the mapper output should be split into.

 We'll address failure tolerance in a later chapter, but at this point an obvious question is what happens to this calculation if a reducer fails. The answer is that the JobTracker will ensure that any failed reduce tasks are reexecuted, potentially on a different node so a transient failure will not be an issue. A more serious issue, such as that caused by a data-sensitive bug or very corrupt data in a split will, unless certain steps are taken, cause the whole job to fail.

The optional partition function

Within the `org.apache.hadoop.mapreduce` package is the `Partitioner` class, an abstract class with the following signature:

```
public abstract class Partitioner<Key, Value>
{
public abstract int getPartition( Key key, Value value,
int numPartitions) ;
}
```

By default, Hadoop will use a strategy that hashes the output key to perform the partitioning. This functionality is provided by the `HashPartitioner` class within the `org.apache.hadoop.mapreduce.lib.partition` package, but it is necessary in some cases to provide a custom subclass of `Partitioner` with application-specific partitioning logic. This would be particularly true if, for example, the data provided a very uneven distribution when the standard hash function was applied.

Reducer input

The reducer TaskTracker receives updates from the JobTracker that tell it which nodes in the cluster hold map output partitions which need to be processed by its local reduce task. It then retrieves these from the various nodes and merges them into a single file that will be fed to the reduce task.

Reducer execution

Our WordCountReducer class is very simple; for each word it simply counts the number of elements in the array and emits the final (Word, count) output for each word.

 We don't worry about any sort of optimization to avoid excess object creation here. The number of reduce invocations is typically smaller than the number of mappers, and consequently the overhead is less of a concern. However, feel free to do so if you find yourself with very tight performance requirements.

For our invocation of WordCount on our sample input, all but one word have only one value in the list of values; is has two.

Note that the word this and This had discrete counts because we did not attempt to ignore case sensitivity. Similarly, ending each sentence with a period would have stopped is having a count of two as is would be different from is.. Always be careful when working with textual data such as capitalization, punctuation, hyphenation, pagination, and other aspects, as they can skew how the data is perceived. In such cases, it's common to have a precursor MapReduce job that applies a normalization or clean-up strategy to the data set.

Reducer output

The final set of reducer output for our example is therefore:

```
(This, 1), (is, 2), (a, 1), (test, 1), (Yes, 1), (this, 1)
```

This data will be output to partition files within the output directory specified in the driver that will be formatted using the specified OutputFormat implementation. Each reduce task writes to a single file with the filename part-r-nnnnn, where nnnnn starts at 00000 and is incremented. This is, of course, what we saw in *Chapter 2, Getting Hadoop Up and Running*; hopefully the part prefix now makes a little more sense.

Shutdown

Once all tasks have completed successfully, the JobTracker outputs the final state of the job to the client, along with the final aggregates of some of the more important counters that it has been aggregating along the way. The full job and task history is available in the log directory on each node or, more accessibly, via the JobTracker web UI; point your browser to port 50030 on the JobTracker node.

That's all there is to it!

As you've seen, each MapReduce program sits atop a significant amount of machinery provided by Hadoop and the sketch provided is in many ways a simplification. As before, much of this isn't hugely valuable for such a small example, but never forget that we can use the same software and mapper/reducer implementations to do a WordCount on a much larger data set across a huge cluster, be it local or on EMR. The work that Hadoop does for you at that point is enormous and is what makes it possible to perform data analysis on such datasets; otherwise, the effort to manually implement the distribution, synchronization, and parallelization of code will be immense.

Apart from the combiner...maybe

There is one additional, and optional, step that we omitted previously. Hadoop allows the use of a combiner class to perform some early sorting of the output from the `map` method before it is retrieved by the reducer.

Why have a combiner?

Much of Hadoop's design is predicated on reducing the expensive parts of a job that usually equate to disk and network I/O. The output of the mapper is often large; it's not infrequent to see it many times the size of the original input. Hadoop does allow configuration options to help reduce the impact of the reducers transferring such large chunks of data across the network. The combiner takes a different approach, where it is possible to perform early aggregation to require less data to be transferred in the first place.

The combiner does not have its own interface; a combiner must have the same signature as the reducer and hence also subclasses the `Reduce` class from the `org.apache.hadoop.mapreduce` package. The effect of this is to basically perform a mini-reduce on the mapper for the output destined for each reducer.

Hadoop does not guarantee whether the combiner will be executed. At times, it may not be executed at all, while at times it may be used once, twice, or more times depending on the size and number of output files generated by the mapper for each reducer.

Time for action – WordCount with a combiner

Let's add a combiner to our first WordCount example. In fact, let's use our reducer as the combiner. Since the combiner must have the same interface as the reducer, this is something you'll often see, though note that the type of processing involved in the reducer will determine if it is a true candidate for a combiner; we'll discuss this later. Since we are looking to count word occurrences, we can do a partial count on the map node and pass these subtotals to the reducer.

1. Copy `WordCount1.java` to `WordCount2.java` and change the driver class to add the following line between the definition of the `Mapper` and `Reducer` classes:

    ```
    job.setCombinerClass(WordCountReducer.class);
    ```

2. Also change the class name to `WordCount2` and then compile it.

    ```
    $ javac WordCount2.java
    ```

3. Create the JAR file.

    ```
    $ jar cvf wc2.jar WordCount2*class
    ```

4. Run the job on Hadoop.

    ```
    $ hadoop jar wc2.jar WordCount2 test.txt output
    ```

5. Examine the output.

    ```
    $ hadoop fs -cat output/part-r-00000
    ```

What just happened?

This output may not be what you expected, as the value for the word `is` is now incorrectly specified as 1 instead of 2.

The problem lies in how the combiner and reducer will interact. The value provided to the reducer, which was previously (`is`, `1`, `1`), is now (`is`, `2`) because our combiner did its own summation of the number of elements for each word. However, our reducer does not look at the actual values in the `Iterable` object, it simply counts how many are there.

When you can use the reducer as the combiner

You need to be careful when writing a combiner. Remember that Hadoop makes no guarantees on how many times it may be applied to map output, it may be 0, 1, or more. It is therefore critical that the operation performed by the combiner can effectively be applied in such a way. Distributive operations such as summation, addition, and similar are usually safe, but, as shown previously, ensure the reduce logic isn't making implicit assumptions that might break this property.

Time for action – fixing WordCount to work with a combiner

Let's make the necessary modifications to WordCount to correctly use a combiner.

Copy `WordCount2.java` to a new file called `WordCount3.java` and change the `reduce` method as follows:

```
public void reduce(Text key, Iterable<IntWritable> values,
Context context) throws IOException, InterruptedException
```

```
{
int total = 0 ;
for (IntWritable val : values))
{
total+= val.get() ;
}
            context.write(key, new IntWritable(total));
}
```

Remember to also change the class name to WordCount3 and then compile, create the JAR file, and run the job as before.

What just happened?

The output is now as expected. Any map-side invocations of the combiner performs successfully and the reducer correctly produces the overall output value.

Would this have worked if the original reducer was used as the combiner and the new reduce implementation as the reducer? The answer is no, though our test example would not have demonstrated it. Because the combiner may be invoked multiple times on the map output data, the same errors would arise in the map output if the dataset was large enough, but didn't occur here due to the small input size. Fundamentally, the original reducer was incorrect, but this wasn't immediately obvious; watch out for such subtle logic flaws. This sort of issue can be really hard to debug as the code will reliably work on a development box with a subset of the data set and fail on the much larger operational cluster. Carefully craft your combiner classes and never rely on testing that only processes a small sample of the data.

Reuse is your friend

In the previous section we took the existing job class file and made changes to it. This is a small example of a very common Hadoop development workflow; use an existing job file as the starting point for a new one. Even if the actual mapper and reducer logic is very different, it's often a timesaver to take an existing working job as this helps you remember all the required elements of the mapper, reducer, and driver implementations.

Pop quiz – MapReduce mechanics

Q1. What do you always have to specify for a MapReduce job?

1. The classes for the mapper and reducer.

2. The classes for the mapper, reducer, and combiner.

3. The classes for the mapper, reducer, partitioner, and combiner.

4. None; all classes have default implementations.

Q2. How many times will a combiner be executed?

1. At least once.

2. Zero or one times.

3. Zero, one, or many times.

4. It's configurable.

Q3. You have a mapper that for each key produces an integer value and the following set of reduce operations:

◆ Reducer A: outputs the sum of the set of integer values.

◆ Reducer B: outputs the maximum of the set of values.

◆ Reducer C: outputs the mean of the set of values.

◆ Reducer D: outputs the difference between the largest and smallest values in the set.

Which of these reduce operations could safely be used as a combiner?

1. All of them.

2. A and B.

3. A, B, and D.

4. C and D.

5. None of them.

Hadoop-specific data types

Up to this point we've glossed over the actual data types used as the input and output of the map and reduce classes. Let's take a look at them now.

The Writable and WritableComparable interfaces

If you browse the Hadoop API for the `org.apache.hadoop.io` package, you'll see some familiar classes such as `Text` and `IntWritable` along with others with the `Writable` suffix.

This package also contains the `Writable` interface specified as follows:

```
import java.io.DataInput ;
import java.io.DataOutput ;
import java.io.IOException ;

public interface Writable
{
void write(DataOutput out) throws IOException ;
void readFields(DataInput in) throws IOException ;
}
```

The main purpose of this interface is to provide mechanisms for the serialization and deserialization of data as it is passed across the network or read and written from the disk. Every data type to be used as a value input or output from a mapper or reducer (that is, V1, V2, or V3) must implement this interface.

Data to be used as keys (K1, K2, K3) has a stricter requirement: in addition to `Writable`, it must also provide an implementation of the standard Java `Comparable` interface. This has the following specifications:

```
public interface Comparable
{
public int compareTO( Object obj) ;
}
```

The compare method returns -1, 0, or 1 depending on whether the compared object is less than, equal to, or greater than the current object.

As a convenience interface, Hadoop provides the `WritableComparable` interface in the `org.apache.hadoop.io` package.

```
public interface WritableComparable extends Writable, Comparable
{}
```

Introducing the wrapper classes

Fortunately, you don't have to start from scratch; as you've already seen, Hadoop provides classes that wrap the Java primitive types and implement `WritableComparable`. They are provided in the `org.apache.hadoop.io` package.

Primitive wrapper classes

These classes are conceptually similar to the primitive wrapper classes, such as Integer and Long found in java.lang. They hold a single primitive value that can be set either at construction or via a setter method.

- BooleanWritable
- ByteWritable
- DoubleWritable
- FloatWritable
- IntWritable
- LongWritable
- VIntWritable – a variable length integer type
- VLongWritable – a variable length long type

Array wrapper classes

These classes provide writable wrappers for arrays of other Writable objects. For example, an instance of either could hold an array of IntWritable or DoubleWritable but not arrays of the raw int or float types. A specific subclass for the required Writable class will be required. They are as follows:

- ArrayWritable
- TwoDArrayWritable

Map wrapper classes

These classes allow implementations of the java.util.Map interface to be used as keys or values. Note that they are defined as Map<Writable, Writable> and effectively manage a degree of internal-runtime-type checking. This does mean that compile type checking is weakened, so be careful.

- AbstractMapWritable: This is a base class for other concrete Writable map implementations
- MapWritable: This is a general purpose map mapping Writable keys to Writable values
- SortedMapWritable: This is a specialization of the MapWritable class that also implements the SortedMap interface

Time for action – using the Writable wrapper classes

Let's write a class to show some of these wrapper classes in action:

1. Create the following as `WritablesTest.java`:

```
import org.apache.hadoop.io.* ;
import java.util.* ;

public class WritablesTest
{
    public static class IntArrayWritable extends ArrayWritable
    {
        public IntArrayWritable()
        {
            super(IntWritable.class) ;
        }
    }

    public static void main(String[] args)
    {
System.out.println("*** Primitive Writables ***") ;
        BooleanWritable bool1 = new BooleanWritable(true) ;
        ByteWritable byte1 = new ByteWritable( (byte)3) ;
        System.out.printf("Boolean:%s Byte:%d\n", bool1, byte1.
get()) ;

        IntWritable i1 = new IntWritable(5) ;
        IntWritable i2 = new IntWritable( 17) ;          System.
out.printf("I1:%d I2:%d\n", i1.get(), i2.get()) ;
        i1.set(i2.get()) ;
        System.out.printf("I1:%d I2:%d\n", i1.get(), i2.get()) ;
        Integer i3 = new Integer( 23) ;
        i1.set( i3) ;
        System.out.printf("I1:%d I2:%d\n", i1.get(), i2.get()) ;

System.out.println("*** Array Writables ***") ;
        ArrayWritable a = new ArrayWritable( IntWritable.class) ;
        a.set( new IntWritable[]{ new IntWritable(1), new
IntWritable(3), new IntWritable(5)}) ;

        IntWritable[] values = (IntWritable[])a.get() ;

        for (IntWritable i: values)
```

```
        System.out.println(i) ;

        IntArrayWritable ia = new IntArrayWritable() ;
        ia.set( new IntWritable[]{ new IntWritable(1), new
IntWritable(3), new IntWritable(5)}) ;

        IntWritable[] ivalues = (IntWritable[])ia.get() ;

        ia.set(new LongWritable[]{new LongWritable(10001)}) ;

System.out.println("*** Map Writables ***") ;
        MapWritable m = new MapWritable() ;
        IntWritable key1 = new IntWritable(5) ;
        NullWritable value1 = NullWritable.get() ;
        m.put(key1, value1) ;
        System.out.println(m.containsKey(key1)) ;
        System.out.println(m.get(key1)) ;
        m.put(new LongWritable(1000000000), key1) ;
        Set<Writable> keys = m.keySet() ;

        for(Writable w: keys)
        System.out.println(w.getClass()) ;
    }
}
```

2. Compile and run the class, and you should get the following output:

```
*** Primitive Writables ***
Boolean:true Byte:3
I1:5 I2:17
I1:17 I2:17
I1:23 I2:17
*** Array Writables ***
1
3
5
*** Map Writables ***
true
(null)
class org.apache.hadoop.io.LongWritable
class org.apache.hadoop.io.IntWritable
```

What just happened?

This output should be largely self-explanatory. We create various `Writable` wrapper objects and show their general usage. There are several key points:

- As mentioned, there is no type-safety beyond `Writable` itself. So it is possible to have an array or map that holds multiple types, as shown previously.

- We can use autounboxing, for example, by supplying an `Integer` object to methods on `IntWritable` that expect an `int` variable.

- The inner class demonstrates what is needed if an `ArrayWritable` class is to be used as an input to a `reduce` function; a subclass with such a default constructor must be defined.

Other wrapper classes

- `CompressedWritable`: This is a base class to allow for large objects that should remain compressed until their attributes are explicitly accessed

- `ObjectWritable`: This is a general-purpose generic object wrapper

- `NullWritable`: This is a singleton object representation of a null value

- `VersionedWritable`: This is a base implementation to allow writable classes to track versions over time

Have a go hero – playing with Writables

Write a class that exercises the `NullWritable` and `ObjectWritable` classes in the same way as it does in the previous examples.

Making your own

As you have seen from the `Writable` and `Comparable` interfaces, the required methods are pretty straightforward; don't be afraid of adding this functionality if you want to use your own custom classes as keys or values within a MapReduce job.

Input/output

There is one aspect of our driver classes that we have mentioned several times without getting into a detailed explanation: the format and structure of the data input into and output from MapReduce jobs.

Files, splits, and records

We have talked about files being broken into splits as part of the job startup and the data in a split being sent to the mapper implementation. However, this overlooks two aspects: how the data is stored in the file and how the individual keys and values are passed to the mapper structure.

InputFormat and RecordReader

Hadoop has the concept of an **InputFormat** for the first of these responsibilities. The InputFormat abstract class in the org.apache.hadoop.mapreduce package provides two methods as shown in the following code:

```
public abstract class InputFormat<K, V>
{
public abstract List<InputSplit> getSplits( JobContext context) ;
RecordReader<K, V> createRecordReader(InputSplit split,
TaskAttemptContext context) ;
}
```

These methods display the two responsibilities of the InputFormat class:

◆ To provide the details on how to split an input file into the splits required for map processing

◆ To create a RecordReader class that will generate the series of key/value pairs from a split

The RecordReader class is also an abstract class within the org.apache.hadoop. mapreduce package:

```
public abstract class RecordReader<Key, Value> implements Closeable
{
public abstract void initialize(InputSplit split, TaskAttemptContext
context) ;
  public abstract boolean nextKeyValue()
throws IOException, InterruptedException ;
public abstract Key getCurrentKey()
throws IOException, InterruptedException ;
public abstract Value getCurrentValue()
throws IOException, InterruptedException ;
public abstract float getProgress()
throws IOException, InterruptedException ;
public abstract close() throws IOException ;
}
```

A `RecordReader` instance is created for each split and calls `getNextKeyValue` to return a Boolean indicating if another key/value pair is available and if so, the `getKey` and `getValue` methods are used to access the key and value respectively.

The combination of the `InputFormat` and `RecordReader` classes therefore are all that is required to bridge between any kind of input data and the key/value pairs required by MapReduce.

Hadoop-provided InputFormat

There are some Hadoop-provided `InputFormat` implementations within the `org.apache.hadoop.mapreduce.lib.input` package:

◆ `FileInputFormat`: This is an abstract base class that can be the parent of any file-based input

◆ `SequenceFileInputFormat`: This is an efficient binary file format that will be discussed in an upcoming section

◆ `TextInputFormat`: This is used for plain text files

> The pre-0.20 API has additional InputFormats defined in the `org.apache.hadoop.mapred` package.
>
> Note that `InputFormats` are not restricted to reading from files; `FileInputFormat` is itself a subclass of `InputFormat`. It is possible to have Hadoop use data that is not based on the files as the input to MapReduce jobs; common sources are relational databases or HBase.

Hadoop-provided RecordReader

Similarly, Hadoop provides a few common `RecordReader` implementations, which are also present within the `org.apache.hadoop.mapreduce.lib.input` package:

◆ `LineRecordReader`: This implementation is the default `RecordReader` class for text files that present the line number as the key and the line contents as the value

◆ `SequenceFileRecordReader`: This implementation reads the key/value from the binary `SequenceFile` container

Again, the pre-0.20 API has additional `RecordReader` classes in the `org.apache.hadoop.mapred` package, such as `KeyValueRecordReader`, that have not yet been ported to the new API.

OutputFormat and RecordWriter

There is a similar pattern for writing the output of a job coordinated by subclasses of OutputFormat and RecordWriter from the org.apache.hadoop.mapreduce package. We'll not explore these in any detail here, but the general approach is similar, though OutputFormat does have a more involved API as it has methods for tasks such as validation of the output specification.

 It is this step that causes a job to fail if a specified output directory already exists. If you wanted different behavior, it would require a subclass of OutputFormat that overrides this method.

Hadoop-provided OutputFormat

The following OutputFormats are provided in the org.apache.hadoop.mapreduce. output package:

- ◆ FileOutputFormat: This is the base class for all file-based OutputFormats
- ◆ NullOutputFormat: This is a dummy implementation that discards the output and writes nothing to the file
- ◆ SequenceFileOutputFormat: This writes to the binary SequenceFile format
- ◆ TextOutputFormat: This writes a plain text file

Note that these classes define their required RecordWriter implementations as inner classes so there are no separately provided RecordWriter implementations.

Don't forget Sequence files

The SequenceFile class within the org.apache.hadoop.io package provides an efficient binary file format that is often useful as an output from a MapReduce job. This is especially true if the output from the job is processed as the input of another job. The Sequence files have several advantages, as follows:

- ◆ As binary files, they are intrinsically more compact than text files
- ◆ They additionally support optional compression, which can also be applied at different levels, that is, compress each record or an entire split
- ◆ The file can be split and processed in parallel

This last characteristic is important, as most binary formats—particularly those that are compressed or encrypted—cannot be split and must be read as a single linear stream of data. Using such files as input to a MapReduce job means that a single mapper will be used to process the entire file, causing a potentially large performance hit. In such a situation, it is preferable to either use a splitable format such as `SequenceFile`, or, if you cannot avoid receiving the file in the other format, do a preprocessing step that converts it into a splitable format. This will be a trade-off, as the conversion will take time; but in many cases—especially with complex map tasks—this will be outweighed by the time saved.

Summary

We have covered a lot of ground in this chapter and we now have the foundation to explore MapReduce in more detail. Specifically, we learned how key/value pairs is a broadly applicable data model that is well suited to MapReduce processing. We also learned how to write mapper and reducer implementations using the 0.20 and above versions of the Java API.

We then moved on and saw how a MapReduce job is processed and how the `map` and `reduce` methods are tied together by significant coordination and task-scheduling machinery. We also saw how certain MapReduce jobs require specialization in the form of a custom partitioner or combiner.

We also learned how Hadoop reads data to and from the filesystem. It uses the concept of `InputFormat` and `OutputFormat` to handle the file as a whole and `RecordReader` and `RecordWriter` to translate the format to and from key/value pairs.

With this knowledge, we will now move on to a case study in the next chapter, which demonstrates the ongoing development and enhancement of a MapReduce application that processes a large data set.

4

Developing MapReduce Programs

Now that we have explored the technology of MapReduce, we will spend this chapter looking at how to put it to use. In particular, we will take a more substantial dataset and look at ways to approach its analysis by using the tools provided by MapReduce.

In this chapter we will cover the following topics:

◆ Hadoop Streaming and its uses

◆ The UFO sighting dataset

◆ Using Streaming as a development/debugging tool

◆ Using multiple mappers in a single job

◆ Efficiently sharing utility files and data across the cluster

◆ Reporting job and task status and log information useful for debugging

Throughout this chapter, the goal is to introduce both concrete tools and ideas about how to approach the analysis of a new data set. We shall start by looking at how to use scripting programming languages to aid MapReduce prototyping and initial analysis. Though it may seem strange to learn the Java API in the previous chapter and immediately move to different languages, our goal here is to provide you with an awareness of different ways to approach the problems you face. Just as many jobs make little sense being implemented in anything but the Java API, there are other situations where using another approach is best suited. Consider these techniques as new additions to your tool belt and with that experience you will know more easily which is the best fit for a given scenario.

Using languages other than Java with Hadoop

We have mentioned previously that MapReduce programs don't have to be written in Java. Most programs are written in Java, but there are several reasons why you may want or need to write your map and reduce tasks in another language. Perhaps you have existing code to leverage or need to use third-party binaries—the reasons are varied and valid.

Hadoop provides a number of mechanisms to aid non-Java development, primary amongst these are **Hadoop Pipes** that provides a native C++ interface to Hadoop and **Hadoop Streaming** that allows any program that uses standard input and output to be used for map and reduce tasks. We will use Hadoop Streaming heavily in this chapter.

How Hadoop Streaming works

With the MapReduce Java API, both map and reduce tasks provide implementations for methods that contain the task functionality. These methods receive the input to the task as method arguments and then output results via the `Context` object. This is a clear and type-safe interface but is by definition Java specific.

Hadoop Streaming takes a different approach. With Streaming, you write a map task that reads its input from standard input, one line at a time, and gives the output of its results to standard output. The reduce task then does the same, again using only standard input and output for its data flow.

Any program that reads and writes from standard input and output can be used in Streaming, such as compiled binaries, Unixshell scripts, or programs written in a dynamic language such as Ruby or Python.

Why to use Hadoop Streaming

The biggest advantage to Streaming is that it can allow you to try ideas and iterate on them more quickly than using Java. Instead of a compile/jar/submit cycle, you just write the scripts and pass them as arguments to the Streaming jar file. Especially when doing initial analysis on a new dataset or trying out new ideas, this can significantly speed up development.

The classic debate regarding dynamic versus static languages balances the benefits of swift development against runtime performance and type checking. These dynamic downsides also apply when using Streaming. Consequently, we favor use of Streaming for up-front analysis and Java for the implementation of jobs that will be executed on the production cluster.

We will use Ruby for Streaming examples in this chapter, but that is a personal preference. If you prefer shell scripting or another language, such as Python, then take the opportunity to convert the scripts used here into the language of your choice.

Time for action – implementing WordCount using Streaming

Let's flog the dead horse of WordCount one more time and implement it using Streaming by performing the following steps:

1. Save the following file to wcmapper.rb:

```ruby
#/bin/env ruby

while line = gets
    words = line.split("\t")
    words.each{ |word| puts word.strip+"\t1"}}
end
```

2. Make the file executable by executing the following command:

```
$ chmod +x wcmapper.rb
```

3. Save the following file to wcreducer.rb:

```ruby
#!/usr/bin/env ruby

current = nil
count = 0

while line = gets
    word, counter = line.split("\t")

    if word == current
        count = count+1
    else
        puts current+"\t"+count.to_s if current
        current = word
        count = 1
    end
end
puts current+"\t"+count.to_s
```

4. Make the file executable by executing the following command:

```
$ chmod +x wcreducer.rb
```

5. Execute the scripts as a Streaming job using the datafile from the previous chapter:

```
$ hadoop jar hadoop/contrib/streaming/hadoop-streaming-1.0.3.jar
-file wcmapper.rb -mapper wcmapper.rb -file wcreducer.rb
-reducer wcreducer.rb -input test.txt -output output
packageJobJar: [wcmapper.rb, wcreducer.rb, /tmp/hadoop-
hadoop/hadoop-unjar1531650352198893161/] [] /tmp/
streamjob937274081293220534.jar tmpDir=null
12/02/05 12:43:53 INFO mapred.FileInputFormat: Total input paths
to process : 1
12/02/05 12:43:53 INFO streaming.StreamJob: getLocalDirs(): [/var/
hadoop/mapred/local]
12/02/05 12:43:53 INFO streaming.StreamJob: Running job:
job_201202051234_0005
...
12/02/05 12:44:01 INFO streaming.StreamJob:  map 100%  reduce 0%
12/02/05 12:44:13 INFO streaming.StreamJob:  map 100%  reduce 100%
12/02/05 12:44:16 INFO streaming.StreamJob: Job complete:
job_201202051234_0005
12/02/05 12:44:16 INFO streaming.StreamJob: Output: wcoutput
```

6. Check the result file:

```
$ hadoop fs -cat output/part-00000
```

What just happened?

Ignore the specifics of Ruby. If you don't know the language, it isn't important here.

Firstly, we created the script that will be our mapper. It uses the `gets` function to read a line from standard input, splits this into words, and uses the `puts` function to write the word and the value `1` to the standard output. We then made the file executable.

Our reducer is a little more complex for reasons we will describe in the next section. However, it performs the job we would expect, it counts the number of occurrences for each word, reads from standard input, and gives the output as the final value to standard output. Again we made sure to make the file executable.

Note that in both cases we are implicitly using Hadoop input and output formats discussed in the earlier chapters. It is the `TextInputFormat` property that processes the source file and provides each line one at a time to the map script. Conversely, the `TextOutputFormat` property will ensure that the output of reduce tasks is also correctly written as textual data. We can of course modify these if required.

Next, we submitted the Streaming job to Hadoop via the rather cumbersome command line shown in the previous section. The reason for each file to be specified twice is that any file not available on each node must be packaged up by Hadoop and shipped across the cluster, which requires it to be specified by the -file option. Then, we also need to tell Hadoop which script performs the mapper and reducer roles.

Finally, we looked at the output of the job, which should be identical to the previous Java-based WordCount implementations

Differences in jobs when using Streaming

The Streaming WordCount mapper looks a lot simpler than the Java version, but the reducer appears to have more logic. Why? The reason is that the implied contract between Hadoop and our tasks changes when we use Streaming.

In Java we knew that our map() method would be invoked once for each input key/value pair and our reduce() method would be invoked for each key and its set of values.

With Streaming we don't have the concept of the map or reduce methods anymore, instead we have written scripts that process streams of received data. This changes how we need to write our reducer. In Java the grouping of values to each key was performed by Hadoop; each invocation of the reduce method would receive a single key and all its values. In Streaming, each instance of the reduce task is given the individual ungathered values one at a time.

Hadoop Streaming does sort the keys, for example, if a mapper emitted the following data:

```
First      1
Word       1
Word       1
A          1
First      1
```

The Streaming reducer would receive this data in the following order:

```
A          1
First      1
First      1
Word       1
Word       1
```

Hadoop still collects the values for each key and ensures that each key is passed only to a single reducer. In other words, a reducer gets all the values for a number of keys and they are grouped together; however, they are not packaged into individual executions of the reducer, that is, one per key, as with the Java API.

This should explain the mechanism used in the Ruby reducer; it first sets empty default values for the current word; then after reading each line it determines if this is another value for the current key, and if so, increments the count. If not, then there will be no more values for the previous key and its final output is sent to standard output and the counting begins again for the new word.

After reading so much in the earlier chapters about how great it is for Hadoop to do so much for us, this may seem a lot more complex, but after you write a few Streaming reducers it's actually not as bad as it may first appear. Also remember that Hadoop does still manage the assignment of splits to individual map tasks and the necessary coordination that sends the values for a given key to the same reducer. This behavior can be modified through configuration settings to change the number of mappers and reducers just as with the Java API.

Analyzing a large dataset

Armed with our abilities to write MapReduce jobs in both Java and Streaming, we'll now explore a more significant dataset than any we've looked at before. In the following section, we will attempt to show how to approach such analysis and the sorts of questions Hadoop allows you to ask of a large dataset.

Getting the UFO sighting dataset

We will use a public domain dataset of over 60,000 UFO sightings. This is hosted by InfoChimps at `http://www.infochimps.com/datasets/60000-documented-ufo-sightings-with-text-descriptions-and-metada`.

You will need to register for a free InfoChimps account to download a copy of the data.

The data comprises a series of UFO sighting records with the following fields:

1. **Sighting date**: This field gives the date when the UFO sighting occurred.
2. **Recorded date**: This field gives the date when the sighting was reported, often different to the sighting date.
3. **Location**: This field gives the location where the sighting occurred.
4. **Shape**: This field gives a brief summary of the shape of the UFO, for example, diamond, lights, cylinder.
5. **Duration**: This field gives the duration of how long the sighting lasted.
6. **Description**: This field gives free text details of the sighting.

Once downloaded, you will find the data in a few formats. We will be using the `.tsv` (tab-separated value) version.

Getting a feel for the dataset

When faced with a new dataset it is often difficult to get a feel for the nature, breadth, and quality of the data involved. There are several questions, the answers to which will affect how you approach the follow-on analysis, in particular:

- How big is the dataset?
- How complete are the records?
- How well do the records match the expected format?

The first is a simple question of scale; are we talking hundreds, thousands, millions, or more records? The second question asks how complete the records are. If you expect each record to have 10 fields (if this is structured or semi-structured data), how many have key fields populated with data? The last question expands on this point, how well do the records match your expectations of format and representation?

Time for action – summarizing the UFO data

Now we have the data, let's get an initial summarization of its size and how many records may be incomplete:

1. With the UFO **tab-separated value (TSV)** file on HDFS saved as `ufo.tsv`, save the following file to `summarymapper.rb`:

```ruby
#!/usr/bin/env ruby

while line = gets
    puts "total\t1"
    parts = line.split("\t")
    puts "badline\t1" if parts.size != 6
    puts "sighted\t1" if !parts[0].empty?
    puts "recorded\t1" if !parts[1].empty?
    puts "location\t1" if !parts[2].empty?
    puts "shape\t1" if !parts[3].empty?
    puts "duration\t1" if !parts[4].empty?
    puts "description\t1" if !parts[5].empty?
end
```

2. Make the file executable by executing the following command:

```
$ chmod +x summarymapper.rb
```

3. Execute the job as follows by using Streaming:

```
$ hadoop jar hadoop/contrib/streaming/hadoop-streaming-1.0.3.jar
-file summarymapper.rb -mapper summarymapper.rb -file wcreducer.rb
-reducer wcreducer.rb -input ufo.tsv -output ufosummary
```

4. Retrieve the summary data:

```
$ hadoop fs -cat ufosummary/part-0000
```

What just happened?

Remember that our UFO sightings should have six fields as described previously. They are listed as follows:

◆ The date of the sighting

◆ The date the sighting was reported

◆ The location of the sighting

◆ The shape of the object

◆ The duration of the sighting

◆ A free text description of the event

The mapper examines the file and counts the total number of records in addition to identifying potentially incomplete records.

We produce the overall count by simply recording how many distinct records are encountered while processing the file. We identify potentially incomplete records by flagging those that either do not contain exactly six fields or have at least one field that has a null value.

Therefore, the implementation of the mapper reads each line and does three things as it proceeds through the file:

◆ It gives the output of a token to be incremented in the total number of records processed

◆ It splits the record on tab boundaries and records any occurrence of lines which do not result in six fields' values

- For each of the six expected fields it reports when the values present are other than an empty string, that is, there is data in the field, though this doesn't actually say anything about the quality of that data

We wrote this mapper intentionally to produce the output of the form (token, count). Doing this allowed us to use our existing WordCount reducer from our earlier implementations as the reducer for this job. There are certainly more efficient implementations, but as this job is unlikely to be frequently executed, the convenience is worth it.

At the time of writing, the result of this job was as follows:

```
badline324
description61372
duration58961
location61377
recorded61377
shape58855
sighted61377
total61377
```

We see from these figures that we have 61,300records. All of these provide values for the sighted date, reported date, and location fields. Around 58,000-59,000 records have values for shape and duration, and almost all have a description.

When split on tab characters there were 372 lines found to not have exactly six fields. However, since only five records had no value for description, this suggests that the bad records typically have too many tabs as opposed to too few. We could of course alter our mapper to gather detailed information on this fact. This is likely due to tabs being used in the free text description, so for now we will do our analysis expecting most records to have correctly placed values for all the six fields, but not make any assumptions regarding further tabs in each record.

Examining UFO shapes

Out of all the fields in these reports, it was shape that immediately interested us most, as it could offer some interesting ways of grouping the data depending on what sort of information we have in that field.

Time for action – summarizing the shape data

Just as we provided a summarization for the overall UFO data set earlier, let's now do a more focused summarization on the data provided for UFO shapes:

1. Save the following to `shapemapper.rb`:

```ruby
#!/usr/bin/env ruby

while line = gets
    parts = line.split("\t")
    if parts.size == 6
        shape = parts[3].strip
        puts shape+"\t1" if !shape.empty?
    end
end
```

2. Make the file executable:

```
$ chmod +x shapemapper.rb
```

3. Execute the job once again using the WordCount reducer:

```
$ hadoop jar hadoop/contrib/streaming/hadoop-streaming-1.0.3.jarr
--file shapemapper.rb -mapper shapemapper.rb -file wcreducer.rb
-reducer wcreducer.rb -input ufo.tsv -output shapes
```

4. Retrieve the shape info:

```
$ hadoop fs -cat shapes/part-00000
```

What just happened?

Our mapper here is pretty simple. It breaks each record into its constituent fields, discards any without exactly six fields, and gives a counter as the output for any non-empty shape value.

For our purposes here, we are happy to ignore any records that don't precisely match the specification we expect. Perhaps one record is the single UFO sighting that will prove it once and for all, but even so it wouldn't likely make much difference to our analysis. Think about the potential value of individual records before deciding to so easily discard some. If you are working primarily on large aggregations where you care mostly about trends, individual records likely don't matter. But in cases where single individual values could materially affect the analysis or must be accounted for, an approach of trying to parse and recover more conservatively rather than discard may be best. We'll talk more about this trade-off in *Chapter 6, When Things Break*.

After the usual routine of making the mapper executable and running the job we produced, data showing 29 different UFO shapes were reported. Here's some sample output tabulated in compact form for space reasons:

```
changed1 changing1533 chevron758 cigar1774
circle5250 cone265 crescent2 cross177
cylinder981 delta8 diamond909 disk4798
dome1 egg661 fireball3437 flare1
flash988 formation1775 hexagon1 light12140
other4574 oval2859 pyramid1 rectangle957
round2 sphere3614 teardrop592 triangle6036
unknown4459
```

As we can see, there is a wide variance in sighting frequency. Some such as pyramid occur only once, while light comprises more than a fifth of all reported shapes. Considering many UFO sightings are at night, it could be argued that a description of light is not terribly useful or specific and when combined with the values for other and unknown we see that around 21000 of our 58000 reported shapes may not actually be of any use. Since we are not about to run out and do additional research, this doesn't matter very much, but what's important is to start thinking of your data in these terms. Even these types of summary analysis can start giving an insight into the nature of the data and indicate what quality of analysis may be possible. In the case of reported shapes, for example, we have already discovered that out of our 61000 sightings only 58000 reported the shape and of these 21000 are of dubious value. We have already determined that our 61000 sample set only provides 37000 shape reports that we may be able to work with. If your analysis is predicated on a minimum number of samples, always be sure to do this sort of summarization up-front to determine if the data set will actually meet your needs.

Time for action – correlating of sighting duration to UFO shape

Let's do a little more detailed analysis in regards to this shape data. We wondered if there was any correlation between the duration of a sighting to the reported shape. Perhaps cigar-shaped UFOs hang around longer than the rest or formations always appear for the exact amount of time.

1. Save the following to `shapetimemapper.rb`:

    ```ruby
    #!/usr/bin/env ruby

    pattern = Regexp.new /\d* ?((min)|(sec))/

    while line = gets
    parts = line.split("\t")
    if parts.size == 6
    ```

```ruby
shape = parts[3].strip
duration = parts[4].strip.downcase
if !shape.empty? && !duration.empty?
match = pattern.match(duration)
time = /\d*/.match(match[0])[0]
unit = match[1]
time = Integer(time)
time = time * 60 if unit == "min"
puts shape+"\t"+time.to_s
end
end
end
```

2. Make the file executable by executing the following command:

```
$ chmod +x shapetimemapper.rb
```

3. Save the following to `shapetimereducer.rb`:

```ruby
#!/usr/bin/env ruby

current = nil
min = 0
max = 0
mean = 0
total = 0
count = 0

while line = gets
word, time = line.split("\t")
time = Integer(time)

if word == current
count = count+1
total = total+time
min = time if time < min
max = time if time > max
else
puts current+"\t"+min.to_s+" "+max.to_s+" "+(total/count).to_s if
current
current = word
count = 1
total = time
min = time
max = time
end
end
puts current+"\t"+min.to_s+" "+max.to_s+" "+(total/count).to_s
```

4. Make the file executable by executing the following command:

```
$ chmod +x shapetimereducer.rb
```

5. Run the job:

```
$ hadoop jar hadoop/contrib/streaminghHadoop-streaming-1.0.3.jar
-file shapetimemapper.rb -mapper shapetimemapper.rb -file
shapetimereducer.rb -reducer shapetimereducer.rb -input ufo.tsv
-output shapetime
```

6. Retrieve the results:

```
$ hadoop fs -cat shapetime/part-00000
```

What just happened?

Our mapper here is a little more involved than previous examples due to the nature of the duration field. Taking a quick look at some sample records, we found values as follows:

```
15 seconds
2 minutes
2 min
2minutes
5-10 seconds
```

In other words, there was a mixture of range and absolute values, different formatting and inconsistent terms for time units. Again for simplicity we decided on a limited interpretation of the data; we will take the absolute value if present, and the upper part of a range if not. We would assume that the strings min or sec would be present for the time units and would convert all timings into seconds. With some regular expression magic, we unpack the duration field into these parts and do the conversion. Note again that we simply discard any record that does not work as we expect, which may not always be appropriate.

The reducer follows the same pattern as our earlier example, starting with a default key and reading values until a new one is encountered. In this case, we want to capture the minimum, maximum, and mean for each shape, so use numerous variables to track the needed data.

Remember that Streaming reducers need to handle a series of values grouped into their associated keys and must identify when a new line has a changed key, and hence indicates the last value for the previous key that has been processed. In contrast, a Java reducer would be simpler as it only deals with the values for a single key in each execution.

After making both files executable we run the job and get the following results, where we removed any shape with less than 10 sightings and again made the output more compact for space reasons. The numbers for each shape are the minimum value, the maximum value, and mean respectively:

```
changing0 5400 670 chevron0 3600 333
cigar0 5400 370 circle0 7200 423
cone0 4500 498 cross2 3600 460
cylinder0 5760 380 diamond0 7800 519
disk0 5400 449 egg0 5400 383
fireball0 5400 236 flash0 7200 303
formation0 5400 434 light0 9000 462
other0 5400 418 oval0 5400 405
rectangle0 4200 352 sphere0 14400 396
teardrop0 2700 335 triangle0 18000 375
unknown0 6000 470
```

It is surprising to see the relatively narrow variance in the mean sighting duration across all shape types; most have the mean value between 350 and 430 seconds. Interestingly, we also see that the shortest mean duration is for fireballs and the maximum for changeable objects, both of which make some degree of intuitive sense. A fireball by definition wouldn't be a long-lasting phenomena and a changeable object would need a lengthy duration for its changes to be noticed.

Using Streaming scripts outside Hadoop

This last example with its more involved mapper and reducer is a good illustration of how Streaming can help MapReduce development in another way; you can execute the scripts outside of Hadoop.

It's generally good practice during MapReduce development to have a sample of the production data against which to test your code. But when this is on HDFS and you are writing Java map and reduce tasks, it can be difficult to debug problems or refine complex logic. With map and reduce tasks that read input from the command line, you can directly run them against some data to get quick feedback on the result. If you have a development environment that provides Hadoop integration or are using Hadoop in standalone mode, the problems are minimized; just remember that Streaming does give you this ability to try the scripts outside of Hadoop; it may be useful some day.

While developing these scripts the author noticed that the last set of records in his UFO datafile had data in a better structured manner than those at the start of the file. Therefore, to do a quick test on the mapper all that was required was:

```
$ tail ufo.tsv | shapetimemapper.rb
```

This principle can be applied to the full workflow to exercise both the map and reduce script.

Time for action – performing the shape/time analysis from the command line

It may not be immediately obvious how to do this sort of local command-line analysis, so let's look at an example.

With the UFO datafile on the local filesystem, execute the following command:

```
$ cat ufo.tsv | shapetimemapper.rb | sort| shapetimereducer.rb
```

What just happened?

With a single Unixcommand line, we produced output identical to our previous full MapReduce job. If you look at what the command line does, this makes sense.

Firstly, the input file is sent—a line at a time—to the mapper. The output of this is passed through the Unix sort utility and this sorted output is passed a line at a time to the reducer. This is of course a very simplified representation of our general MapReduce job workflow.

Then the obvious question is why should we bother with Hadoop if we can do equivalent analysis at the command line. The answer of course is our old friend, scale. This simple approach works fine for a file such as the UFO sightings, which though non-trivial, is only 71MB in size. To put this into context we could hold thousands of copies of this dataset on a single modern disk drive.

So what if the dataset was 71GB in size instead, or even 71TB? In the latter case, at least we would have to spread the data across multiple hosts, and then decide how to split the data, combine partial answers, and deal with the inevitable failures along the way. In other words,we would need something like Hadoop.

However, don't discount the use of command-line tools like this, such approaches should be well used during MapReduce development.

Java shape and location analysis

Let's return to the Java MapReduce API and consider some analysis of the shape and location data within the reports.

However, before we start writing code, let's think about how we've been approaching the per-field analysis of this dataset. The previous mappers have had a common pattern:

- Discard records determined to be corrupt
- Process valid records to extract the field of interest
- Output a representation of the data we care about for the record

Now if we were to write Java mappers to analyze location and then perhaps the sighting and reported time columns, we would follow a similar pattern. So can we avoid any of the consequent code duplication?

The answer is yes, through the use of `org.apache.hadoop.mapred.lib.ChainMapper`. This class provides a means by which multiple mappers are executed in sequence and it is the output of the final mapper that is passed to the reducer. `ChainMapper` is applicable not just for this type of data clean-up; when analyzing particular jobs, it is not an uncommon pattern that is useful to perform multiple map-type tasks before applying a reducer.

An example of this approach would be to write a validation mapper that could be used by all future field analysis jobs. This mapper would discard lines deemed corrupt, passing only valid lines to the actual business logic mapper that can now be focused on analyzing data instead of worrying about coarse-level validation.

An alternative approach here would be to do the validation within a custom `InputFormat` class that discards non-valid records; which approach makes the most sense will depend on your particular situation.

Each mapper in the chain is executed within a single JVM so there is no need to worry about the use of multiple mappers increasing our filesystem I/O load.

Time for action – using ChainMapper for field validation/ analysis

Let's use this principle and employ the `ChainMapper` class to help us provide some record validation within our job:

1. Create the following class as `UFORecordValidationMapper.java`:

```java
import java.io.IOException;

import org.apache.hadoop.io.* ;
import org.apache.hadoop.mapred.* ;
import org.apache.hadoop.mapred.lib.* ;

public class UFORecordValidationMapper extends MapReduceBase
implements Mapper<LongWritable, Text, LongWritable, Text>
{

    public void map(LongWritable key, Text value,
        OutputCollector<LongWritable, Text> output,
        Reporter reporter) throws IOException
{
String line = value.toString();
```

```
        if (validate(line))
            output.collect(key, value);
    }

    private boolean validate(String str)
    {
        String[] parts = str.split("\t") ;

        if (parts.length != 6)
        return false ;

        return true ;
    }
}
```

2. Create the following as UFOLocation.java:

```
import java.io.IOException;
import java.util.Iterator ;
import java.util.regex.* ;

import org.apache.hadoop.conf.* ;
import org.apache.hadoop.fs.Path;
import org.apache.hadoop.io.* ;
import org.apache.hadoop.mapred.* ;
import org.apache.hadoop.mapred.lib.* ;

public class UFOLocation
{

    public static class MapClass extends MapReduceBase
implements Mapper<LongWritable, Text, Text, LongWritable>
    {

private final static LongWritable one = new LongWritable(1);
private static Pattern locationPattern = Pattern.compile(
"[a-zA-Z]{2}[^a-zA-Z]*$") ;

public void map(LongWritable key, Text value,
OutputCollector<Text, LongWritable> output,
Reporter reporter) throws IOException
{
String line = value.toString();
        String[] fields = line.split("\t") ;
        String location = fields[2].trim() ;
```

```
        if (location.length() >= 2)
        {

            Matcher matcher = locationPattern.matcher(location) ;
            if (matcher.find() )
            {
                int start = matcher.start() ;
                String state = location.substring(start,start+2);

                output.collect(new Text(state.toUpperCase()),
                        One);
            }
        }
    }
}

public static void main(String[] args) throws Exception
{
    Configuration config = new Configuration() ;
JobConf conf = new JobConf(config, UFOLocation.class);
conf.setJobName("UFOLocation");

conf.setOutputKeyClass(Text.class);
conf.setOutputValueClass(LongWritable.class);

JobConf mapconf1 = new JobConf(false) ;
ChainMapper.addMapper( conf, UFORecordValidationMapper.class,
LongWritable.class, Text.class, LongWritable.class,
Text.class, true, mapconf1) ;

JobConf mapconf2 = new JobConf(false) ;
ChainMapper.addMapper( conf, MapClass.class,
LongWritable.class, Text.class,
Text.class, LongWritable.class, true, mapconf2) ;
conf.setMapperClass(ChainMapper.class);
conf.setCombinerClass(LongSumReducer.class);
conf.setReducerClass(LongSumReducer.class);

FileInputFormat.setInputPaths(conf,args[0]) ;
FileOutputFormat.setOutputPath(conf, new Path(args[1])) ;

JobClient.runJob(conf);
}
}
```

3. Compile both files:

```
$ javac UFORecordValidationMapper.java UFOLocation.java
```

4. Jar up the class files and submit the job to Hadoop:

```
$ Hadoop jar ufo.jar UFOLocation ufo.tsv output
```

5. Copy the output file to the local filesystem and examine it:

```
$ Hadoop fs -get output/part-00000 locations.txt
$ more locations.txt
```

What just happened?

There's quite a bit happening here, so let's look at it one piece at a time.

The first mapper is our simple validation mapper. The class follows the same interface as the standard MapReduce API and the map method simply returns the result of a utility validation method. We split this out into a separate method to highlight the functionality of the mapper, but the checks could easily have been within the main map method itself. For simplicity, we keep to our previous validation strategy of looking for the number of fields and discarding lines that don't break into exactly six tab-delimited fields.

Note that the ChainMapper class has unfortunately been one of the last components to be migrated to the context object API and as of Hadoop 1.0, it can only be used with the older API. It remains a valid concept and useful tool but until Hadoop 2.0, where it will finally be migrated into the org.apache.hadoop.mapreduce.lib.chain package, its current use requires the older approach.

The other file contains another mapper implementation and an updated driver in the main method. The mapper looks for a two-letter sequence at the end of the location field in a UFO sighting report. From some manual examination of data, it is obvious that most location fields are of the form city, state, where the standard two-character abbreviation is used for the state.

Some records, however, add trailing parenthesis, periods, or other punctuation. Some others are simply not in this format. For our purposes, we are happy to discard those records and focus on those that have the trailing two-character state abbreviation we are looking for.

The map method extracts this from the location field using another regular expression and gives the output as the capitalized form of the abbreviation along with a simple count.

The driver for the job has the most changes as the previous configuration involving a single map class is replaced with multiple calls on the ChainMapper class.

The general model is to create a new configuration object for each mapper, then add the mapper to the `ChainMapper` class along with a specification of its input and output, and a reference to the overall job configuration object.

Notice that the two mappers have different signatures. Both input a key of type `LongWritable` and value of type `Text` which are also the output types of `UFORecordValidationMapper`. `UFOLocationMapper` however outputs the reverse with a key of type Text and a value of type `LongWritable`.

The important thing here is to match the input from the final mapper in the chain (`UFOLocationMapper`) with the inputs expected by the `reduce` class (`LongSumReducer`). When using the`ChainMapper` class the mappers in the chain can have different input and output as long as the following are true:

- For all but the final mapper each map output matches the input of the subsequent mapper in the chain
- For the final mapper, its output matches the input of the reducer

We compile these classes and put them in the same jar file. This is the first time we have bundled the output from more than one Java source file together. As may be expected, there is no magic here; the usual rules on jar files, path, and class names apply. Because in this case we have both our classes in the same package, we don't have to worry about an additional import in the driver class file.

We then run the MapReduce job and examine the output, which is not quite as expected.

Have a go hero

Use the Java API and the previousChainMapper example to reimplement the mappers previously written in Ruby that produce the shape frequency and duration reports.

Too many abbreviations

The following are the first few entries from our result file of the previous job:

```
AB      286
AD      6
AE      7
AI      6
AK      234
AL      548
AM      22
AN      161
...
```

The file had 186 different two-character entries. Plainly, our approach of extracting the final character digraph from the location field was not sufficiently robust.

We have a number of issues with the data which becomes apparent after a manual analysis of the source file:

♦ There is inconsistency in the capitalization of the state abbreviations

♦ A non-trivial number of sightings are from outside the U.S. and though they may follow a similar (city, area) pattern, the abbreviation is not one of the 50 we'd expect

♦ Some fields simply don't follow the pattern at all, yet would still be captured by our regular expression

We need to filter these results, ideally by normalizing the U.S. records into correct state output and by gathering everything else into a broader category.

To perform this task we need to add to the mapper some notion of what the valid U.S. state abbreviations are. We could of course hardcode this into the mapper but that does not seem right. Although we are for now going to treat all non-U.S. sightings as a single category, we may wish to extend that over time and perhaps do a breakdown by country. If we hardcode the abbreviations, we would need to recompile our mapper each time.

Using the Distributed Cache

Hadoop gives us an alternative mechanism to achieve the goal of sharing reference data across all tasks in the job, the Distributed Cache. This can be used to efficiently make available common read-only files that are used by the map or reduce tasks to all nodes. The files can be text data as in this case but could also be additional jars, binary data, or archives; anything is possible.

The files to be distributed are placed on HDFS and added to the DistributedCache within the job driver. Hadoop copies the files onto the local filesystem of each node prior to job execution, meaning every task has local access to the files.

An alternative is to bundle needed files into the job jar submitted to Hadoop. This does tie the data to the job jar making it more difficult to share across jobs and requires the jar to be rebuilt if the data changes.

Time for action – using the Distributed Cache to improve location output

Let's now use the Distributed Cache to share a list of U.S. state names and abbreviations across the cluster:

1. Create a datafile called `states.txt` on the local filesystem. It should have the state abbreviation and full name tab separated, one per line. Or retrieve the file from this book's homepage. The file should start like the following:

   ```
   AL      Alabama
   AK      Alaska
   AZ      Arizona
   AR      Arkansas
   CA      California
   ```

   ...

2. Place the file on HDFS:

   ```
   $ hadoop fs -put states.txt states.txt
   ```

3. Copy the previous `UFOLocation.java` file to UFOLocation2.java file and make the changes by adding the following import statements:

   ```
   import java.io.* ;
   import java.net.* ;
   import java.util.* ;
   import org.apache.hadoop.fs.Path;
   import org.apache.hadoop.filecache.DistributedCache ;
   ```

4. Add the following line to the driver main method after the job name is set:

   ```
   DistributedCache.addCacheFile(new URI ("/user/hadoop/states.txt"),
   conf) ;
   ```

5. Replace the map class as follows:

   ```
       public static class MapClass extends MapReduceBase
   implements Mapper<LongWritable, Text, Text, LongWritable>
       {

           private final static LongWritable one = new
   LongWritable(1);
           private static Pattern locationPattern = Pattern.compile(
   "[a-zA-Z]{2}[^a-zA-Z]*$") ;
           private Map<String, String> stateNames ;

           @Override
   ```

```
public void configure( JobConf job)
{
    try
    {
        Path[] cacheFiles = DistributedCache.
getLocalCacheFiles(job) ;
        setupStateMap( cacheFiles[0].toString()) ;
    } catch (IOException e)
{
System.err.println("Error reading state file.") ;
        System.exit(1) ;
}
    }


    private void setupStateMap(String filename)
throws IOException
    {
        Map<String, String> states = new HashMap<String,
String>() ;
        BufferedReader reader = new BufferedReader( new
FileReader(filename)) ;
        String line = reader.readLine() ;
        while (line != null)
        {
            String[] split = line.split("\t") ;
            states.put(split[0], split[1]) ;
            line = reader.readLine() ;
        }

        stateNames = states ;
    }

    public void map(LongWritable key, Text value,
        OutputCollector<Text, LongWritable> output,
        Reporter reporter) throws IOException
    {
        String line = value.toString();
String[] fields = line.split("\t") ;
String location = fields[2].trim() ;
if (location.length() >= 2)
{

        Matcher matcher = locationPattern.matcher(location) ;
        if (matcher.find() )
```

```
            {
                int start = matcher.start() ;
                String state = location.substring(start, start+2)
;

                output.collect(newText(lookupState(state.
toUpperCase())), one);
            }
        }
    }

    private String lookupState( String state)
    {
        String fullName = stateNames.get(state) ;

        return fullName == null? "Other": fullName ;
    }
}
```

6. Compile these classes and submit the job to Hadoop. Then retrieve the result file.

What just happened?

We first created the lookup file we will use in our job and placed it on HDFS. Files to be added to the Distributed Cache must initially be copied onto the HDFS filesystem.

After creating our new job file, we added the required class imports. Then we modified the driver class to add the file we want on each node to be added to the DistributedCache. The filename can be specified in multiple ways, but the easiest way is with an absolute path to the file location on HDFS.

There were a number of changes to our mapper class. We added an overridden configure method, which we use to populate a map that will be used to associate state abbreviations with their full name.

The configure method is called on task startup and the default implementation does nothing. In our overridden version, we retrieve the array of files that have been added to the Distributed Cache. As we know there is only one file in the cache we feel safe in using the first index in this array, and pass that to a utility method that parses the file and uses the contents to populate the state abbreviation lookup map. Notice that once the file reference is retrieved, we can access the file with standard Java I/O classes; it is after all just a file on the local filesystem.

We add another method to perform the lookup that takes the string extracted from the location field and returns either the full name of the state if there is a match or the string `Other` otherwise. This is called prior to the map result being written via the `OutputCollector` class.

The result of this job should be similar to the following data:

```
Alabama     548
Alaska      234
Arizona     2097
Arkansas    534
California          7679
...
Other       4531...
...
```

This works fine but we have been losing some information along the way. In our validation mapper, we simply drop any lines which don't meet our six field criteria. Though we don't care about individual lost records, we may care if the number of dropped records is very large. Currently, our only way of determining that is to sum the number of records for each recognized state and subtract from the total number of records in the file. We could also try to have this data flow through the rest of the job to be gathered in a special reduced key but that also seems wrong. Fortunately, there is a better way.

Counters, status, and other output

At the end of every MapReducejob, we see output related to counters such as the following output:

```
12/02/12 06:28:51 INFO mapred.JobClient: Counters: 22
12/02/12 06:28:51 INFO mapred.JobClient:   Job Counters
12/02/12 06:28:51 INFO mapred.JobClient:     Launched reduce tasks=1
12/02/12 06:28:51 INFO mapred.JobClient:     Launched map tasks=18
12/02/12 06:28:51 INFO mapred.JobClient:     Data-local map tasks=18
12/02/12 06:28:51 INFO mapred.JobClient:   SkippingTaskCounters
12/02/12 06:28:51 INFO mapred.JobClient:     MapProcessedRecords=61393
...
```

It is possible to add user-defined counters that will likewise be aggregated from all tasks and reported in this final output as well as in the MapReduce web UI.

Time for action – creating counters, task states, and writing log output

We'll modify our UFORecordValidationMapper to report statistics about skipped records and also highlight some other facilities for recording information about a job:

1. Create the following as the UFOCountingRecordValidationMapper.java file:

```
import java.io.IOException;

import org.apache.hadoop.io.* ;
import org.apache.hadoop.mapred.* ;
import org.apache.hadoop.mapred.lib.* ;

public class UFOCountingRecordValidationMapper extends
MapReduceBase
implements Mapper<LongWritable, Text, LongWritable, Text>
{

    public enum LineCounters
    {
        BAD_LINES,
        TOO_MANY_TABS,
        TOO_FEW_TABS
    } ;

    public void map(LongWritable key, Text value,
        OutputCollector<LongWritable, Text> output,
        Reporter reporter) throws IOException
    {
        String line = value.toString();

        if (validate(line, reporter))
Output.collect(key, value);
    }

    private boolean validate(String str, Reporter reporter)
    {
        String[] parts = str.split("\t") ;

        if (parts.length != 6)
        {
            if (parts.length < 6)
            {
```

```
reporter.incrCounter(LineCounters.TOO_FEW_TABS, 1) ;
            }
            else
            {
                reporter.incrCounter(LineCounters.TOO_MANY_TABS,
    1) ;
            }

            reporter.incrCounter(LineCounters.BAD_LINES, 1) ;

    if((reporter.getCounter(
    LineCounters.BAD_LINES).getCounter()%10)
    == 0)
            {
                reporter.setStatus("Got 10 bad lines.") ;
                System.err.println("Read another 10 bad lines.") ;
            }

            return false ;
        }
        return true ;
    }
        }
```

2. Make a copy of the UFOLocation2.java file as the UFOLocation3.java file to use this new mapper instead of UFORecordValidationMapper:

    ...

```
        JobConf mapconf1 = new JobConf(false) ;
        ChainMapper.addMapper( conf,
UFOCountingRecordValidationMapper.class,
            LongWritable.class, Text.class, LongWritable.class,
Text.class,
            true, mapconf1) ;
```

3. Compile the files, jar them up, and submit the job to Hadoop:

    ...

```
12/02/12 06:28:51 INFO mapred.JobClient: Counters: 22
12/02/12 06:28:51 INFO mapred.JobClient:    UFOCountingRecordValida
tionMapper$LineCounters
12/02/12 06:28:51 INFO mapred.JobClient:       TOO_MANY_TABS=324
12/02/12 06:28:51 INFO mapred.JobClient:       BAD_LINES=326
12/02/12 06:28:51 INFO mapred.JobClient:       TOO_FEW_TABS=2
12/02/12 06:28:51 INFO mapred.JobClient:    Job Counters
```

4. Use a web browser to go to the MapReduce web UI (remember by default it is on port 50030 on the JobTracker host). Select the job at the bottom of the **Completed Jobs** list and you should see a screen similar to the following screenshot:

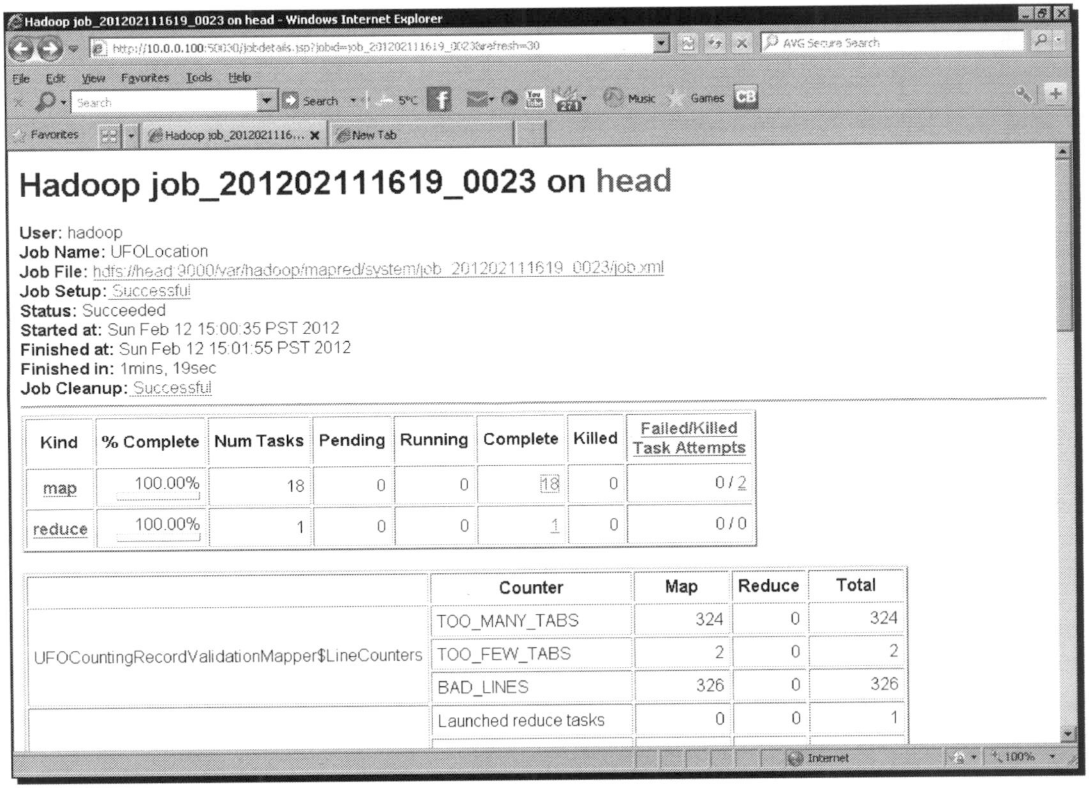

5. Click on the link to the map tasks and you should see an overview screen like the following screenshot:

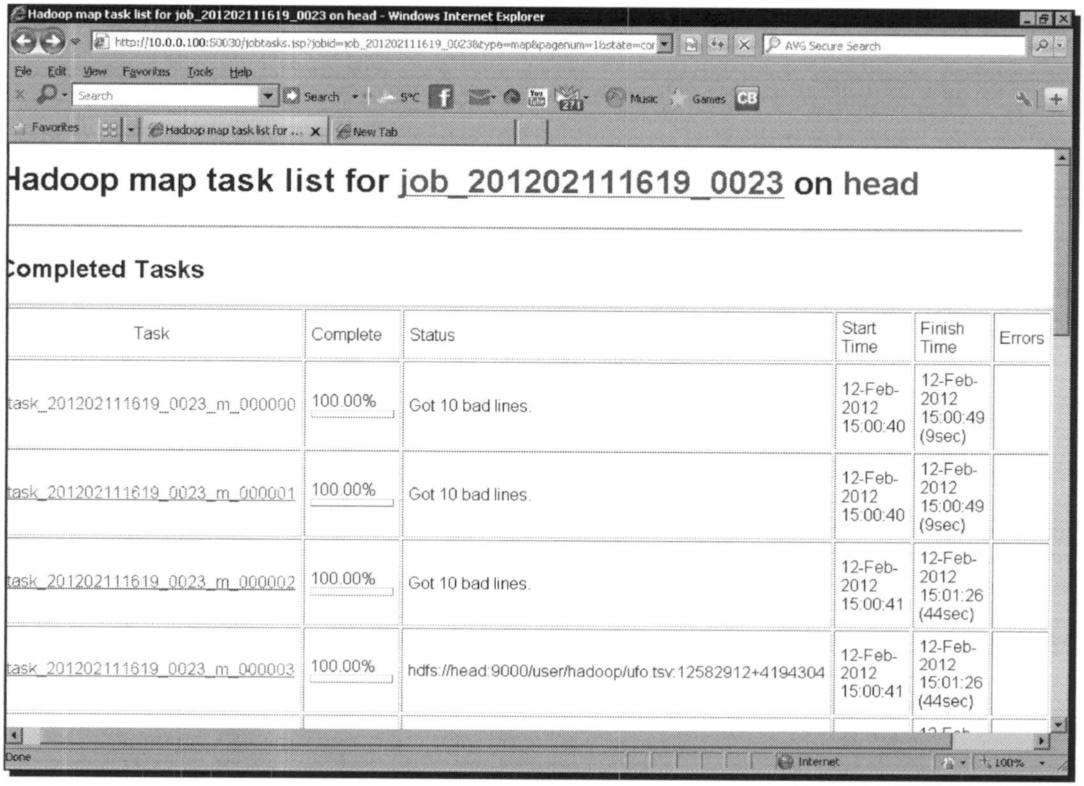

6. For one of the tasks with our custom status message, click on the link to its counters. This should give a screen similar to the one shown as follows:

Counters for task_201202111619_0023_m_000000 - Windows Internet Explorer

http://10.0.0.100:50030/taskstats.jsp?jobid=job_201202111619_0023&tipid=task_201202111619_0023_... | AVG Secure Search

File Edit View Favorites Tools Help

Search | Search | 5°C | Music | Games | CB

Favorites | Counters for task_20120... x | New Tab

Counters for task_201202111619_0023_m_000000

UFOCountingRecordValidationMapper$LineCounters

TOO_MANY_TABS	19
BAD_LINES	19

SkippingTaskCounters

MapProcessedRecords	4,411

FileSystemCounters

HDFS_BYTES_READ	4,198,400
FILE_BYTES_WRITTEN	1,065

Map-Reduce Framework

Combine output records	52
Map input records	4,411
Spilled Records	52
Map output bytes	76,359
Map input bytes	4,195,420
Combine input records	4,386
Map output records	4,386

Go back to the job
Go back to JobTracker

Done | Internet | 100%

7. Go back to the task list and click on the task ID to get the task overview similar to the following screenshot:

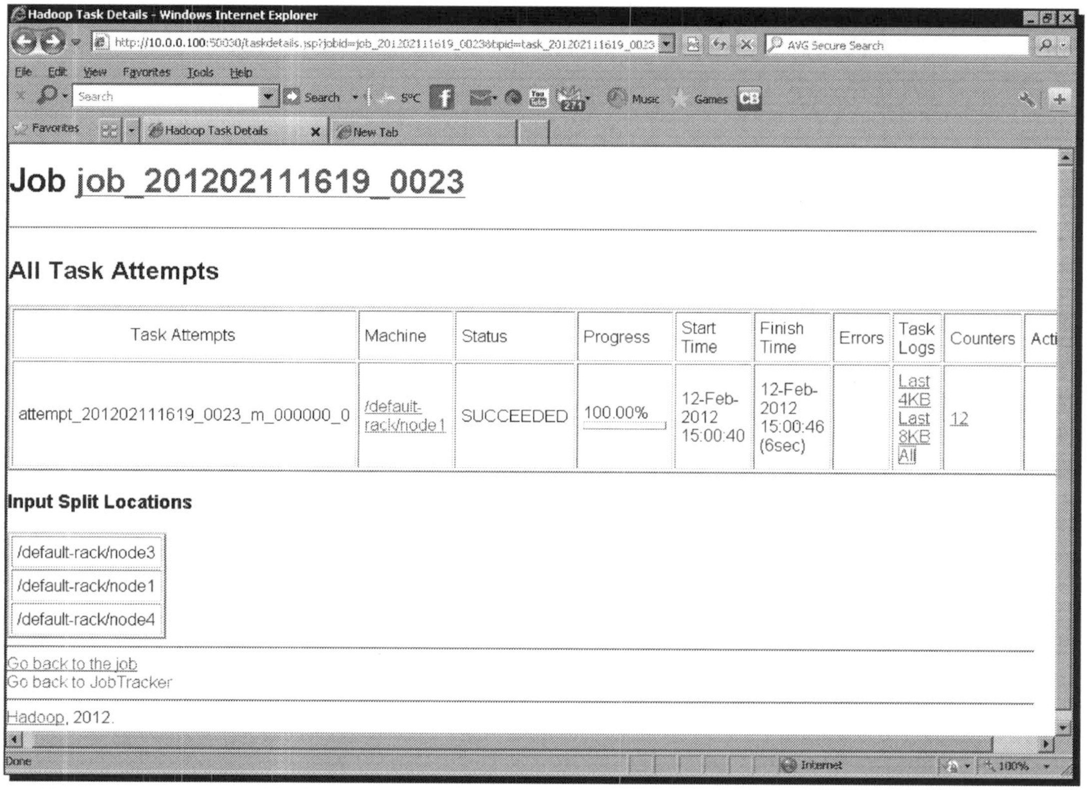

8. Under the **Task Logs** column are options for the amount of data to be displayed. Click on **All** and the following screenshot should be displayed:

9. Now log into one of the task nodes and look through the files stored under `hadoop/logs/userlogs`. There is a directory for each task attempt and several files within each; the one to look for is `stderr`.

What just happened?

The first thing we need to do in order to add new counters is to create a standard Java enumeration that will hold them. In this case we created what Hadoop would consider a counter group called **LineCounters** and within that there are three counters for the total number of bad lines, and finer grained counters for the number of lines with either too few or too many fields. This is all you need to do to create a new set of counters; define the enumeration and once you start setting the counter values, they will be automatically understood by the framework.

To add to a counter we simply increment it via the `Reporter` object, in each case here we add one each time we encounter a bad line, one with fewer than six fields, and one with more than six fields.

We also retrieve the `BAD_LINE` counter for a task and if it is a multiple of 10, do the following:

- Set the task status to reflect this fact
- Write a similar message to `stderr` with the standard Java `System.err.println` mechanism

We then go to the MapReduce UI and validate whether we can see both the counter totals in the job overview as well as tasks with the custom state message in the task list.

We then explored the web UI, looking at the counters for an individual job, then under the detail page for a task we saw, we can click on through the log files for the task.

We then looked at one of the nodes to see that Hadoop also captures the logs from each task in a directory on the filesystem under the `{HADOOP_HOME}/logs/userlogs` directory. Under subdirectories for each task attempt, there are files for the standard streams as well as the general task logs. As you will see, a busy node can end up with a large number of task log directories and it is not always easy to identify the task directories of interest. The web interface proved itself to be a more efficient view on this data.

 If you are using the Hadoop `context` object API, then counters are accessed through the `Context.getCounter().increment()` method.

Too much information!

After not worrying much about how to get status and other information out of our jobs, it may suddenly seem like we've got too many confusing options. The fact of the matter is that when running a fully distributed cluster in particular, there really is no way around the fact that the data may be spread across every node. With Java code we can't as easily mock its usage on the command line as we did with our Ruby Streaming tasks; so care needs to be taken to think about what information will be needed at runtime. This should include details concerning both the general job operation (additional statistics) as well as indicators of problems that may need further investigation.

Counters, task status messages, and good old-fashioned Java logging can work together. If there is a situation you care about, set it as a counter that will record each time it occurs and consider setting the status message of the task that encountered it. If there is some specific data, write that to `stderr`. Since counters are so easily visible, you can know pretty quickly post job completion if the situation of interest occurred. From this, you can go to the web UI and see all the tasks in which the situation was encountered at a glance. From here, you can click through to examine the more detailed logs for the task.

In fact, you don't need to wait until the job completes; counters and task status messages are updated in the web UI as the job proceeds, so you can start the investigation as soon as either counters or task status messages alert you to the situation. This is particularly useful in very long running jobs where the errors may cause you to abort the job.

Summary

This chapter covered development of a MapReduce job, highlighting some of the issues and approaches you are likely to face frequently. In particular, we learned how Hadoop Streaming provides a means to use scripting languages to write map and reduce tasks, and how using Streaming can be an effective tool for early stages of job prototyping and initial data analysis.

We also learned that writing tasks in a scripting language can provide the additional benefit of using command-line tools to directly test and debug the code. Within the Java API, we looked at the `ChainMapper` class that provides an efficient way of decomposing a complex map task into a series of smaller, more focused ones.

We then saw how the Distributed Cache provides a mechanism for efficient sharing of data across all nodes. It copies files from HDFS onto the local filesystem on each node, providing local access to the data. We also learned how to add job counters by defining a Java enumeration for the counter group and using framework methods to increment their values, and how to use a combination of counters, task status messages, and debug logs to develop an efficient job analysis workflow.

We expect most of these techniques and ideas to be the ones that you will encounter frequently as you develop MapReduce jobs. In the next chapter, we will explore a series of more advanced techniques that are less often encountered but are invaluable when they are.

5

Advanced MapReduce Techniques

Now that we have looked at a few details of the fundamentals of MapReduce and its usage, it's time to examine some more techniques and concepts involved in MapReduce. This chapter will cover the following topics:

+ Performing joins on data

+ Implementing graph algorithms in MapReduce

+ How to represent complex datatypes in a language-independent fashion

Along the way, we'll use the case studies as examples in order to highlight other aspects such as tips and tricks and identifying some areas of best practice.

Simple, advanced, and in-between

Including the word "advanced" in a chapter title is a little dangerous, as complexity is a subjective concept. So let's be very clear about the material covered here. We don't, for even a moment, suggest that this is the pinnacle of distilled wisdom that would otherwise take years to acquire. Conversely, we also don't claim that some of the techniques and problems covered in this chapter will have occurred to someone new to the world of Hadoop.

For the purposes of this chapter, therefore, we use the term "advanced" to cover things that you don't see in the first days or weeks, or wouldn't necessarily appreciate if you did. These are some techniques that provide both specific solutions to particular problems but also highlight ways in which the standard Hadoop and related APIs can be employed to address problems that are not obviously suited to the MapReduce processing model. Along the way, we'll also point out some alternative approaches that we don't implement here but which may be useful sources for further research.

Our first case study is a very common example of this latter case; performing join-type operations within MapReduce.

Joins

Few problems use a single set of data. In many cases, there are easy ways to obviate the need to try and process numerous discrete yet related data sets within the MapReduce framework.

The analogy here is, of course, to the concept of **join** in a relational database. It is very natural to segment data into numerous tables and then use SQL statements that join tables together to retrieve data from multiple sources. The canonical example is where a main table has only ID numbers for particular facts, and joins against other tables are used to extract data about the information referred to by the unique ID.

When this is a bad idea

It is possible to implement joins in MapReduce. Indeed, as we'll see, the problem is less about the ability to do it and more the choice of which of many potential strategies to employ.

However, MapReduce joins are often difficult to write and easy to make inefficient. Work with Hadoop for any length of time, and you will come across a situation where you need to do it. However, if you very frequently need to perform MapReduce joins, you may want to ask yourself if your data is well structured and more relational in nature than you first assumed. If so, you may want to consider **Apache Hive** (the main topic of *Chapter 8, A Relational View on Data with Hive*) or **Apache Pig** (briefly mentioned in the same chapter). Both provide additional layers atop Hadoop that allow data processing operations to be expressed in high-level languages; in the case of Hive, through a variant of SQL.

Map-side versus reduce-side joins

That caveat out of the way, there are two basic approaches to join data in Hadoop and these are given their names depending on where in the job execution the join occurs. In either case, we need to bring multiple data streams together and perform the join through some logic. The basic difference between these two approaches is whether the multiple data streams are combined within the mapper or reducer functions.

Map-side joins, as the name implies, read the data streams into the mapper and uses logic within the mapper function to perform the join. The great advantage of a map-side join is that by performing all joining—and more critically data volume reduction—within the mapper, the amount of data transferred to the reduce stage is greatly minimized. The drawback of map-side joins is that you either need to find a way of ensuring one of the data sources is very small or you need to define the job input to follow very specific criteria. Often, the only way to do that is to preprocess the data with another MapReduce job whose sole purpose is to make the data ready for a map-side join.

In contrast, a **reduce-side join** has the multiple data streams processed through the map stage without performing any join logic and does the joining in the reduce stage. The potential drawback of this approach is that all the data from each source is pulled through the shuffle stage and passed into the reducers, where much of it may then be discarded by the join operation. For large data sets, this can become a very significant overhead.

The main advantage of the reduce-side join is its simplicity; you are largely responsible for how the jobs are structured and it is often quite straightforward to define a reduce-side join approach for related data sets. Let's look at an example.

Matching account and sales information

A common situation in many companies is that sales records are kept separate from the client data. There is, of course, a relationship between the two; usually a sales record contains the unique ID of the user account through which the sale was performed.

In the Hadoop world, these would be represented by two types of data files: one containing records of the user IDs and information for sales, and the other would contain the full data for each user account.

Frequent tasks require reporting that uses data from both these sources; say, for example, we wanted to see the total number of sales and total value for each user but do not want to associate it with an anonymous ID number, but rather with a name. This may be valuable when customer service representatives wish to call the most frequent customers—data from the sales records—but want to be able to refer to the person by name and not just a number.

Time for action – reduce-side join using MultipleInputs

We can perform the report explained in the previous section using a reduce-side join by performing the following steps:

1. Create the following tab-separated file and name it `sales.txt`:

```
00135.992012-03-15
00212.492004-07-02
00413.422005-12-20
003499.992010-12-20
00178.952012-04-02
00221.992006-11-30
00293.452008-09-10
0019.992012-05-17
```

2. Create the following tab-separated file and name it `accounts.txt`:

```
001John AllenStandard2012-03-15
002Abigail SmithPremium2004-07-13
003April StevensStandard2010-12-20
004Nasser HafezPremium2001-04-23
```

3. Copy the datafiles onto HDFS.

```
$ hadoop fs -mkdir sales
$ hadoop fs -put sales.txt sales/sales.txt
$ hadoop fs -mkdir accounts
$ hadoop fs -put accounts/accounts.txt
```

4. Create the following file and name it `ReduceJoin.java`:

```java
import java.io.* ;

import org.apache.hadoop.conf.Configuration;
import org.apache.hadoop.fs.Path;
import org.apache.hadoop.io.Text;
import org.apache.hadoop.mapreduce.*;
import org.apache.hadoop.mapreduce.lib.input.*;
import org.apache.hadoop.mapreduce.lib.input.*;

public class ReduceJoin
{

    public static class SalesRecordMapper
extends Mapper<Object, Text, Text, Text>
    {

        public void map(Object key, Text value, Context context)
throws IOException, InterruptedException
        {
            String record = value.toString() ;
            String[] parts = record.split("\t") ;

            context.write(new Text(parts[0]), new
Text("sales\t"+parts[1])) ;
        }
    }

    public static class AccountRecordMapper
extends Mapper<Object, Text, Text, Text>
    {
```

```
        public void map(Object key, Text value, Context context)
throws IOException, InterruptedException
        {
            String record = value.toString() ;
            String[] parts = record.split("\t") ;

            context.write(new Text(parts[0]), new
Text("accounts\t"+parts[1])) ;
        }
    }

    public static class ReduceJoinReducer
    extends Reducer<Text, Text, Text, Text>
    {

        public void reduce(Text key, Iterable<Text> values,
            Context context)
            throws IOException, InterruptedException
        {
            String name = "" ;
double total = 0.0 ;
            int count = 0 ;

            for(Text t: values)
            {
                String parts[] = t.toString().split("\t") ;

                if (parts[0].equals("sales"))
                {
                    count++ ;
                    total+= Float.parseFloat(parts[1]) ;
                }
                else if (parts[0].equals("accounts"))
                {
                    name = parts[1] ;
                }
            }

            String str = String.format("%d\t%f", count, total) ;
            context.write(new Text(name), new Text(str)) ;
        }
    }
```

```
        public static void main(String[] args) throws Exception
{
        Configuration conf = new Configuration();
        Job job = new Job(conf, "Reduce-side join");
        job.setJarByClass(ReduceJoin.class);
        job.setReducerClass(ReduceJoinReducer.class);
        job.setOutputKeyClass(Text.class);
        job.setOutputValueClass(Text.class);
MultipleInputs.addInputPath(job, new Path(args[0]),
TextInputFormat.class, SalesRecordMapper.class) ;
MultipleInputs.addInputPath(job, new Path(args[1]),
TextInputFormat.class, AccountRecordMapper.class) ;
        Path outputPath = new Path(args[2]);
        FileOutputFormat.setOutputPath(job, outputPath);
outputPath.getFileSystem(conf).delete(outputPath);

        System.exit(job.waitForCompletion(true) ? 0 : 1);
    }
}
```

5. Compile the file and add it to a JAR file.

    ```
    $ javac ReduceJoin.java
    $ jar -cvf join.jar *.class
    ```

6. Run the job by executing the following command:

    ```
    $ hadoop jar join.jarReduceJoin sales accounts outputs
    ```

7. Examine the result file.

    ```
    $ hadoop fs -cat /user/garry/outputs/part-r-00000
    John Allen     3        124.929998
    Abigail Smith3           127.929996
    April Stevens1           499.989990
    Nasser Hafez  1          13.420000
    ```

What just happened?

Firstly, we created the datafiles to be used in this example. We created two small data sets as this makes it easier to track the result output. The first data set we defined was the account details with four columns, as follows:

◆ The account ID

◆ The client name

- The type of account
- The date the account was opened

We then created a sales record with three columns:

- The account ID of the purchaser
- The value of the sale
- The date of the sale

Naturally, real account and sales records would have many more fields than the ones mentioned here. After creating the files, we placed them onto HDFS.

We then created the `ReduceJoin.java` file, which looks very much like the previous MapReduce jobs we have used. There are a few aspects to this job that make it special and allow us to implement a join.

Firstly, the class has two defined mappers. As we have seen before, jobs can have multiple mappers executed in a chain; but in this case, we wish to apply different mappers to each of the input locations. Accordingly, we have the sales and account data defined into the `SalesRecordMapper` and `AccountRecordMapper` classes. We used the `MultipleInputs` class from the `org.apache.hadoop.mapreduce.lib.io` package as follows:

```
MultipleInputs.addInputPath(job, new Path(args[0]),
TextInputFormat.class, SalesRecordMapper.class) ;
MultipleInputs.addInputPath(job, new Path(args[1]),
TextInputFormat.class, AccountRecordMapper.class) ;
```

As you can see, unlike in previous examples where we add a single input location, the `MultipleInputs` class allows us to add multiple sources and associate each with a distinct input format and mapper.

The mappers are pretty straightforward; the `SalesRecordMapper` class emits an output of the form `<account number>, <sales value>` while the `AccountRecordMapper` class emits an output of the form `<account number>, <client name>`. We therefore have the order value and client name for each sale being passed into the reducer where the actual join will happen.

Notice that both mappers actually emit more than the required values. The `SalesRecordMapper` class prefixes its value output with `sales` while the `AccountRecordMapper` class uses the tag `account`.

If we look at the reducer, we can see why this is so. The reducer retrieves each record for a given key, but without these explicit tags we would not know if a given value came from the sales or account mapper and hence would not understand how to treat the data value.

The `ReduceJoinReducer` class therefore treats the values in the `Iterator` object differently, depending on which mapper they came from. Values from the `AccountRecordMapper` class—and there should be only one—are used to populate the client name in the final output. For each sales record—likely to be multiple, as most clients buy more than a single item—the total number of orders is counted as is the overall combined value. The output from the reducer is therefore a key of the account holder name and a value string containing the number of orders and the total order value.

We compile and execute the class; notice how we provide three arguments representing the two input directories as well as the single output source. Because of how the `MultipleInputs` class is configured, we must also ensure we specify the directories in the right order; there is no dynamic mechanism to determine which type of file is in which location.

After execution, we examine the output file and confirm that it does indeed contain the overall totals for named clients as expected.

DataJoinMapper and TaggedMapperOutput

There is a way of implementing a reduce-side join in a more sophisticated and object-oriented fashion. Within the `org.apache.hadoop.contrib.join` package are classes such as `DataJoinMapperBase` and `TaggedMapOutput` that provide an encapsulated means of deriving the tags for map output and having them processed at the reducer. This mechanism means you don't have to define explicit tag strings as we did previously and then carefully parse out the data received at the reducer to determine from which mapper the data came; there are methods in the provided classes that encapsulate this functionality.

This capability is particularly valuable when using numeric or other non-textual data. For creating our own explicit tags as in the previous example, we would have to convert types such as integers into strings to allow us to add the required prefix tag. This will be more inefficient than using the numeric types in their normal form and relying on the additional classes to implement the tag.

The framework allows for quite sophisticated tag generation as well as concepts such as tag grouping that we didn't implement previously. There is additional work required to use this mechanism that includes overriding additional methods and using a different map base class. For straightforward joins such as in the previous example, this framework may be overkill, but if you find yourself implementing very complex tagging logic, it may be worth a look.

Implementing map-side joins

For a join to occur at a given point, we must have access to the appropriate records from each data set at that point. This is where the simplicity of the reduce-side join comes into its own; though it incurs the expense of additional network traffic, processing it by definition ensures that the reducer has all records associated with the join key.

If we wish to perform our join in the mapper, it isn't as easy to make this condition hold true. We can't assume that our input data is sufficiently well structured to allow associated records to be read simultaneously. We generally have two classes of approach here: obviate the need to read from multiple external sources or preprocess the data so that it is amenable for map-side joining.

Using the Distributed Cache

The simplest way of realizing the first approach is to take all but one data set and make it available in the Distributed Cache that we used in the previous chapter. The approach can be used for multiple data sources, but for simplicity let's discuss just two.

If we have one large data set and one smaller one, such as with the sales and account info earlier, one option would be to package up the account info and push it into the Distributed Cache. Each mapper would then read this data into an efficient data structure, such as a hash table that uses the join key as the hash key. The sales records are then processed, and during the processing of record each the needed account information can be retrieved from the hash table.

This mechanism is very effective and when one of the smaller data sets can easily fit into memory, it is a great approach. However, we are not always that lucky, and sometimes the smallest data set is still too large to be copied to every worker machine and held in memory.

Have a go hero - Implementing map-side joins

Take the previous sales/account record example and implement a map-side join using the Distributed Cache. If you load the account records into a hash table that maps account ID numbers to client names, you can use the account ID to retrieve the client name. Do this within the mapper while processing the sales records.

Pruning data to fit in the cache

If the smallest data set is still too big to be used in the Distributed Cache, all is not necessarily lost. Our earlier example, for instance, extracted only two fields from each record and discarded the other fields not required by the job. In reality, an account will be described by many attributes, and this sort of reduction will limit the data size dramatically. Often the data available to Hadoop is this full data set, but what we need is only a subset of the fields.

In such a case, therefore, it may be possible to extract from the full data set only the fields that are needed during the MapReduce job, and in doing so create a pruned data set that is small enough to be used in the cache.

 This is a very similar concept to the underlying **column-oriented databases**. Traditional relational databases store data a row at a time, meaning that the full row needs to be read to extract a single column. A column-based database instead stores each column separately, allowing a query to read only the columns in which it is interested.

If you take this approach, you need to consider what mechanism will be used to generate the data subset and how often this will be done. The obvious approach is to write another MapReduce job that does the necessary filtering and this output is then used in the Distributed Cache for the follow-on job. If the smaller data set changes only rarely, you may be able to get away with generating the pruned data set on a scheduled basis; for example, refresh it every night. Otherwise, you will need to make a chain of two MapReduce jobs: one to produce the pruned data set and the other to perform the join operation using the large set and the data in the Distributed Cache.

Using a data representation instead of raw data

Sometimes, one of the data sources is not used to retrieve additional data but is instead used to derive some fact that is then used in a decision process. We may, for example, be looking to filter sales records to extract only those for which the shipping address was in a specific locale.

In such a case, we can reduce the required data size down to a list of the applicable sales records that may more easily fit into the cache. We can again store it as a hash table, where we are just recording the fact that the record is valid, or even use something like a sorted list or a tree. In cases where we can accept some false positives while still guaranteeing no false negatives, a **Bloom filter** provides an extremely compact way of representing such information.

As can be seen, applying this approach to enable a map-side join requires creativity and not a little luck in regards to the nature of the data set and the problem at hand. But remember that the best relational database administrators spend significant time optimizing queries to remove unnecessary data processing; so it's never a bad idea to ask if you truly need to process all that data.

Using multiple mappers

Fundamentally, the previous techniques are trying to remove the need for a full cross data set join. But sometimes this is what you have to do; you may simply have very large data sets that cannot be combined in any of these clever ways.

There are classes within the `org.apache.hadoop.mapreduce.lib.join` package that support this situation. The main class of interest is `CompositeInputFormat`, which applies a user-defined function to combine records from multiple data sources.

The main limitation of this approach is that the data sources must already be indexed based on the common key, in addition to being both sorted and partitioned in the same way. The reason for this is simple: when reading from each source, the framework needs to know if a given key is present at each location. If we know that each partition is sorted and contains the same key range, simple iteration logic can do the required matching.

This situation is obviously not going to happen by accident, so again you may find yourself writing preprocess jobs to transform all the input data sources into the correct sort and partition structure.

 This discussion starts to touch on distributed and parallel join algorithms; both topics are of extensive academic and commercial research. If you are interested in the ideas and want to learn more of the underlying theory, go searching on `http://scholar.google.com`.

To join or not to join...

After our tour of joins in the MapReduce world, let's come back to the original question: are you really sure you want to be doing this? The choice is often between a relatively easily implemented yet inefficient reduce-side join, and more efficient but more complex map-side alternatives. We have seen that joins can indeed be implemented in MapReduce, but they aren't always pretty. This is why we advise the use of something like Hive or Pig if these types of problems comprise a large portion of your workload. Obviously, we can use tools such as those that do their own translation into MapReduce code under the hood and directly implement both map-side and reduce-side joins, but it's often better to use a well-engineered and well-optimized library for such workloads instead of building your own. That is after all why you are using Hadoop and not writing your own distributed processing framework!

Graph algorithms

Any good computer scientist will tell you that the graph data structure is one of the most powerful tools around. Many complex systems are best represented by graphs and a body of knowledge going back at least decades (centuries if you get more mathematical about it) provides very powerful algorithms to solve a vast variety of graph problems. But by their very nature, graphs and their algorithms are often very difficult to imagine in a MapReduce paradigm.

Graph 101

Let's take a step back and define some terminology. A graph is a structure comprising of nodes (also called vertices) that are connected by links called **edges**. Depending on the type of graph, the edges may be bidirectional or unidirectional and may have weights associated with them. For example, a city road network can be seen as a graph where the roads are the edges, and intersections and points of interest are nodes. Some streets are one-way and some are not, some have tolls, some are closed at certain times of day, and so forth.

For transportation companies, there is much money to be made by optimizing the routes taken from one point to another. Different graph algorithms can derive such routes by taking into account attributes such as one-way streets and other costs expressed as weights that make a given road more attractive or less so.

For a more current example, think of the social graph popularized by sites such as Facebook where the nodes are people and the edges are the relationships between them.

Graphs and MapReduce – a match made somewhere

The main reason graphs don't look like many other MapReduce problems is due to the stateful nature of graph processing, which can be seen in the path-based relationship between elements and often between the large number of nodes processed together for a single algorithm. Graph algorithms tend to use notions of the global state to make determinations about which elements to process next and modify such global knowledge at each step.

In particular, most of the well-known algorithms often execute in an incremental or reentrant fashion, building up structures representing processed and pending nodes, and working through the latter while reducing the former.

MapReduce problems, on the other hand, are conceptually stateless and typically based upon a divide-and-conquer approach where each Hadoop worker host processes a small subset of the data, writing out a portion of the final result where the total job output is viewed as the simple collection of these smaller outputs. Therefore, when implementing graph algorithms in Hadoop, we need to express algorithms that are fundamentally stateful and conceptually single-threaded in a stateless parallel and distributed framework. That's the challenge!

Most of the well-known graph algorithms are based upon search or traversal of the graph, often to find routes—frequently ranked by some notion of cost—between nodes. The most fundamental graph traversal algorithms are **depth-first search (DFS)** and **breadth-first search (BFS)**.The difference between the algorithms is the ordering in which a node is processed in relationship to its neighbors.

We will look at representing an algorithm that implements a specialized form of such a traversal; for a given starting node in the graph, determine the distance between it and every other node in the graph.

 As can be seen, the field of graph algorithms and theory is a huge one that we barely scratch the surface of here. If you want to find out more, the Wikipedia entry on graphs is a good starting point; it can be found at `http://en.wikipedia.org/wiki/Graph_(abstract_data_type)`.

Representing a graph

The first problem we face is how to represent the graph in a way we can efficiently process using MapReduce. There are several well-known graph representations known as pointer-based, adjacency matrix, and adjacency list. In most implementations, these representations often assume a single process space with a global view of the whole graph; we need to modify the representation to allow individual nodes to be processed in discrete map and reduce tasks.

We'll use the graph shown here in the following examples. The graph does have some extra information that will be explained later.

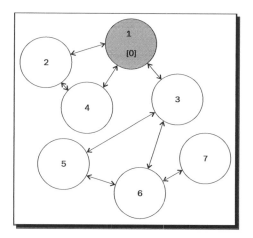

Our graph is quite simple; it has only seven nodes, and all but one of the edges is bidirectional. We are also using a common coloring technique that is used in standard graph algorithms, as follows:

◆ White nodes are yet to be processed
◆ Gray nodes are currently being processed
◆ Black nodes have been processed

As we process our graph in the following steps, we will expect to see the nodes move through these stages.

Time for action – representing the graph

Let's define a textual representation of the graph that we'll use in the following examples.

Create the following as `graph.txt`:

```
12,3,40C
21,4
31,5,6
41,2
53,6
63,5
76
```

What just happened?

We defined a file structure that will represent our graph, based somewhat on the adjacency list approach. We assumed that each node has a unique ID and the file structure has four fields, as follows:

- The node ID
- A comma-separated list of neighbors
- The distance from the start node
- The node status

In the initial representation, only the starting node has values for the third and fourth columns: its distance from itself is 0 and its status is "C", which we'll explain later.

Our graph is directional—more formally referred to as a directed graph—that is to say, if node 1 lists node 2 as a neighbor, there is only a return path if node 2 also lists node 1 as its neighbor. We see this in the graphical representation where all but one edge has an arrow on both ends.

Overview of the algorithm

Because this algorithm and corresponding MapReduce job is quite involved, we'll explain it before showing the code, and then demonstrate it in use later.

Given the previous representation, we will define a MapReduce job that will be executed multiple times to get the final output; the input to a given execution of the job will be the output from the previous execution.

Based on the color code described in the previous section, we will define three states for a node:

◆ **Pending**: The node is yet to be processed; it is in the default state (white)

◆ **Currently processing**: The node is being processed (gray)

◆ **Done**: The final distance for the node has been determined (black)

The mapper

The mapper will read in the current representation of the graph and treat each node as follows:

◆ If the node is marked as Done, it gives output with no changes.

◆ If the node is marked as Currently processing, its state is changed to Done and gives output with no other changes. Each of its neighbors gives output as per the current record with its distance incremented by one, but with no neighbors; node 1 doesn't know node 2's neighbors, for example.

◆ If the node is marked Pending, its state is changed to Currently processing and it gives output with no further changes.

The reducer

The reducer will receive one or more records for each node ID, and it will combine their values into the final output node record for that stage.

The general algorithm for the reducer is as follows:

◆ A Done record is the final output and no further processing of the values is performed

◆ For other nodes, the final output is built up by taking the list of neighbors, where it is to be found, and the highest distance and state

Iterative application

If we apply this algorithm once, we will get node 1 marked as Done, several more (its immediate neighbors) as Current, and a few others as Pending. Successive applications of the algorithm will see all nodes move to their final state; as each node is encountered, its neighbors are brought into the processing pipeline. We will show this later.

Time for action – creating the source code

We'll now see the source code to implement our graph traversal. Because the code is lengthy, we'll break it into multiple steps; obviously they should all be together in a single source file.

1. Create the following as `GraphPath.java` with these imports:

```
import java.io.* ;

import org.apache.hadoop.conf.Configuration;
import org.apache.hadoop.fs.Path;
import org.apache.hadoop.io.Text;
import org.apache.hadoop.mapreduce.Job;
import org.apache.hadoop.mapreduce.*;
import org.apache.hadoop.mapreduce.lib.input.*;
import org.apache.hadoop.mapreduce.lib.output.*;


public class GraphPath
{
```

2. Create an inner class to hold an object-oriented representation of a node:

```
// Inner class to represent a node
    public static class Node
    {
// The integer node id
        private String id ;
// The ids of all nodes this node has a path to
        private String neighbours ;
// The distance of this node to the starting node
        private int distance ;
// The current node state
        private String state ;

// Parse the text file representation into a Node object
        Node( Text t)
        {
            String[] parts = t.toString().split("\t") ;
this.id = parts[0] ;
this.neighbours = parts[1] ;
            if (parts.length<3 || parts[2].equals(""))
this.distance = -1 ;
            else
this.distance = Integer.parseInt(parts[2]) ;
```

```
                    if (parts.length< 4 || parts[3].equals(""))
this.state = "P" ;
                    else
this.state = parts[3] ;
            }

// Create a node from a key and value object pair
            Node(Text key, Text value)
            {
                this(new Text(key.toString()+"\t"+value.toString())) ;
            }

            Public String getId()
            {return this.id ;
            }

            public String getNeighbours()
            {
                return this.neighbours ;
            }

            public int getDistance()
            {
                return this.distance ;
            }

            public String getState()
            {
                return this.state ;
            }
        }
```

3. Create the mapper for the job. The mapper will create a new Node object for its input and then examine it, and based on its state do the appropriate processing.

```
    public static class GraphPathMapper
extends Mapper<Object, Text, Text, Text>
{

        public void map(Object key, Text value, Context context)
throws IOException, InterruptedException
{
            Node n = new Node(value) ;

            if (n.getState().equals("C"))
```

```
                {
// Output the node with its state changed to Done
            context.write(new Text(n.getId()), new
Text(n.getNeighbours()+"\t"+n.getDistance()+"\t"+"D")) ;

                for (String neighbour:n.getNeighbours().
split(","))
                {
// Output each neighbour as a Currently processing node
// Increment the distance by 1; it is one link further away
                    context.write(new Text(neighbour), new
Text("\t"+(n.getDistance()+1)+"\tC")) ;
                }
            }
            else
            {
// Output a pending node unchanged
            context.write(new Text(n.getId()), new
Text(n.getNeighbours()+"\t"+n.getDistance()
+"\t"+n.getState())) ;
            }

        }
    }
```

4. Create the reducer for the job. As with the mapper, this reads in a representation of a node and gives as output a different value depending on the state of the node. The basic approach is to collect from the input the largest value for the state and distance columns, and through this converge to the final solution.

```
    public static class GraphPathReducer
extends Reducer<Text, Text, Text, Text>
{

        public void reduce(Text key, Iterable<Text> values,
            Context context)
            throws IOException, InterruptedException
{
// Set some default values for the final output
            String neighbours = null ;
int distance = -1 ;
String state = "P" ;

            for(Text t: values)
{
                Node n = new Node(key, t) ;
```

```
                if (n.getState().equals("D"))
                {
// A done node should be the final output; ignore the remaining
// values
neighbours = n.getNeighbours() ;
                    distance = n.getDistance() ;
                    state = n.getState() ;
                    break ;
                }

// Select the list of neighbours when found
                if (n.getNeighbours() != null)
neighbours = n.getNeighbours() ;

// Select the largest distance
                if (n.getDistance() > distance)
distance = n.getDistance() ;

// Select the highest remaining state
                if (n.getState().equals("D") ||
(n.getState().equals("C") &&state.equals("P")))
state=n.getState() ;
                }

// Output a new node representation from the collected parts
            context.write(key, new
Text(neighbours+"\t"+distance+"\t"+state)) ;
        }
    }
```

5. Create the job driver:

```
    public static void main(String[] args) throws Exception
{
        Configuration conf = new Configuration();
        Job job = new Job(conf, "graph path");
        job.setJarByClass(GraphPath.class);
        job.setMapperClass(GraphPathMapper.class);
        job.setReducerClass(GraphPathReducer.class);
        job.setOutputKeyClass(Text.class);
        job.setOutputValueClass(Text.class);
        FileInputFormat.addInputPath(job, new Path(args[0]));
        FileOutputFormat.setOutputPath(job, new Path(args[1]));
        System.exit(job.waitForCompletion(true) ? 0 : 1);
    }
}
```

What just happened?

The job here implements the previously described algorithm that we'll execute in the following sections. The job setup is pretty standard, and apart from the algorithm definition the only new thing here is the use of an inner class to represent nodes.

The input to a mapper or reducer is often a flattened representation of a more complex structure or object. We could just use that representation, but in this case this would result in the mapper and reducer bodies being full of text and string manipulation code that would obscure the actual algorithm.

The use of the Node inner class allows the mapping from the flat file to object representation that is to be encapsulated in an object that makes sense in terms of the business domain. This also makes the mapper and reducer logic clearer as comparisons between object attributes are more semantically meaningful than comparisons with slices of a string identified only by absolute index positions.

Time for action – the first run

Let's now perform the initial execution of this algorithm on our starting representation of the graph:

1. Put the previously created graph.txt file onto HDFS:

   ```
   $ hadoop fs -mkdirgraphin
   $ hadoop fs -put graph.txtgraphin/graph.txt
   ```

2. Compile the job and create the JAR file:

   ```
   $ javac GraphPath.java
   $ jar -cvf graph.jar *.class
   ```

3. Execute the MapReduce job:

   ```
   $ hadoop jar graph.jarGraphPathgraphingraphout1
   ```

4. Examine the output file:

   ```
   $ hadoop fs -cat /home/user/hadoop/graphout1/part-r00000
   12,3,40D
   21,41C
   31,5,61C
   41,21C
   53,6-1P
   63,5-1P
   76-1P
   ```

What just happened?

After putting the source file onto HDFS and creating the job JAR file, we executed the job in Hadoop. The output representation of the graph shows a few changes, as follows:

- Node 1 is now marked as Done; its distance from itself is obviously 0
- Nodes 2, 3, and 4 – the neighbors of node 1 — are marked as Currently processing
- All other nodes are Pending

Our graph now looks like the following figure:

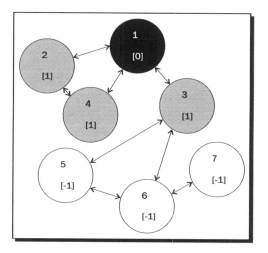

Given the algorithm, this is to be expected; the first node is complete and its neighboring nodes, extracted through the mapper, are in progress. All other nodes are yet to begin processing.

Time for action – the second run

If we take this representation as the input to another run of the job, we would expect nodes 2, 3, and 4 to now be complete, and for their neighbors to now be in the Current state. Let's see; execute the following steps:

1. Execute the MapReduce job by executing the following command:

```
$ hadoop jar graph.jarGraphPathgraphout1graphout2
```

2. Examine the output file:

```
$ hadoop fs -cat /home/user/hadoop/graphout2/part-r000000
12,3,40D
21,41D
```

```
31,5,61D
41,21D
53,62C
63,52C
76-1P
```

What just happened?

As expected, nodes 1 through 4 are complete, nodes 5 and 6 are in progress, and node 7 is still pending, as seen in the following figure:

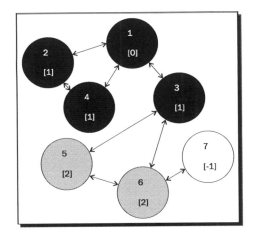

If we run the job again, we should expect nodes 5 and 6 to be Done and any unprocessed neighbors to become Current.

Time for action – the third run

Let's validate that assumption by running the algorithm for the third time.

1. Execute the MapReduce job:

   ```
   $ hadoop jar graph.jarGraphPathgraphout2graphout3
   ```

2. Examine the output file:

   ```
   $ hadoop fs -cat /user/hadoop/graphout3/part-r-00000
   12,3,40D
   21,41D
   31,5,61D
   ```

```
41,21D
53,62D
63,52D
76-1P
```

What just happened?

We now see nodes 1 through 6 are complete. But node 7 is still pending and no nodes are currently being processed, as shown in the following figure:

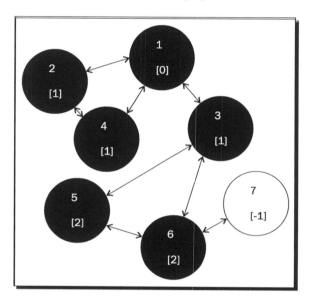

The reason for this state is that though node 7 has a link to node 6, there is no edge in the reverse direction. Node 7 is therefore effectively unreachable from node 1. If we run the algorithm one final time, we should expect to see the graph unchanged.

Time for action – the fourth and last run

Let's perform the fourth execution to validate that the output has now reached its final stable state.

1. Execute the MapReduce job:

```
$ hadoop jar graph.jarGraphPathgraphout3graphout4
```

2. Examine the output file:

```
$ hadoop fs -cat /user/hadoop/graphout4/part-r-00000
12,3,40D
21,41D
31,5,61D
41,21D
53,62D
63,52D
76-1P
```

What just happened?

The output is as expected; since node 7 is not reachable by node 1 or any of its neighbors, it will remain Pending and never be processed further. Consequently, our graph is unchanged as shown in the following figure:

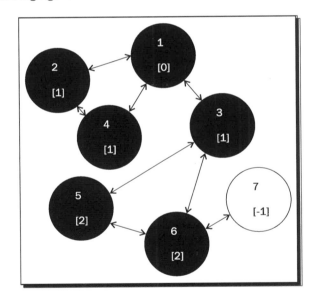

The one thing we did not build into our algorithm was an understanding of a terminating condition; the process is complete if a run does not create any new D or C nodes.

The mechanism we use here is manual, that is, we knew by examination that the graph representation had reached its final stable state. There are ways of doing this programmatically, however. In a later chapter, we will discuss custom job counters; we can, for example, increment a counter every time a new D or C node is created and only reexecute the job if that counter is greater than zero after the run.

Running multiple jobs

The previous algorithm is the first time we have explicitly used the output of one MapReduce job as the input to another. In most cases, the jobs are different; but, as we have seen, there is value in repeatedly applying an algorithm until the output reaches a stable state.

Final thoughts on graphs

For anyone familiar with graph algorithms, the previous process will seem very alien. This is simply a consequence of the fact that we are implementing a stateful and potentially recursive global and reentrant algorithm as a series of serial stateless MapReduce jobs. The important fact is not in the particular algorithm used; the lesson is in how we can take flat text structures and a series of MapReduce jobs, and from this implement something like graph traversal. You may have problems that at first don't appear to have any way of being implemented in the MapReduce paradigm; consider some of the techniques used here and remember that many algorithms can be modeled in MapReduce. They may look very different from the traditional approach, but the goal is the correct output and not an implementation of a known algorithm.

Using language-independent data structures

A criticism often leveled at Hadoop, and which the community has been working hard to address, is that it is very Java-centric. It may appear strange to accuse a project fully implemented in Java of being Java-centric, but the consideration is from a client's perspective.

We have shown how Hadoop Streaming allows the use of scripting languages to implement map and reduce tasks and how Pipes provides similar mechanisms for C++. However, one area that does remain Java-only is the nature of the input formats supported by Hadoop MapReduce. The most efficient format is SequenceFile, a binary splittable container that supports compression. However, SequenceFiles have only a Java API; they cannot be written or read in any other language.

We could have an external process creating data to be ingested into Hadoop for MapReduce processing, and the best way we could do this is either have it simply as an output of text type or do some preprocessing to translate the output format into SequenceFiles to be pushed onto HDFS. We also struggle here to easily represent complex data types; we either have to flatten them to a text format or write a converter across two binary formats, neither of which is an attractive option.

Candidate technologies

Fortunately, there have been several technologies released in recent years that address the question of cross-language data representations. They are **Protocol Buffers** (created by Google and hosted at `http://code.google.com/p/protobuf`), **Thrift** (originally created by Facebook and now an Apache project at `http://thrift.apache.org`), and **Avro** (created by Doug Cutting, the original creator of Hadoop). Given its heritage and tight Hadoop integration, we will use Avro to explore this topic. We won't cover Thrift or Protocol Buffers in this book, but both are solid technologies; if the topic of data serialization interests you, check out their home pages for more information.

Introducing Avro

Avro, with its home page at `http://avro.apache.org`, is a data-persistence framework with bindings for many programming languages. It creates a binary structured format that is both compressible and splittable, meaning it can be efficiently used as the input to MapReduce jobs.

Avro allows the definition of hierarchical data structures; so, for example, we can create a record that contains an array, an enumerated type, and a subrecord. We can create these files in any programming language, process them in Hadoop, and have the result read by a third language.

We'll talk about these aspects of language independence over the next sections, but this ability to express complex structured types is also very valuable. Even if we are using only Java, we could employ Avro to allow us to pass complex data structures in and out of mappers and reducers. Even things like graph nodes!

Time for action – getting and installing Avro

Let's download Avro and get it installed on our system.

1. Download the latest stable version of Avro from `http://avro.apache.org/releases.html`.

2. Download the latest version of the ParaNamer library from `http://paranamer.codehaus.org`.

3. Add the classes to the build classpath used by the Java compiler.

```
$ export CLASSPATH=avro-1.7.2.jar:${CLASSPATH}
$ export CLASSPATH=avro-mapred-1.7.2.jar:${CLASSPATH}
$ export CLASSPATH=paranamer-2.5.jar:${CLASSPATH
```

4. Add existing JAR files from the Hadoop distribution to the `build` classpath.

```
Export CLASSPATH=${HADOOP_HOME}/lib/Jackson-core-asl-
1.8.jar:${CLASSPATH}
```

```
Export CLASSPATH=${HADOOP_HOME}/lib/Jackson-mapred-asl-
1.8.jar:${CLASSPATH}
```

```
Export CLASSPATH=${HADOOP_HOME}/lib/commons-cli-
1.2.jar:${CLASSPATH}
```

5. Add the new JAR files to the Hadoop `lib` directory.

```
$cpavro-1.7.2.jar ${HADOOP_HOME}/lib
```

```
$cpavro-1.7.2.jar ${HADOOP_HOME}/lib
```

```
$cpavro-mapred-1.7.2.jar ${HADOOP_HOME}/lib
```

What just happened?

Setting up Avro is a little involved; it is a much newer project than the other Apache tools we'll be using, so it requires more than a single download of a tarball.

We download the Avro and Avro-mapred JAR files from the Apache website. There is also a dependency on ParaNamer that we download from its home page at codehaus.org.

> The ParaNamer home page has a broken download link at the time of writing; as an alternative, try the following link:
>
> http://search.maven.org/remotecontent?filepath=com/
> thoughtworks/paranamer/paranamer/2.5/paranamer-2.5.jar

After downloading these JAR files, we need to add them to the classpath used by our environment; primarily for the Java compiler. We add these files, but we also need to add to the `build` classpath several packages that ship with Hadoop because they are required to compile and run Avro code.

Finally, we copy the three new JAR files into the Hadoop `lib` directory on each host in the cluster to enable the classes to be available for the map and reduce tasks at runtime. We could distribute these JAR files through other mechanisms, but this is the most straightforward means.

Avro and schemas

One advantage Avro has over tools such as Thrift and Protocol Buffers, is the way it approaches the schema describing an Avro datafile. While the other tools always require the schema to be available as a distinct resource, Avro datafiles encode the schema in their header, which allows for the code to parse the files without ever seeing a separate schema file.

Avro supports but does not require code generation that produces code tailored to a specific data schema. This is an optimization that is valuable when possible but not a necessity.

We can therefore write a series of Avro examples that never actually use the datafile schema, but we'll only do that for parts of the process. In the following examples, we will define a schema that represents a cut-down version of the UFO sighting records we used previously.

Time for action – defining the schema

Let's now create this simplified UFO schema in a single Avro schema file.

Create the following as `ufo.avsc`:

```
{ "type": "record",
  "name": "UFO_Sighting_Record",
  "fields" : [
     {"name": "sighting_date", "type": "string"},
     {"name": "city", "type": "string"},
     {"name": "shape", "type": ["null", "string"]},
     {"name": "duration", "type": "float"}
  ]
}
```

What just happened?

As can be seen, Avro uses JSON in its schemas, which are usually saved with the `.avsc` extension. We create here a schema for a format that has four fields, as follows:

- The **Sighting_date** field of type string to hold a date of the form `yyyy-mm-dd`
- The **City** field of type string that will contain the city's name where the sighting occurred
- The **Shape** field, an optional field of type string, that represents the UFO's shape
- The **Duration** field gives a representation of the sighting duration in fractional minutes

With the schema defined, we will now create some sample data.

Time for action – creating the source Avro data with Ruby

Let's create the sample data using Ruby to demonstrate the cross-language capabilities of Avro.

1. Add the rubygems package:

```
$ sudo apt-get install rubygems
```

2. Install the Avro gem:

```
$ gem install avro
```

3. Create the following as generate.rb:

```ruby
require 'rubygems'
require 'avro'

file = File.open('sightings.avro', 'wb')
schema = Avro::Schema.parse(
File.open("ufo.avsc", "rb").read)

writer = Avro::IO::DatumWriter.new(schema)
dw = Avro::DataFile::Writer.new(file, writer, schema)
dw<< {"sighting_date" => "2012-01-12", "city" => "Boston", "shape"
=> "diamond", "duration" => 3.5}
dw<< {"sighting_date" => "2011-06-13", "city" => "London", "shape"
=> "light", "duration" => 13}
dw<< {"sighting_date" => "1999-12-31", "city" => "New York",
"shape" => "light", "duration" => 0.25}
dw<< {"sighting_date" => "2001-08-23", "city" => "Las Vegas",
"shape" => "cylinder", "duration" => 1.2}
dw<< {"sighting_date" => "1975-11-09", "city" => "Miami",
"duration" => 5}
dw<< {"sighting_date" => "2003-02-27", "city" => "Paris", "shape"
=> "light", "duration" => 0.5}
dw<< {"sighting_date" => "2007-04-12", "city" => "Dallas", "shape"
=> "diamond", "duration" => 3.5}
dw<< {"sighting_date" => "2009-10-10", "city" => "Milan", "shape"
=> "formation", "duration" => 0}
dw<< {"sighting_date" => "2012-04-10", "city" => "Amsterdam",
"shape" => "blur", "duration" => 6}
dw<< {"sighting_date" => "2006-06-15", "city" => "Minneapolis",
"shape" => "saucer", "duration" => 0.25}
dw.close
```

4. Run the program and create the datafile:

```
$ ruby generate.rb
```

What just happened?

Before we use Ruby, we ensure the `rubygems` package is installed on our Ubuntu host. We then install the preexisting Avro gem for Ruby. This provides the libraries we need to read and write Avro files from, within the Ruby language.

The Ruby script itself simply reads the previously created schema and creates a datafile with 10 test records. We then run the program to create the data.

This is not a Ruby tutorial, so I will leave analysis of the Ruby API as an exercise for the reader; its documentation can be found at `http://rubygems.org/gems/avro`.

Time for action – consuming the Avro data with Java

Now that we have some Avro data, let's write some Java code to consume it:

1. Create the following as `InputRead.java`:

```
import java.io.File;
import java.io.IOException;

import org.apache.avro.file.DataFileReader;
import org.apache.avro.generic.GenericData;
import org.apache.avro. generic.GenericDatumReader;
import org.apache.avro.generic.GenericRecord;
import org.apache.avro.io.DatumReader;

public class InputRead
{
    public static void main(String[] args) throws IOException
    {
        String filename = args[0] ;

        File file=new File(filename) ;
DatumReader<GenericRecord> reader= new
GenericDatumReader<GenericRecord>();
DataFileReader<GenericRecord>dataFileReader=new
DataFileReader<GenericRecord>(file,reader);

        while (dataFileReader.hasNext())
        {
GenericRecord result=dataFileReader.next();
            String output = String.format("%s %s %s %f",
result.get("sighting_date"), result.get("city"),
result.get("shape"), result.get("duration")) ;
```

```
System.out.println(output) ;
        }
    }
}
```

2. Compile and run the program:

   $ **javacInputRead.java**

   $ **java InputReadsightings.avro**

   The output will be as shown in the following screenshot:

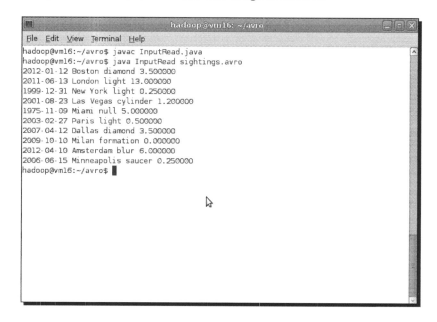

What just happened?

We created the Java class InputRead, which takes the filename passed as a command-line argument and parses this as an Avro datafile. When Avro reads from a datafile, each individual element is called a **datum** and each datum will follow the structure defined in the schema.

In this case, we don't use an explicit schema; instead, we read each datum into the GenericRecord class, and from this extract each field by explicitly retrieving it by name.

The GenericRecord class is a very flexible class in Avro; it can be used to wrap any record structure, such as our UFO-sighting type. Avro also supports primitive types such as integers, floats, and booleans as well as other structured types such as arrays and enums. In these examples, we'll use records as the most common structure, but this is only a convenience.

Using Avro within MapReduce

Avro's support for MapReduce revolves around several Avro-specific variants of other familiar classes, whereas we'd normally expect a new datafile format to be supported in Hadoop through new `InputFormat` and `OutputFormat` classes, we'll use **AvroJob**, **AvroMapper**, and **AvroReducer** instead of the non-Avro versions. AvroJob expects Avro datafiles as its input and output, so instead of specifying input and output format types, we configure it with details of the input and output Avro schemas.

The main difference for our mapper and reducer implementations are the types used. Avro, by default, has a single input and output, whereas we're used to our `Mapper` and `Reducer` classes having a key/value input and a key/value output. Avro also introduces the `Pair` class, which is often used to emit intermediate key/value data.

Avro does also support **AvroKey** and **AvroValue**, which can wrap other types, but we'll not use those in the following examples.

Time for action – generating shape summaries in MapReduce

In this section we will write a mapper that takes as input the UFO sighting record we defined earlier. It will output the shape and a count of `1`, and the reducer will take this shape and count records and produce a new structured Avro datafile type containing the final counts for each UFO shape. Perform the following steps:

1. Copy the `sightings.avro` file to HDFS.

```
$ hadoopfs -mkdiravroin
$ hadoopfs -put sightings.avroavroin/sightings.avro
```

2. Create the following as `AvroMR.java`:

```
import java.io.IOException;
import org.apache.avro.Schema;
import org.apache.avro.generic.*;
import org.apache.avro.Schema.Type;
import org.apache.avro.mapred.*;
import org.apache.avro.reflect.ReflectData;
import org.apache.avro.util.Utf8;
import org.apache.hadoop.conf.*;
import org.apache.hadoop.fs.Path;
import org.apache.hadoop.mapred.*;
import org.apache.hadoop.mapreduce.Job;
import org.apache.hadoop.io.* ;
import org.apache.hadoop.util.*;

// Output record definition
```

```
class UFORecord
{
UFORecord()
    {
    }

    public String shape ;
    public long count ;
}

public class AvroMR extends Configured  implements Tool
{
// Create schema for map output
    public static final Schema PAIR_SCHEMA =
Pair.getPairSchema(Schema.create(Schema.Type.STRING),
Schema.create(Schema.Type.LONG));
// Create schema for reduce output
    public final static Schema OUTPUT_SCHEMA =
ReflectData.get().getSchema(UFORecord.class);

    @Override
    public int run(String[] args) throws Exception
    {
JobConfconf = new JobConf(getConf(), getClass());
conf.setJobName("UFO count");

        String[] otherArgs = new GenericOptionsParser(conf, args).
getRemainingArgs();
        if (otherArgs.length != 2)
        {
System.err.println("Usage: avro UFO counter <in><out>");
System.exit(2);

        }

FileInputFormat.addInputPath(conf, new Path(otherArgs[0]));
        Path outputPath = new Path(otherArgs[1]);
FileOutputFormat.setOutputPath(conf, outputPath);
outputPath.getFileSystem(conf).delete(outputPath);
        Schema input_schema =
Schema.parse(getClass().getResourceAsStream("ufo.avsc"));
AvroJob.setInputSchema(conf, input_schema);
AvroJob.setMapOutputSchema(conf,
Pair.getPairSchema(Schema.create(Schema.Type.STRING),
```

```
Schema.create(Schema.Type.LONG)));

AvroJob.setOutputSchema(conf, OUTPUT_SCHEMA);
AvroJob.setMapperClass(conf, AvroRecordMapper.class);
AvroJob.setReducerClass(conf, AvroRecordReducer.class);
conf.setInputFormat(AvroInputFormat.class) ;
JobClient.runJob(conf);


        return 0 ;
    }

    public static class AvroRecordMapper extends
AvroMapper<GenericRecord, Pair<Utf8, Long>>
    {
        @Override
        public void map(GenericRecord in, AvroCollector<Pair<Utf8,
Long>> collector, Reporter reporter) throws IOException
        {
            Pair<Utf8,Long> p = new Pair<Utf8,Long>(PAIR_SCHEMA) ;
Utf8 shape = (Utf8)in.get("shape") ;
            if (shape != null)
            {
p.set(shape, 1L) ;
collector.collect(p);
            }
        }
    }

    public static class AvroRecordReducer extends
AvroReducer<Utf8,
Long, GenericRecord>
    {
        public void reduce(Utf8 key, Iterable<Long> values,
AvroCollector<GenericRecord> collector,
            Reporter reporter) throws IOException
        {
            long sum = 0;
            for (Long val : values)
            {
                sum += val;
            }

GenericRecord value = new
GenericData.Record(OUTPUT_SCHEMA);
```

```
value.put("shape", key);
value.put("count", sum);

collector.collect(value);
        }
    }

    public static void main(String[] args) throws Exception
    {
int res = ToolRunner.run(new Configuration(), new AvroMR(),
args);
System.exit(res);
    }
}
```

3. Compile and run the job:

```
$ javacAvroMR.java
$ jar -cvfavroufo.jar *.class ufo.avsc
    $ hadoop jar ~/classes/avroufo.jarAvroMRavroinavroout
```

4. Examine the output directory:

```
$ hadoopfs -1savroout
Found 3 items
-rw-r--r--    1 … /user/hadoop/avroout/_SUCCESS
drwxr-xr-x    - hadoopsupergroup           0 … /user/hadoop/
avroout/_logs
-rw-r--r--    1 …   /user/hadoop/avroout/part-00000.avro
```

5. Copy the output file to the local filesystem:

```
$ hadoopfs -get /user/hadoop/avroout/part-00000.avroresult.avro
```

What just happened?

We created the Job class and examined its various components. The actual logic within the Mapper and Reducer classes is relatively straightforward: the Mapper class just extracts the shape column and emits it with a count of 1; the reducer then counts the total number of entries for each shape. The interesting aspects are around the defined input and output types to the Mapper and Reducer classes and how the job is configured.

The Mapper class has an input type of GenericRecord and an output type of Pair. The Reducer class has a corresponding input type of Pair and output type of GenericRecord.

The GenericRecord class passed to the Mapper class wraps a datum that is the UFO sighting record represented in the input file. This is how the Mapper class is able to retrieve the **Shape** field by name.

Recall that GenericRecords may or may not be explicitly created with a schema, and in either case the structure can be determined from the datafile. For the GenericRecord output by the Reducer class, we do pass a schema but use a new mechanism for its creation.

Within the previously mentioned code, we created the additional UFORecord class and used Avro reflection to generate its schema dynamically at runtime. We were then able to use this schema to create a GenericRecord class specialized to wrap that particular record type.

Between the Mapper and Reducer classes we use the Avro Pair type to hold a key and value pair. This allows us to express the same logic for the Mapper and Reducer classes that we used in the original WordCount example back in *Chapter 2, Getting Hadoop Up and Running*; the Mapper class emits singleton counts for each value and the reducer sums these into an overall total for each shape.

In addition to the Mapper and Reducer classes' input and output, there is some configuration unique to a job processing Avro data:

```
Schema input_schema = Schema.parse(getClass().
getResourceAsStream("ufo.avsc")) ;
AvroJob.setInputSchema(conf, input_schema);
AvroJob.setMapOutputSchema(conf,              Pair.getPairSchema(Schema.
create(Schema.Type.STRING), Schema.create(Schema.Type.LONG)));

AvroJob.setOutputSchema(conf, OUTPUT_SCHEMA);
AvroJob.setMapperClass(conf, AvroRecordMapper.class);
AvroJob.setReducerClass(conf, AvroRecordReducer.class);
```

These configuration elements demonstrate the criticality of schema definition to Avro; though we can do without it, we must set the expected input and output schema types. Avro will validate the input and output against the specified schemas, so there is a degree of data type safety. For the other elements, such as setting up the Mapper and Reducer classes, we simply set those on AvroJob instead of the more generic classes, and once done, the MapReduce framework will perform appropriately.

This example is also the first time we've explicitly implemented the Tool interface. When running the Hadoop command-line program, there are a series of arguments (such as -D) that are common across all the multiple subcommands. If a job class implements the Tool interface as mentioned in the previous section, it automatically gets access to any of these standard options passed on the command line. It's a useful mechanism that prevents lots of code duplication.

Time for action – examining the output data with Ruby

Now that we have the output data from the job, let's examine it again using Ruby.

1. Create the following as `read.rb`:

```ruby
require 'rubygems'
require 'avro'

file = File.open('res.avro', 'rb')
reader = Avro::IO::DatumReader.new()
dr = Avro::DataFile::Reader.new(file, reader)

dr.each {|record|
print record["shape"]," ",record["count"],"\n"
}
dr.close
```

2. Examine the created result file.

```
$ ruby read.rb
blur 1
cylinder 1
diamond 2
formation 1
light 3
saucer 1
```

What just happened?

As before, we'll not analyze the Ruby Avro API. The example created a Ruby script that opens an Avro datafile, iterates through each datum, and displays it based on explicitly named fields. Note that the script does not have access to the schema for the datafile; the information in the header provides enough data to allow each field to be retrieved.

Time for action – examining the output data with Java

To show that the data is accessible from multiple languages, let's also display the job output using Java.

1. Create the following as `OutputRead.java`:

```java
import java.io.File;
import java.io.IOException;
```

```
import org.apache.avro.file.DataFileReader;
import org.apache.avro.generic.GenericData;
import org.apache.avro. generic.GenericDatumReader;
import org.apache.avro.generic.GenericRecord;
import org.apache.avro.io.DatumReader;

public class OutputRead
{
    public static void main(String[] args) throws IOException
    {
        String filename = args[0] ;

        File file=new File(filename) ;
DatumReader<GenericRecord> reader= new
GenericDatumReader<GenericRecord>();
DataFileReader<GenericRecord>dataFileReader=new
DataFileReader<GenericRecord>(file,reader);

        while (dataFileReader.hasNext())
        {
GenericRecord result=dataFileReader.next();
            String output = String.format("%s %d",
result.get("shape"), result.get("count")) ;
System.out.println(output) ;
        }
    }
}
```

2. Compile and run the program:

    ```
    $ javacOutputResult.java
    $ java OutputResultresult.avro
    blur 1
    cylinder 1
    diamond 2
    formation 1
    light 3
    saucer 1
    ```

What just happened?

We added this example to show the Avro data being read by more than one language. The code is very similar to the earlier InputRead class; the only difference is that the named fields are used to display each datum as it is read from the datafile.

Have a go hero – graphs in Avro

As previously mentioned, we worked hard to reduce representation-related complexity in our GraphPath class. But with mappings to and from flat lines of text and objects, there was an overhead in managing these transformations.

With its support for nested complex types, Avro can natively support a representation of a node that is much closer to the runtime object. Modify the GraphPath class job to read and write the graph representation to an Avro datafile comprising of datums for each node. The following example schema may be a good starting point, but feel free to enhance it:

```
{ "type": "record",
  "name": "Graph_representation",
  "fields" : [
{"name": "node_id", "type": "int"},
    {"name": "neighbors", "type": "array", "items:"int" },
    {"name": "distance", "type": "int"},
  {"name": "status", "type": "enum",
"symbols": ["PENDING", "CURRENT", "DONE"
},]
]
}
```

Going forward with Avro

There are many features of Avro we did not cover in this case study. We focused only on its value as an at-rest data representation. It can also be used within a **remote procedure call (RPC)** framework and can optionally be used as the default RPC format in Hadoop 2.0. We didn't use Avro's code generation facilities that produce a much more domain-focused API. Nor did we cover issues such as Avro's ability to support schema evolution that, for example, allows new fields to be added to recent records without invalidating old datums or breaking existing clients. It's a technology you are very likely to see more of in the future.

Summary

This chapter has used three case studies to highlight some more advanced aspects of Hadoop and its broader ecosystem. In particular, we covered the nature of join-type problems and where they are seen, how reduce-side joins can be implemented with relative ease but with an efficiency penalty, and how to use optimizations to avoid full joins in the map-side by pushing data into the Distributed Cache.

We then learned how full map-side joins can be implemented, but require significant input data processing; how other tools such as Hive and Pig should be investigated if joins are a frequently encountered use case; and how to think about complex types like graphs and how they can be represented in a way that can be used in MapReduce.

We also saw techniques for breaking graph algorithms into multistage MapReduce jobs, the importance of language-independent data types, how Avro can be used for both language independence as well as complex Java-consumed types, and the Avro extensions to the MapReduce APIs that allow structured types to be used as the input and output to MapReduce jobs.

This now concludes our coverage of the programmatic aspects of the Hadoop MapReduce framework. We will now move on in the next two chapters to explore how to manage and scale a Hadoop environment.

6
When Things Break

One of the main promises of Hadoop is resilience to failure and an ability to survive failures when they do happen. Tolerance to failure will be the focus of this chapter.

In particular, we will cover the following topics:

◆ How Hadoop handles failures of DataNodes and TaskTrackers

◆ How Hadoop handles failures of the NameNode and JobTracker

◆ The impact of hardware failure on Hadoop

◆ How to deal with task failures caused by software bugs

◆ How dirty data can cause tasks to fail and what to do about it

Along the way, we will deepen our understanding of how the various components of Hadoop fit together and identify some areas of best practice.

Failure

With many technologies, the steps to be taken when things go wrong are rarely covered in much of the documentation and are often treated as topics only of interest to the experts. With Hadoop, it is much more front and center; much of the architecture and design of Hadoop is predicated on executing in an environment where failures are both frequent and expected.

Embrace failure

In recent years, a different mindset than the traditional one has been described by the term **embrace failure**. Instead of hoping that failure does not happen, accept the fact that it will and know how your systems and processes will respond when it does.

Or at least don't fear it

That's possibly a stretch, so instead, our goal in this chapter is to make you feel more comfortable about failures in the system. We'll be killing the processes of a running cluster, intentionally causing the software to fail, pushing bad data into our jobs, and generally causing as much disruption as we can.

Don't try this at home

Often when trying to break a system, a test instance is abused, leaving the operational system protected from the disruption. We will not advocate doing the things given in this chapter to an operational Hadoop cluster, but the fact is that apart from one or two very specific cases, you could. The goal is to understand the impact of the various types of failures so that when they do happen on the business-critical system, you will know whether it is a problem or not. Fortunately, the majority of cases are handled for you by Hadoop.

Types of failure

We will generally categorize failures into the following five types:

- Failure of a node, that is, DataNode or TaskTracker process
- Failure of a cluster's masters, that is, NameNode or JobTracker process
- Failure of hardware, that is, host crash, hard drive failure, and so on
- Failure of individual tasks within a MapReduce job due to software errors
- Failure of individual tasks within a MapReduce job due to data problems

We will explore each of these in turn in the following sections.

Hadoop node failure

The first class of failure that we will explore is the unexpected termination of the individual DataNode and TaskTracker processes. Given Hadoop's claims of managing system availability through survival of failures on its commodity hardware, we can expect this area to be very solid. Indeed, as clusters grow to hundreds or thousands of hosts, failures of individual nodes are likely to become quite commonplace.

Before we start killing things, let's introduce a new tool and set up the cluster properly.

The dfsadmin command

As an alternative tool to constantly viewing the HDFS web UI to determine the cluster status, we will use the dfsadmin command-line tool:

```
$ Hadoop dfsadmin
```

This will give a list of the various options the command can take; for our purposes we'll be using the -report option. This gives an overview of the overall cluster state, including configured capacity, nodes, and files as well as specific details about each configured node.

Cluster setup, test files, and block sizes

We will need a fully distributed cluster for the following activities; refer to the setup instructions given earlier in the book. The screenshots and examples that follow use a cluster of one host for the JobTracker and NameNode and four slave nodes for running the DataNode and TaskTracker processes.

Remember that you don't need physical hardware for each node, we use virtual machines for our cluster.

In normal usage, 64 MB is the usual configured block size for a Hadoop cluster. For our testing purposes, that is terribly inconvenient as we'll need pretty large files to get meaningful block counts across our multinode cluster.

What we can do is reduce the configured block size; in this case, we will use 4 MB. Make the following modifications to the hdfs-site.xml file within the Hadoop conf directory:

```
<property>
<name>dfs.block.size</name>
<value>4194304</value>
;</property>
<property>
<name>dfs.namenode.logging.level</name>
<value>all</value>
</property>
```

The first property makes the required changes to the block size and the second one increases the NameNode logging level to make some of the block operations more visible.

Both these settings are appropriate for this test setup but would rarely be seen on a production cluster. Though the higher NameNode logging may be required if a particularly difficult problem is being investigated, it is highly unlikely you would ever want a block size as small as 4 MB. Though the smaller block size will work fine, it will impact Hadoop's efficiency.

We also need a reasonably-sized test file that will comprise of multiple 4 MB blocks. We won't actually be using the content of the file, so the type of file is irrelevant. But you should copy the largest file you can onto HDFS for the following sections. We used a CD ISO image:

```
$ Hadoop fs -put cd.iso file1.data
```

Fault tolerance and Elastic MapReduce

The examples in this book are for a local Hadoop cluster because this allows some of the failure mode details to be more explicit. EMR provides exactly the same failure tolerance as the local cluster, so the failure scenarios described here apply equally to a local Hadoop cluster and the one hosted by EMR.

Time for action – killing a DataNode process

Firstly, we'll kill a DataNode. Recall that the DataNode process runs on each host in the HDFS cluster and is responsible for the management of blocks within the HDFS filesystem. Because Hadoop, by default, uses a replication factor of 3 for blocks, we should expect a single DataNode failure to have no direct impact on availability, rather it will result in some blocks temporarily falling below the replication threshold. Execute the following steps to kill a DataNode process:

1. Firstly, check on the original status of the cluster and check whether everything is healthy. We'll use the dfsadmin command for this:

```
$ Hadoop dfsadmin -report
Configured Capacity: 81376493568 (75.79 GB)
Present Capacity: 61117323920 (56.92 GB)
DFS Remaining: 59576766464 (55.49 GB)
DFS Used: 1540557456 (1.43 GB)
DFS Used%: 2.52%
Under replicated blocks: 0
Blocks with corrupt replicas: 0
Missing blocks: 0

------------------------------------------------
```

```
Datanodes available: 4 (4 total, 0 dead)


Name: 10.0.0.102:50010
Decommission Status : Normal
Configured Capacity: 20344123392 (18.95 GB)
DFS Used: 403606906 (384.91 MB)
Non DFS Used: 5063119494 (4.72 GB)
DFS Remaining: 14877396992(13.86 GB)
DFS Used%: 1.98%
DFS Remaining%: 73.13%
Last contact: Sun Dec 04 15:16:27 PST 2011
...
```

Now log onto one of the nodes and use the `jps` command to determine the process ID of the DataNode process:

```
$ jps
2085 TaskTracker
2109 Jps
1928 DataNode
```

2. Use the **process ID (PID)** of the DataNode process and kill it:

```
$ kill -9  1928
```

3. Check that the DataNode process is no longer running on the host:

```
$ jps
2085 TaskTracker
```

4. Check the status of the cluster again by using the `dfsadmin` command:

```
$ Hadoop dfsadmin -report
Configured Capacity: 81376493568 (75.79 GB)
Present Capacity: 61117323920 (56.92 GB)
DFS Remaining: 59576766464 (55.49 GB)
DFS Used: 1540557456 (1.43 GB)
DFS Used%: 2.52%
Under replicated blocks: 0
Blocks with corrupt replicas: 0
Missing blocks: 0
```

```
-------------------------------------------------
Datanodes available: 4 (4 total, 0 dead)
...
```

5. The key lines to watch are the lines reporting on blocks, live nodes, and the last contact time for each node. Once the last contact time for the dead node is around 10 minutes, use the command more frequently until the block and live node values change:

```
$ Hadoop dfsadmin -report
Configured Capacity: 61032370176 (56.84 GB)
Present Capacity: 46030327050 (42.87 GB)
DFS Remaining: 44520288256 (41.46 GB)
DFS Used: 1510038794 (1.41 GB)
DFS Used%: 3.28%
Under replicated blocks: 12
Blocks with corrupt replicas: 0
Missing blocks: 0


-------------------------------------------------
Datanodes available: 3 (4 total, 1 dead)
...
```

6. Repeat the process until the count of under-replicated blocks is once again 0:

```
$ Hadoop dfsadmin -report
...
Under replicated blocks: 0
Blocks with corrupt replicas: 0
Missing blocks: 0


-------------------------------------------------
Datanodes available: 3 (4 total, 1 dead)
...
```

What just happened?

The high-level story is pretty straightforward; Hadoop recognized the loss of a node and worked around the problem. However, quite a lot is going on to make that happen.

When we killed the DataNode process, the process on that host was no longer available to serve or receive data blocks as part of the read/write operations. However, we were not actually accessing the filesystem at the time, so how did the NameNode process know this particular DataNode was dead?

NameNode and DataNode communication

The answer lies in the constant communication between the NameNode and DataNode processes that we have alluded to once or twice but never really explained. This occurs through a constant series of heartbeat messages from the DataNode reporting on its current state and the blocks it holds. In return, the NameNode gives instructions to the DataNode, such as notification of the creation of a new file or an instruction to retrieve a block from another node.

It all begins when the NameNode process starts up and begins receiving status messages from the DataNode. Recall that each DataNode knows the location of its NameNode and will continuously send status reports. These messages list the blocks held by each DataNode and from this, the NameNode is able to construct a complete mapping that allows it to relate files and directories to the blocks from where they are comprised and the nodes on which they are stored.

The NameNode process monitors the last time it received a heartbeat from each DataNode and after a threshold is reached, it assumes the DataNode is no longer functional and marks it as dead.

> The exact threshold after which a DataNode is assumed to be dead is not configurable as a single HDFS property. Instead, it is calculated from several other properties such as defining the heartbeat interval. As we'll see later, things are a little easier in the MapReduce world as the timeout for TaskTrackers is controlled by a single configuration property.

Once a DataNode is marked as dead, the NameNode process determines the blocks which were held on that node and have now fallen below their replication target. In the default case, each block held on the killed node would have been one of the three replicas, so each block for which the node held a replica will now have only two replicas across the cluster.

In the preceding example, we captured the state when 12 blocks were still under-replicated, that is they did not have enough replicas across the cluster to meet the replication target. When the NameNode process determines the under-replicated blocks, it assigns other DataNodes to copy these blocks from the hosts where the existing replicas reside. In this case we only had to re-replicate a very small number of blocks; in a live cluster, the failure of a node can result in a period of high network traffic as the affected blocks are brought up to their replication factor.

Note that if a failed node returns to the cluster, we have the situation of blocks having more than the required number of replicas; in such a case the NameNode process will send instructions to remove the surplus replicas. The specific replica to be deleted is chosen randomly, so the result will be that the returned node will end up retaining some of its blocks and deleting the others.

Have a go hero – NameNode log delving

We configured the NameNode process to log all its activities. Have a look through these very verbose logs and attempt to identify the replication requests being sent.

The final output shows the status after the under-replicated blocks have been copied to the live nodes. The cluster is down to only three live nodes but there are no under-replicated blocks.

 A quick way to restart the dead nodes across all hosts is to use the start-all.sh script. It will attempt to start everything but is smart enough to detect the running services, which means you get the dead nodes restarted without the risk of duplicates.

Time for action – the replication factor in action

Let's repeat the preceding process, but this time, kill two DataNodes out of our cluster of four. We will give an abbreviated walk-through of the activity as it is very similar to the previous *Time for action* section:

1. Restart the dead DataNode and monitor the cluster until all nodes are marked as live.

2. Pick two DataNodes, use the process ID, and kill the DataNode processes.

3. As done previously, wait for around 10 minutes then actively monitor the cluster state via dfsadmin, paying particular attention to the reported number of under-replicated blocks.

4. Wait until the cluster has stabilized with an output similar to the following:

    ```
    Configured Capacity: 61032370176 (56.84 GB)
    Present Capacity: 45842373555 (42.69 GB)
    DFS Remaining: 44294680576 (41.25 GB)
    DFS Used: 1547692979 (1.44 GB)
    DFS Used%: 3.38%
    Under replicated blocks: 125
    Blocks with corrupt replicas: 0
    ```

```
Missing blocks: 0


------------------------------------------------
Datanodes available: 2 (4 total, 2 dead)
...
```

What just happened?

This is the same process as before; the difference is that due to two DataNode failures there were significantly more blocks that fell below the replication factor, many going down to a single remaining replica. Consequently, you should see more activity in the reported number of under-replicated blocks as it first increase because nodes fail and then drop as re-replication occurs. These events can also be seen in the NameNode logs.

Note that though Hadoop can use re-replication to bring those blocks with only a single remaining replica up to two replicas, this still leaves the blocks in an under-replicated state. With only two live nodes in the cluster, it is now impossible for any block to meet the default replication target of three.

We have been truncating the dfsadmin output for space reasons; in particular, we have been omitting the reported information for each node. However, let's take a look at the first node in our cluster through the previous stages. Before we started killing any DataNode, it reported the following:

```
Name: 10.0.0.101:50010
Decommission Status : Normal
Configured Capacity: 20344123392 (18.95 GB)
DFS Used: 399379827 (380.88 MB)
Non DFS Used: 5064258189 (4.72 GB)
DFS Remaining: 14880485376(13.86 GB)
DFS Used%: 1.96%
DFS Remaining%: 73.14%
Last contact: Sun Dec 04 15:16:27 PST 2011
```

After a single DataNode was killed and all blocks had been re-replicated as necessary, it reported the following:

```
Name: 10.0.0.101:50010
Decommission Status : Normal
Configured Capacity: 20344123392 (18.95 GB)
DFS Used: 515236022 (491.37 MB)
Non DFS Used: 5016289098 (4.67 GB)
DFS Remaining: 14812598272(13.8 GB)
```

```
DFS Used%: 2.53%
DFS Remaining%: 72.81%
Last contact: Sun Dec 04 15:31:22 PST 2011
```

The thing to note is the increase in the local DFS storage on the node. This shouldn't be a surprise. With a dead node, the others in the cluster need to add some additional block replicas and that will translate to a higher storage utilization on each.

Finally, the following is the node's report after two other DataNodes were killed:

```
Name: 10.0.0.101:50010
Decommission Status : Normal
Configured Capacity: 20344123392 (18.95 GB)
DFS Used: 514289664 (490.46 MB)
Non DFS Used: 5063868416 (4.72 GB)
DFS Remaining: 14765965312(13.75 GB)
DFS Used%: 2.53%
DFS Remaining%: 72.58%
Last contact: Sun Dec 04 15:43:47 PST 2011
```

With two dead nodes it may seem as if the remaining live nodes should consume even more local storage space, but this isn't the case and it's yet again a natural consequence of the replication factor.

If we have four nodes and a replication factor of 3, each block will have a replica on three of the live nodes in the cluster. If a node dies, the blocks living on the other nodes are unaffected, but any blocks with a replica on the dead node will need a new replica created. However, with only three live nodes, each node will hold a replica of every block. If a second node fails, the situation will result into under-replicated blocks and Hadoop does not have anywhere to put the additional replicas. Since both remaining nodes already hold a replica of each block, their storage utilization does not increase.

Time for action – intentionally causing missing blocks

The next step should be obvious; let's kill three DataNodes in quick succession.

 This is the first of the activities we mentioned that you really should not do on a production cluster. Although there will be no data loss if the steps are followed properly, there is a period when the existing data is unavailable.

The following are the steps to kill three DataNodes in quick succession:

1. Restart all the nodes by using the following command:

```
$ start-all.sh
```

2. Wait until Hadoop dfsadmin -report shows four live nodes.

3. Put a new copy of the test file onto HDFS:

```
$ Hadoop fs -put file1.data file1.new
```

4. Log onto three of the cluster hosts and kill the DataNode process on each.

5. Wait for the usual 10 minutes then start monitoring the cluster via dfsadmin until you get output similar to the following that reports the missing blocks:

```
...

Under replicated blocks: 123

Blocks with corrupt replicas: 0

Missing blocks: 33


-------------------------------------------------

Datanodes available: 1 (4 total, 3 dead)

...
```

6. Try and retrieve the test file from HDFS:

```
$ hadoop fs -get file1.new  file1.new

11/12/04 16:18:05 INFO hdfs.DFSClient: No node available for
block: blk_1691554429626293399_1003 file=/user/hadoop/file1.new

11/12/04 16:18:05 INFO hdfs.DFSClient: Could not obtain block
blk_1691554429626293399_1003 from any node:  java.io.IOException:
No live nodes contain current block

...

get: Could not obtain block: blk_1691554429626293399_1003 file=/
user/hadoop/file1.new
```

7. Restart the dead nodes using the start-all.sh script:

```
$ start-all.sh
```

8. Repeatedly monitor the status of the blocks:

```
$ Hadoop dfsadmin -report | grep -i blocks

Under replicated blockss: 69

Blocks with corrupt replicas: 0

Missing blocks: 35
```

```
$ Hadoop dfsadmin -report | grep -i blocks
Under replicated blockss: 0
Blocks with corrupt replicas: 0
Missing blocks: 30
```

9. Wait until there are no reported missing blocks then copy the test file onto the local filesystem:

```
$ Hadoop fs -get file1.new file1.new
```

10. Perform an MD5 check on this and the original file:

```
$ md5sum file1.*
f1f30b26b40f8302150bc2a494c1961d  file1.data
f1f30b26b40f8302150bc2a494c1961d  file1.new
```

What just happened?

After restarting the killed nodes, we copied the test file onto HDFS again. This isn't strictly necessary as we could have used the existing file but due to the shuffling of the replicas, a clean copy gives the most representative results.

We then killed three DataNodes as before and waited for HDFS to respond. Unlike the previous examples, killing these many nodes meant it was certain that some blocks would have all of their replicas on the killed nodes. As we can see, this is exactly the result; the remaining single node cluster shows over a hundred blocks that are under-replicated (obviously only one replica remains) but there are also 33 missing blocks.

Talking of blocks is a little abstract, so we then try to retrieve our test file which, as we know, effectively has 33 holes in it. The attempt to access the file fails as Hadoop could not find the missing blocks required to deliver the file.

We then restarted all the nodes and tried to retrieve the file again. This time it was successful, but we took an added precaution of performing an MD5 cryptographic check on the file to confirm that it was bitwise identical to the original one — which it is.

This is an important point: though node failure may result in data becoming unavailable, there may not be a permanent data loss if the node recovers.

When data may be lost

Do not assume from this example that it's impossible to lose data in a Hadoop cluster. For general use it is very hard, but disaster often has a habit of striking in just the wrong way.

As seen in the previous example, a parallel failure of a number of nodes equal to or greater than the replication factor has a chance of resulting in missing blocks. In our example of three dead nodes in a cluster of four, the chances were high; in a cluster of 1000, it would be much lower but still non-zero. As the cluster size increases, so does the failure rate and having three node failures in a narrow window of time becomes less and less unlikely. Conversely, the impact also decreases but rapid multiple failures will always carry a risk of data loss.

Another more insidious problem is recurring or partial failures, for example, when power issues across the cluster cause nodes to crash and restart. It is possible for Hadoop to end up chasing replication targets, constantly asking the recovering hosts to replicate under-replicated blocks, and also seeing them fail mid-way through the task. Such a sequence of events can also raise the potential of data loss.

Finally, never forget the human factor. Having a replication factor equal to the size of the cluster—ensuring every block is on every node—won't help you when a user accidentally deletes a file or directory.

The summary is that data loss through system failure is pretty unlikely but is possible through almost inevitable human action. Replication is not a full alternative to backups; ensure that you understand the importance of the data you process and the impact of the types of loss discussed here.

 The most catastrophic losses in a Hadoop cluster are actually caused by NameNode failure and filesystem corruption; we'll discuss this topic in some detail in the next chapter.

Block corruption

The reports from each DataNode also included a count of the corrupt blocks, which we have not referred to. When a block is first stored, there is also a hidden file written to the same HDFS directory containing cryptographic checksums for the block. By default, there is a checksum for each 512-byte chunk within the block.

Whenever any client reads a block, it will also retrieve the list of checksums and compare these to the checksums it generates on the block data it has read. If there is a checksum mismatch, the block on that particular DataNode will be marked as corrupt and the client will retrieve a different replica. On learning of the corrupt block, the NameNode will schedule a new replica to be made from one of the existing uncorrupted replicas.

If the scenario seems unlikely, consider that faulty memory, disk drive, storage controller, or numerous issues on an individual host could cause some corruption to a block as it is initially being written while being stored or when being read. These are rare events and the chances of the same corruption occurring on all DataNodes holding replicas of the same block become exceptionally remote. However, remember as previously mentioned that replication is not a full alternative to backup and if you need 100 percent data availability, you likely need to think about off-cluster backup.

Time for action – killing a TaskTracker process

We've abused HDFS and its DataNode enough; now let's see what damage we can do to MapReduce by killing some TaskTracker processes.

Though there is an `mradmin` command, it does not give the sort of status reports we are used to with HDFS. So we'll use the MapReduce web UI (located by default on port 50070 on the JobTracker host) to monitor the MapReduce cluster health.

Perform the following steps:

1. Ensure everything is running via the `start-all.sh` script then point your browser at the MapReduce web UI. The page should look like the following screenshot:

2. Start a long-running MapReduce job; the example pi estimator with large values is great for this:

```
$ Hadoop jar Hadoop/Hadoop-examples-1.0.4.jar pi 2500 2500
```

3. Now log onto a cluster node and use `jps` to identify the TaskTracker process:

```
$ jps
21822 TaskTracker
3918 Jps
3891 DataNode
```

4. Kill the TaskTracker process:

```
$ kill -9 21822
```

5. Verify that the TaskTracker is no longer running:

```
$jps
3918 Jps
3891 DataNode
```

6. Go back to the MapReduce web UI and after 10 minutes you should see that the number of nodes and available map/reduce slots change as shown in the following screenshot:

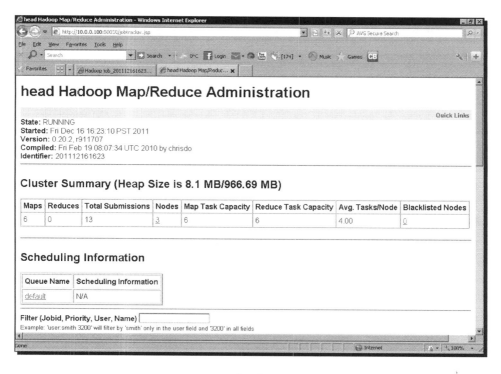

7. Monitor the job progress in the original window; it should be proceeding, even if it is slow.

8. Restart the dead TaskTracker process:

```
$ start-all.sh
```

9. Monitor the MapReduce web UI. After a little time the number of nodes should be back to its original number as shown in the following screenshot:

What just happened?

The MapReduce web interface provides a lot of information on both the cluster as well as the jobs it executes. For our interests here, the important data is the cluster summary that shows the currently executing number of map and reduce tasks, the total number of submitted jobs, the number of nodes and their map and reduce capacity, and finally, any blacklisted nodes.

The relationship of the JobTracker process to the TaskTracker process is quite different than that between NameNode and DataNode but a similar heartbeat/monitoring mechanism is used.

The TaskTracker process frequently sends heartbeats to the JobTracker, but instead of status reports of block health, they contain progress reports of the assigned task and available capacity. Each node has a configurable number of map and reduce task slots (the default for each is two), which is why we see four nodes and eight map and reduce slots in the first web UI screenshot.

When we kill the TaskTracker process, its lack of heartbeats is measured by the JobTracker process and after a configurable amount of time, the node is assumed to be dead and we see the reduced cluster capacity reflected in the web UI.

> The timeout for a TaskTracker process to be considered dead is modified by the `mapred.tasktracker.expiry.interval` property, configured in `mapred-site.xml`.

When a TaskTracker process is marked as dead, the JobTracker process also considers its in-progress tasks as failed and re-assigns them to the other nodes in the cluster. We see this implicitly by watching the job proceed successfully despite a node being killed.

After the TaskTracker process is restarted it sends a heartbeat to the JobTracker, which marks it as alive and reintegrates it into the MapReduce cluster. This we see through the cluster node and task slot capacity returning to their original values as can be seen in the final screenshot.

Comparing the DataNode and TaskTracker failures

We'll not perform similar two or three node killing activities with TaskTrackers as the task execution architecture renders individual TaskTracker failures relatively unimportant. Because the TaskTracker processes are under the control and coordination of JobTracker, their individual failures have no direct effect other than to reduce the cluster execution capacity. If a TaskTracker instance fails, the JobTracker will simply schedule the failed tasks on a healthy TaskTracker process in the cluster. The JobTracker is free to reschedule tasks around the cluster because TaskTracker is conceptually stateless; a single failure does not affect other parts of the job.

In contrast, loss of a DataNode—which is intrinsically stateful—can affect the persistent data held on HDFS, potentially making it unavailable.

This highlights the nature of the various nodes and their relationship to the overall Hadoop framework. The DataNode manages data, and the TaskTracker reads and writes that data. Catastrophic failure of every TaskTracker would still leave us with a completely functional HDFS; a similar failure of the NameNode process would leave a live MapReduce cluster that is effectively useless (unless it was configured to use a different storage system).

Permanent failure

Our recovery scenarios so far have assumed that the dead node can be restarted on the same physical host. But what if it can't due to the host having a critical failure? The answer is simple; you can remove the host from the slave's file and Hadoop will no longer try to start a DataNode or TaskTracker on that host. Conversely, if you get a replacement machine with a different hostname, add this new host to the same file and run `start-all.sh`.

> Note that the slave's file is only used by tools such as the `start`/`stop` and `slaves.sh` scripts. You don't need to keep it updated on every node, but only on the hosts where you generally run such commands. In practice, this is likely to be either a dedicated head node or the host where the NameNode or JobTracker processes run. We'll explore these setups in *Chapter 7, Keeping Things Running*.

Killing the cluster masters

Though the failure impact of DataNode and TaskTracker processes is different, each individual node is relatively unimportant. Failure of any single TaskTracker or DataNode is not a cause for concern and issues only occur if multiple others fail, particularly in quick succession. But we only have one JobTracker and NameNode; let's explore what happens when they fail.

Time for action – killing the JobTracker

We'll first kill the JobTracker process which we should expect to impact our ability to execute MapReduce jobs but not affect the underlying HDFS filesystem.

1. Log on to the JobTracker host and kill its process.

2. Attempt to start a test MapReduce job such as Pi or WordCount:

```
$ Hadoop jar wc.jar WordCount3 test.txt output

Starting Job

11/12/11 16:03:29 INFO ipc.Client: Retrying connect to server:
/10.0.0.100:9001. Already tried 0 time(s).

11/12/11 16:03:30 INFO ipc.Client: Retrying connect to server:
/10.0.0.100:9001. Already tried 1 time(s).

...

11/12/11 16:03:38 INFO ipc.Client: Retrying connect to server:
/10.0.0.100:9001. Already tried 9 time(s).
```

```
java.net.ConnectException: Call to /10.0.0.100:9001 failed on
connection exception: java.net.ConnectException: Connection
refused
    at org.apache.hadoop.ipc.Client.wrapException(Client.java:767)
    at org.apache.hadoop.ipc.Client.call(Client.java:743)
    at org.apache.hadoop.ipc.RPC$Invoker.invoke(RPC.java:220)
...
```

3. Perform some HDFS operations:

```
$ hadoop fs -ls /
Found 2 items
drwxr-xr-x    - hadoop supergroup           0 2011-12-11 19:19 /user
drwxr-xr-x    - hadoop supergroup           0 2011-12-04 20:38 /var
$ hadoop fs -cat test.txt
This is a test file
```

What just happened?

After killing the JobTracker process we attempted to launch a MapReduce job. From the walk-through in *Chapter 2, Getting Hadoop Up and Running*, we know that the client on the machine where we are starting the job attempts to communicate with the JobTracker process to initiate the job scheduling activities. But in this case there was no running JobTracker, this communication did not happen and the job failed.

We then performed a few HDFS operations to highlight the point in the previous section; a non-functional MapReduce cluster will not directly impact HDFS, which will still be available to all clients and operations.

Starting a replacement JobTracker

The recovery of the MapReduce cluster is also pretty straightforward. Once the JobTracker process is restarted, all the subsequent MapReduce jobs are successfully processed.

Note that when the JobTracker was killed, any jobs that were in flight are lost and need to be restarted. Watch out for temporary files and directories on HDFS; many MapReduce jobs write temporary data to HDFS that is usually cleaned up on job completion. Failed jobs— especially the ones failed due to a JobTracker failure—are likely to leave such data behind and this may require a manual clean-up.

Have a go hero – moving the JobTracker to a new host

But what happens if the host on which the JobTracker process was running has a fatal hardware failure and cannot be recovered? In such situations you will need to start a new JobTracker process on a different host. This requires all nodes to have their `mapred-site.xml` file updated with the new location and the cluster restarted. Try this! We'll talk about it more in the next chapter.

Time for action – killing the NameNode process

Let's now kill the NameNode process, which we should expect to directly stop us from accessing HDFS and by extension, prevent the MapReduce jobs from executing:

 Don't try this on an operationally important cluster. Though the impact will be short-lived, it effectively kills the entire cluster for a period of time.

1. Log onto the NameNode host and list the running processes:

```
$ jps
2372 SecondaryNameNode
2118 NameNode
2434 JobTracker
5153 Jps
```

2. Kill the NameNode process. Don't worry about SecondaryNameNode, it can keep running.

3. Try to access the HDFS filesystem:

```
$ hadoop fs -ls /
11/12/13 16:00:05 INFO ipc.Client: Retrying connect to server:
/10.0.0.100:9000. Already tried 0 time(s).

11/12/13 16:00:06 INFO ipc.Client: Retrying connect to server:
/10.0.0.100:9000. Already tried 1 time(s).

11/12/13 16:00:07 INFO ipc.Client: Retrying connect to server:
/10.0.0.100:9000. Already tried 2 time(s).

11/12/13 16:00:08 INFO ipc.Client: Retrying connect to server:
/10.0.0.100:9000. Already tried 3 time(s).

11/12/13 16:00:09 INFO ipc.Client: Retrying connect to server:
/10.0.0.100:9000. Already tried 4

time(s).

…

Bad connection to FS. command aborted.
```

4. Submit the MapReduce job:

```
$ hadoop jar hadoop/hadoop-examples-1.0.4.jar  pi 10 100

Number of Maps  = 10

Samples per Map = 100

11/12/13 16:00:35 INFO ipc.Client: Retrying connect to server:
/10.0.0.100:9000. Already tried 0 time(s).

11/12/13 16:00:36 INFO ipc.Client: Retrying connect to server:
/10.0.0.100:9000. Already tried 1 time(s).

11/12/13 16:00:37 INFO ipc.Client: Retrying connect to server:
/10.0.0.100:9000. Already tried 2 time(s).

...

java.lang.RuntimeException: java.net.ConnectException: Call
to /10.0.0.100:9000 failed on connection exception: java.net.
ConnectException: Connection refused

   at org.apache.hadoop.mapred.JobConf.getWorkingDirectory(JobConf.
java:371)

   at org.apache.hadoop.mapred.FileInputFormat.
setInputPaths(FileInputFormat.java:309)

...

Caused by: java.net.ConnectException: Call to /10.0.0.100:9000
failed on connection exception: java.net.ConnectException:
Connection refused

...
```

5. Check the running processes:

```
$ jps

2372 SecondaryNameNode

5253 Jps

2434 JobTracker

Restart the NameNode

$ start-all.sh
```

6. Access HDFS:

```
$ Hadoop fs -ls /

Found 2 items


drwxr-xr-x   - hadoop supergroup          0 2011-12-16 16:18 /user


drwxr-xr-x   - hadoop supergroup          0 2011-12-16 16:23 /var
```

What just happened?

We killed the NameNode process and tried to access the HDFS filesystem. This of course failed; without the NameNode there is no server to receive our filesystem commands.

We then tried to submit a MapReduce job and this also failed. From the abbreviated exception stack trace you can see that while trying to set up the input paths for the job data, the JobTracker also tried and failed to connect to NameNode.

We then confirmed that the JobTracker process is healthy and it was the NameNode's unavailability that caused the MapReduce task to fail.

Finally, we restarted the NameNode and confirmed that we could once again access the HDFS filesystem.

Starting a replacement NameNode

With the differences identified so far between the MapReduce and HDFS clusters, it shouldn't be a surprise to learn that restarting a new NameNode on a different host is not as simple as moving the JobTracker. To put it more starkly, having to move NameNode due to a hardware failure is probably the worst crisis you can have with a Hadoop cluster. Unless you have prepared carefully, the chance of losing all your data is very high.

That's quite a statement and we need to explore the nature of the NameNode process to understand why this is the case.

The role of the NameNode in more detail

So far we've spoken of the NameNode process as the coordinator between the DataNode processes and the service responsible for ensuring the configuration parameters, such as block replication values, are honored. This is an important set of tasks but it's also very operationally focused. The NameNode process also has the responsibility of managing the HDFS filesystem metadata; a good analogy is to think of it holding the equivalent of the file allocation table in a traditional filesystem.

File systems, files, blocks, and nodes

When accessing HDFS you rarely care about blocks. You want to access a given file at a certain location in the filesystem. To facilitate this, the NameNode process is required to maintain numerous pieces of information:

- The actual filesystem contents, the names of all the files, and their containing directories
- Additional metadata about each of these elements, such as size, ownership, and replication factor

+ The mapping of which blocks hold the data for each file
+ The mapping of which nodes in the cluster hold which blocks and from this, the current replication state of each

All but the last of the preceding points is persistent data that must be maintained across restarts of the NameNode process.

The single most important piece of data in the cluster – fsimage

The NameNode process stores two data structures to disk, the `fsimage` file and the edits log of changes to it. The `fsimage` file holds the key filesystem attributes mentioned in the previous section; the name and details of each file and directory on the filesystem and the mapping of the blocks that correspond to each.

If the `fsimage` file is lost, you have a series of nodes holding blocks of data without any knowledge of which blocks correspond to which part of which file. In fact, you don't even know which files are supposed to be constructed in the first place. Loss of the `fsimage` file leaves you with all the filesystem data but renders it effectively useless.

The `fsimage` file is read by the NameNode process at startup and is held and manipulated in memory for performance reasons. To avoid changes to the filesystem being lost, any modifications made are written to the edits log throughout the NameNode's uptime. The next time it restarts, it looks for this log at startup and uses it to update the `fsimage` file which it then reads into memory.

This process can be optimized by the use of the SecondaryNameNode which we'll mention later.

DataNode startup

When a DataNode process starts up, it commences its heartbeat process by reporting to the NameNode process on the blocks it holds. As explained earlier in this chapter, this is how the NameNode process knows which node should be used to service a request for a given block. If the NameNode process itself restarts, it uses the re-establishment of the heartbeats with all the DataNode processes to construct its mapping of blocks to nodes.

With the DataNode processes potentially coming in and out of the cluster, there is little use in this mapping being stored persistently as the on-disk state would often be out-of-date with the current reality. This is why the NameNode process does not persist the location of which blocks are held on which nodes.

Safe mode

If you look at the HDFS web UI or the output of `dfsadmin` shortly after starting an HDFS cluster, you will see a reference to the cluster being in **safe mode** and the required threshold of the reported blocks before it will leave safe mode. This is the DataNode block reporting mechanism at work.

As an additional safeguard, the NameNode process will hold the HDFS filesystem in a read-only mode until it has confirmed that a given percentage of blocks meet their replication threshold. In the usual case this will simply require all the DataNode processes to report in, but if some have failed, the NameNode process will need to schedule some re-replication before safe mode can be left.

SecondaryNameNode

The most unfortunately named entity in Hadoop is the **SecondaryNameNode**. When one learns of the critical `fsimage` file for the first time, this thing called SecondaryNameNode starts to sound like a helpful mitigation. Is it perhaps, as the name suggests, a second copy of the NameNode process running on another host that can take over when the primary fails? No, it isn't. SecondaryNameNode has a very specific role; it periodically reads in the state of the `fsimage` file and the edits log and writes out an updated `fsimage` file with the changes in the log applied. This is a major time saver in terms of NameNode startup. If the NameNode process has been running for a significant period of time, the edits log will be huge and it will take a very long time (easily several hours) to apply all the changes to the old `fsimage` file's state stored on the disk. The SecondaryNameNode facilitates a faster startup.

So what to do when the NameNode process has a critical failure?

Would it help to say don't panic? There are approaches to NameNode failure and this is such an important topic that we have an entire section on it in the next chapter. But for now, the main point is that you can configure the NameNode process to write its `fsimage` file and edits log to multiple locations. Typically, a network filesystem is added as a second location to ensure a copy of the `fsimage` file outside the NameNode host.

But the process of moving to a new NameNode process on a new host requires manual effort and your Hadoop cluster is dead in the water until you do. This is something you want to have a process for and that you have tried (successfully!) in a test scenario. You really don't want to be learning how to do this when your operational cluster is down, your CEO is shouting at you, and the company is losing money.

BackupNode/CheckpointNode and NameNode HA

Hadoop 0.22 replaced SecondaryNameNode with two new components, **BackupNode** and **CheckpointNode**. The latter of these is effectively a renamed SecondaryNameNode; it is responsible for updating the `fsimage` file at regular checkpoints to decrease the NameNode startup time.

The BackupNode, however, is a step closer to the goal of a fully functional hot-backup for the NameNode. It receives a constant stream of filesystem updates from the NameNode and its in-memory state is up-to-date at any point in time, with the current state held in the master NameNode. If the NameNode dies, the BackupNode is much more capable of being brought into service as a new NameNode. The process isn't automatic and requires manual intervention and a cluster restart, but it takes some of the pain out of a NameNode failure.

Remember that Hadoop 1.0 is a continuation of the Version 0.20 branch, so it does not contain the features mentioned previously.

Hadoop 2.0 will take these extensions to the next logical step: a fully automatic NameNode failover from the current master NameNode to an up-to-date backup NameNode. This NameNode **High Availability (HA)** is one of the most long-requested changes to the Hadoop architecture and will be a welcome addition when complete.

Hardware failure

When we killed the various Hadoop components earlier, we were—in most cases—using termination of the Hadoop processes as a proxy for the failure of the hosting physical hardware. From experience, it is quite rare to see the Hadoop processes fail without some underlying host issue causing the problem.

Host failure

Actual failure of the host is the simplest case to consider. A machine could fail due to a critical hardware issue (failed CPU, blown power supply, stuck fans, and so on), causing sudden failure of the Hadoop processes running on the host. Critical bugs in system-level software (kernel panics, I/O locks, and so on) can also have the same effect.

Generally speaking, if the failure causes a host to crash, reboot, or otherwise become unreachable for a period of time, we can expect Hadoop to act just as demonstrated throughout this chapter.

Host corruption

A more insidious problem is when a host appears to be functioning but is in reality producing corrupt results. Examples of this could be faulty memory resulting in corruption of data or disk sector errors, resulting in data on the disk being damaged.

For HDFS, this is where the status reports of corrupted blocks that we discussed earlier come into play.

For MapReduce there is no equivalent mechanism. Just as with most other software, the TaskTracker relies on data being written and read correctly by the host and has no means to detect corruption in either task execution or during the shuffle stage.

The risk of correlated failures

There is a phenomenon that most people don't consider until it bites them; sometimes the cause of a failure will also result in subsequent failures and greatly increase the chance of encountering a data loss scenario.

As an example, I once worked on a system that used four networking devices. One of these failed and no one cared about it; there were three remaining devices, after all. Until they all failed in an 18-hour period. Turned out they all contained hard drives from a faulty batch.

It doesn't have to be quite this exotic; more frequent causes will be due to faults in the shared services or facilities. Network switches can fail, power distribution can spike, air conditioning can fail, and equipment racks can short-circuit. As we'll see in the next chapter Hadoop doesn't assign blocks to random locations, it actively seeks to adopt a placement strategy that provides some protection from such failures in shared services.

We are again talking about unlikely scenarios, most often a failed host is just that and not the tip of a failure-crisis iceberg. However, remember to never discount the unlikely scenarios, especially when taking clusters to progressively larger scale.

Task failure due to software

As mentioned earlier, it is actually relatively rare to see the Hadoop processes themselves crash or otherwise spontaneously fail. What you are likely to see more of in practice are failures caused by the tasks, that is faults in the map or reduce tasks that you are executing on the cluster.

Failure of slow running tasks

We will first look at what happens if tasks hang or otherwise appear to Hadoop to have stopped making progress.

Time for action – causing task failure

Let's cause a task to fail; before we do, we will need to modify the default timeouts:

1. Add this configuration property to `mapred-site.xml`:

```
<property>
<name>mapred.task.timeout</name>
<value>30000</value>
</property>
```

2. We will now modify our old friend WordCount from *Chapter 3, Understanding MapReduce*. Copy `WordCount3.java` to a new file called `WordCountTimeout.java` and add the following imports:

```
import java.util.concurrent.TimeUnit ;
import org.apache.hadoop.fs.FileSystem ;
import org.apache.hadoop.fs.FSDataOutputStream ;
```

3. Replace the `map` method with the following one:

```
    public void map(Object key, Text value, Context context
                        ) throws IOException, InterruptedException {
String lockfile = "/user/hadoop/hdfs.lock" ;
  Configuration config = new Configuration() ;
FileSystem hdfs = FileSystem.get(config) ;
Path path = new Path(lockfile) ;
if (!hdfs.exists(path))
{
byte[] bytes = "A lockfile".getBytes() ;
  FSDataOutputStream out = hdfs.create(path) ;
out.write(bytes, 0, bytes.length);
out.close() ;
TimeUnit.SECONDS.sleep(100) ;
}

String[] words = value.toString().split(" ") ;

for (String str: words)
{
        word.set(str);
        context.write(word, one);

    }
    }
  }
```

4. Compile the file after changing the class name, jar it up, and execute it on the cluster:

```
$ Hadoop jar wc.jar WordCountTimeout test.txt output

...

11/12/11 19:19:51 INFO mapred.JobClient:  map 50% reduce 0%

11/12/11 19:20:25 INFO mapred.JobClient:  map 0% reduce 0%

11/12/11 19:20:27 INFO mapred.JobClient: Task Id : attempt_2011121
11821_0004_m_000000_0, Status : FAILED

Task attempt_201112111821_0004_m_000000_0 failed to report status
for 32 seconds. Killing!

11/12/11 19:20:31 INFO mapred.JobClient:  map 100% reduce 0%

11/12/11 19:20:43 INFO mapred.JobClient:  map 100% reduce 100%

11/12/11 19:20:45 INFO mapred.JobClient: Job complete:
job_201112111821_0004

11/12/11 19:20:45 INFO mapred.JobClient: Counters: 18

11/12/11 19:20:45 INFO mapred.JobClient:   Job Counters

...
```

What just happened?

We first modified a default Hadoop property that manages how long a task can seemingly make no progress before the Hadoop framework considers it for termination.

Then we modified WordCount3 to add some logic that causes the task to sleep for 100 seconds. We used a lock file on HDFS to ensure that only a single task instance sleeps. If we just had the sleep statement in the map operation without any checks, every mapper would timeout and the job would fail.

Have a go hero – HDFS programmatic access

We said we would not really deal with programmatic access to HDFS in this book. However, take a look at what we have done here and browse through the Javadoc for these classes. You will find that the interface largely follows the patterns for access to a standard Java filesystem.

Then we compile, jar up the classes, and execute the job on the cluster. The first task goes to sleep and after exceeding the threshold we set (the value was specified in milliseconds), Hadoop kills the task and reschedules another mapper to process the split assigned to the failed task.

Hadoop's handling of slow-running tasks

Hadoop has a balancing act to perform here. It wants to terminate tasks that have got stuck or, for other reasons, are running abnormally slowly; but sometimes complex tasks simply take a long time. This is especially true if the task relies on any external resources to complete its execution.

Hadoop looks for evidence of progress from a task when deciding how long it has been idle/quiet/stuck. Generally this could be:

- Emitting results
- Writing values to counters
- Explicitly reporting progress

For the latter, Hadoop provides the `Progressable` interface which contains one method of interest:

```
Public void progress() ;
```

The `Context` class implements this interface, so any mapper or reducer can call `context.progress()` to show it is alive and continuing to process.

Speculative execution

Typically, a MapReduce job will comprise of many discrete maps and reduce task executions. When run across a cluster, there is a real risk that a misconfigured or ill host will cause its tasks to run significantly slower than the others.

To address this, Hadoop will assign duplicate maps or reduce tasks across the cluster towards the end of the map or reduce phase. This speculative task execution is aimed at preventing one or two slow running tasks from causing a significant impact on the overall job execution time.

Hadoop's handling of failing tasks

Tasks won't just hang; sometimes they'll explicitly throw exceptions, abort, or otherwise stop executing in a less silent way than the ones mentioned previously.

Hadoop has three configuration properties that control how it responds to task failures, all set in `mapred-site.xml`:

- `mapred.map.max.attempts`: A given map task will be retried this many times before causing the job to fail

- ◆ `mapred.reduce.max.attempts`: A given reduce task will be retried these many times before causing the job to fail
- ◆ `mapred.max.tracker.failures`: The job will fail if this many individual task failures are recorded

The default value for all of these is 4.

> Note that it does not make sense for `mapred.tracker.max.failures` to be set to a value smaller than either of the other two properties.
>
> Which of these you consider setting will depend on the nature of your data and jobs. If your jobs access external resources that may occasionally cause transient errors, increasing the number of repeat failures of a task may be useful. But if the task is very data-specific, these properties may be less applicable as a task that fails once will do so again. However, note that a default value higher than 1 does make sense as in a large complex system various transient failures are always possible.

Have a go hero – causing tasks to fail

Modify the WordCount example; instead of sleeping, have it throw a RuntimeException based on a random number. Modify the cluster configuration and explore the relationship between the configuration properties that manage how many failed tasks will cause the whole job to fail.

Task failure due to data

The final types of failure that we will explore are those related to data. By this, we mean tasks that crash because a given record had corrupt data, used the wrong data types or formats, or a wide variety of related problems. We mean those cases where the data received diverges from expectations.

Handling dirty data through code

One approach to dirty data is to write mappers and reducers that deal with data defensively. So, for example, if the value received by the mapper should be a comma-separated list of values, first validate the number of items before processing the data. If the first value should be a string representation of an integer, ensure that the conversion into a numerical type has solid error handling and default behavior.

The problem with this approach is that there will always be some type of weird data input that was not considered, no matter how careful you were. Did you consider receiving values in a different unicode character set? What about multiple character sets, null values, badly terminated strings, wrongly encoded escape characters, and so on?

If the data input to your jobs is something you generate and/or control, these possibilities are less of a concern. However, if you are processing data received from external sources, there will always be grounds for surprise.

Using Hadoop's skip mode

The alternative is to configure Hadoop to approach task failures differently. Instead of looking upon a failed task as an atomic event, Hadoop can instead attempt to identify which records may have caused the problem and exclude them from future task executions. This mechanism is known as **skip mode**. This can be useful if you are experiencing a wide variety of data issues where coding around them is not desirable or practical. Alternatively, you may have little choice if, within your job, you are using third-party libraries for which you may not have the source code.

Skip mode is currently available only for jobs written to the pre 0.20 version of API, which is another consideration.

Time for action – handling dirty data by using skip mode

Let's see skip mode in action by writing a MapReduce job that receives the data that causes it to fail:

1. Save the following Ruby script as `gendata.rb`:

    ```ruby
    File.open("skipdata.txt", "w") do |file|
      3.times do
        500000.times{file.write("A valid record\n")}
        5.times{file.write("skiptext\n")}
      end
      500000.times{file.write("A valid record\n")}
    End
    ```

2. Run the script:

    ```
    $ ruby gendata.rb
    ```

3. Check the size of the generated file and its number of lines:

    ```
    $ ls -lh skipdata.txt
    -rw-rw-r-- 1 hadoop hadoop 29M 2011-12-17 01:53 skipdata.txt
    ~$ cat skipdata.txt | wc -l
    2000015
    ```

4. Copy the file onto HDFS:

    ```
    $ hadoop fs -put skipdata.txt skipdata.txt
    ```

5. Add the following property definition to `mapred-site.xml`:

```
<property>
<name>mapred.skip.map.max.skip.records</name>
<value5</value>
</property>
```

6. Check the value set for `mapred.max.map.task.failures` and set it to 20 if it is lower.

7. Save the following Java file as `SkipData.java`:

```java
import java.io.IOException;

import org.apache.hadoop.conf.* ;
import org.apache.hadoop.fs.Path;
import org.apache.hadoop.io.* ;
import org.apache.hadoop.mapred.* ;
import org.apache.hadoop.mapred.lib.* ;

public class SkipData
{

    public static class MapClass extends MapReduceBase
    implements Mapper<LongWritable, Text, Text, LongWritable>
    {

        private final static LongWritable one = new
LongWritable(1);
        private Text word = new Text("totalcount");

        public void map(LongWritable key, Text value,
            OutputCollector<Text, LongWritable> output,
                Reporter reporter) throws IOException
                {
                    String line = value.toString();

                    if (line.equals("skiptext"))
                    throw new RuntimeException("Found skiptext") ;
                    output.collect(word, one);
                }
        }

        public static void main(String[] args) throws Exception
        {
                Configuration config = new Configuration() ;
```

```
            JobConf conf = new JobConf(config, SkipData.class);
            conf.setJobName("SkipData");

            conf.setOutputKeyClass(Text.class);
            conf.setOutputValueClass(LongWritable.class);

            conf.setMapperClass(MapClass.class);
            conf.setCombinerClass(LongSumReducer.class);
            conf.setReducerClass(LongSumReducer.class);

            FileInputFormat.setInputPaths(conf,args[0]) ;
            FileOutputFormat.setOutputPath(conf, new
    Path(args[1])) ;

            JobClient.runJob(conf);
        }
    }
```

8. Compile this file and jar it into `skipdata.jar`.

9. Run the job:

```
$ hadoop jar skip.jar SkipData skipdata.txt output
...
11/12/16 17:59:07 INFO mapred.JobClient:  map 45% reduce 8%
11/12/16 17:59:08 INFO mapred.JobClient: Task Id : attempt_2011121
61623_0014_m_000003_0, Status : FAILED
java.lang.RuntimeException: Found skiptext
   at SkipData$MapClass.map(SkipData.java:26)
   at SkipData$MapClass.map(SkipData.java:12)
   at org.apache.hadoop.mapred.MapRunner.run(MapRunner.java:50)
   at org.apache.hadoop.mapred.MapTask.runOldMapper(MapTask.
java:358)
   at org.apache.hadoop.mapred.MapTask.run(MapTask.java:307)
   at org.apache.hadoop.mapred.Child.main(Child.java:170)


11/12/16 17:59:11 INFO mapred.JobClient:  map 42% reduce 8%
...
11/12/16 18:01:26 INFO mapred.JobClient:  map 70% reduce 16%
11/12/16 18:01:35 INFO mapred.JobClient:  map 71% reduce 16%
11/12/16 18:01:43 INFO mapred.JobClient: Task Id : attempt_2011111
61623_0014_m_000003_2, Status : FAILED
java.lang.RuntimeException: Found skiptext
...
11/12/16 18:12:44 INFO mapred.JobClient:  map 99% reduce 29%
11/12/16 18:12:50 INFO mapred.JobClient:  map 100% reduce 29%
```

```
11/12/16 18:13:00 INFO mapred.JobClient:  map 100% reduce 100%
11/12/16 18:13:02 INFO mapred.JobClient: Job complete:
job_201112161623_0014
...
```

10. Examine the contents of the job output file:

```
$ hadoop fs -cat output/part-00000
totalcount   2000000
```

11. Look in the output directory for skipped records:

```
$ hadoop fs -ls output/_logs/skip
Found 15 items
-rw-r--r--    3 hadoop supergroup          203 2011-12-16 18:05 /
user/hadoop/output/_logs/skip/attempt_201112161623_0014_m_000001_3
-rw-r--r--    3 hadoop supergroup          211 2011-12-16 18:06 /
user/hadoop/output/_logs/skip/attempt_201112161623_0014_m_000001_4
...
```

12. Check the job details from the MapReduce UI to observe the recorded statistics as shown in the following screenshot:

Kind	% Complete	Num Tasks	Pending	Running	Complete	Killed	Failed/Killed Task Attempts
map	100.00%	8	0	0	8	0	22 / 1
reduce	100.00%	1	0	0	1	0	0 / 0

	Counter	Map	Reduce	Total
Job Counters	Launched reduce tasks	0	0	1
	Rack-local map tasks	0	0	16
	Launched map tasks	0	0	31
	Data-local map tasks	0	0	15
SkippingTaskCounters	MapProcessedRecords	2,000,000	0	2,000,000
FileSystemCounters	FILE_BYTES_READ	378	321	699
	HDFS_BYTES_READ	30,028,814	0	30,028,814
	FILE_BYTES_WRITTEN	997	321	1,318
	HDFS_BYTES_WRITTEN	670	19	689
	Reduce input groups	0	1	1
	Map skipped records	15	0	15
	Combine output records	15	0	15

What just happened?

We had to do a lot of setup here so let's walk through it a step at a time.

Firstly, we needed to configure Hadoop to use skip mode; it is disabled by default. The key configuration property was set to 5, meaning that we didn't want the framework to skip any set of records greater than this number. Note that this includes the invalid records, and by setting this property to 0 (the default) Hadoop will not enter skip mode.

We also check to ensure that Hadoop is configured with a sufficiently high threshold for repeated task attempt failures, which we will explain shortly.

Next we needed a test file that we could use to simulate dirty data. We wrote a simple Ruby script that generated a file with 2 million lines that we would treat as valid with three sets of five bad records interspersed through the file. We ran this script and confirmed that the generated file did indeed have 2,000,015 lines. This file was then put on HDFS where it would be the job input.

We then wrote a simple MapReduce job that effectively counts the number of valid records. Every time the line reads from the input as the valid text we emit an additional count of 1 to what will be aggregated as a final total. When the invalid lines are encountered, the mapper fails by throwing an exception.

We then compile this file, jar it up, and run the job. The job takes a while to run and as seen from the extracts of the job status, it follows a pattern that we have not seen before. The map progress counter will increase but when a task fails, the progress will drop back then start increasing again. This is skip mode in action.

Every time a key/value pair is passed to the mapper, Hadoop by default increments a counter that allows it to keep track of which record caused a failure.

> If your map or reduce tasks process their input through mechanisms other than directly receiving all data via the arguments to the map or reduce method (for example, from asynchronous processes or caches) you will need to ensure you explicitly update this counter manually.

When a task fails, Hadoop retries it on the same block but attempts to work around the invalid records. Through a binary search approach, the framework performs retries across the data until the number of skipped records is no greater than the maximum value we configured earlier, that is 5. This process does require multiple task retries and failures as the framework seeks the optimal batch to skip, which is why we had to ensure the framework was configured to be tolerant of a higher-than-usual number of repeated task failures.

We watched the job continue following this back and forth process and on completion checked the contents of the output file. This showed 2,000,000 processed records, that is the correct number of valid records in our input file. Hadoop successfully managed to skip only the three sets of five invalid records.

We then looked within the `_logs` directory in the job output directory and saw that there is a skip directory containing the sequence files of the skipped records.

Finally, we looked at the MapReduce web UI to see the overall job status, which included both the number of records processed while in skip mode as well as the number of records skipped. Note that the total number of failed tasks was 22, which is greater than our threshold for failed map attempts, but this number is aggregate failures across multiple tasks.

To skip or not to skip...

Skip mode can be very effective but as we have seen previously, there is a performance penalty caused by Hadoop having to determine which record range to skip. Our test file was actually quite helpful to Hadoop; the bad records were nicely grouped in three groups and only accounted for a tiny fraction of the overall data set. If there were many more invalid records in the input data and they were spread much more widely across the file, a more effective approach may have been to use a precursor MapReduce job to filter out all the invalid records.

This is why we have presented the topics of writing code to handle bad data and using skip mode consecutively. Both are valid techniques that you should have in your tool belt. There is no single answer to when one or the other is the best approach, you need to consider the input data, performance requirements, and opportunities for hardcoding before making a decision.

Summary

We have caused a lot of destruction in this chapter and I hope you never have to deal with this much failure in a single day with an operational Hadoop cluster. There are some key learning points from the experience.

In general, component failures are not something to fear in Hadoop. Particularly with large clusters, failure of some component or host will be pretty commonplace and Hadoop is engineered to handle this situation. HDFS, with its responsibility to store data, actively manages the replication of each block and schedules new copies to be made when the DataNode processes die.

MapReduce has a stateless approach to TaskTracker failure and in general simply schedules duplicate jobs if one fails. It may also do this to prevent the misbehaving hosts from slowing down the whole job.

Failure of the HDFS and MapReduce master nodes is a more significant failure. In particular, the NameNode process holds critical filesystem data and you must actively ensure you have it set up to allow a new NameNode process to take over.

In general, hardware failures will look much like the previous process failures, but always be aware of the possibility of correlated failures. If tasks fail due to software errors, Hadoop will retry them within configurable thresholds. Data-related errors can be worked around by employing skip mode, though it will come with a performance penalty.

Now that we know how to handle failures in our cluster, we will spend the next chapter working through the broader issues of cluster setup, health, and maintenance.

7
Keeping Things Running

Having a Hadoop cluster is not all about writing interesting programs to do clever data analysis. You also need to maintain the cluster, and keep it tuned and ready to do the data crunching you want.

In this chapter we will cover:

- ◆ More about Hadoop configuration properties
- ◆ How to select hardware for your cluster
- ◆ How Hadoop security works
- ◆ Managing the NameNode
- ◆ Managing HDFS
- ◆ Managing MapReduce
- ◆ Scaling the cluster

Although these topics are operationally focused, they do give us an opportunity to explore some aspects of Hadoop we have not looked at before. Therefore, even if you won't be personally managing the cluster, there should be useful information here for you too.

A note on EMR

One of the main benefits of using cloud services such as those offered by Amazon Web Services is that much of the maintenance overhead is borne by the service provider. Elastic MapReduce can create Hadoop clusters tied to the execution of a single task (non-persistent job flows) or allow long-running clusters that can be used for multiple jobs (persistent job flows). When non-persistent job flows are used, the actual mechanics of how the underlying Hadoop cluster is configured and run are largely invisible to the user. Consequently, users employing non-persistent job flows will not need to consider many of the topics in this chapter. If you are using EMR with persistent job flows, many topics (but not all) do become relevant.

We will generally talk about local Hadoop clusters in this chapter. If you need to reconfigure a persistent job flow, use the same Hadoop properties but set them as described in *Chapter 3, Writing MapReduce Jobs*.

Hadoop configuration properties

Before we look at running the cluster, let's talk a little about Hadoop's configuration properties. We have been introducing many of these along the way, and there are a few additional points worth considering.

Default values

One of the most mystifying things to a new Hadoop user is the large number of configuration properties. Where do they come from, what do they mean, and what are their default values?

If you have the full Hadoop distribution—that is, not just the binary distribution—the following XML files will answer your questions:

- `Hadoop/src/core/core-default.xml`
- `Hadoop/src/hdfs/hdfs-default.xml`
- `Hadoop/src/mapred/mapred-default.xml`

Time for action – browsing default properties

Fortunately, the XML documents are not the only way of looking at the default values; there are also more readable HTML versions, which we'll now take a quick look at.

These files are not included in the Hadoop binary-only distribution; if you are using that, you can also find these files on the Hadoop website.

1. Point your browser at the `docs/core-default.html` file within your Hadoop distribution directory and browse its contents. It should look like the next screenshot:

2. Now, similarly, browse these other files:

- ❑ `Hadoop/docs/hdfs-default.html`

- ❑ `Hadoop/docs/mapred-default.html`

What just happened?

As you can see, each property has a name, default value, and a brief description. You will also see there are indeed a very large number of properties. Do not expect to understand all of these now, but do spend a little time browsing to get a flavor for the type of customization allowed by Hadoop.

Additional property elements

When we have previously set properties in the configuration files, we have used an XML element of the following form:

```
<property>
<name>the.property.name</name>
<value>The property value</value>
</property>
```

There are an additional two optional XML elements we can add, description and final. A fully described property using these additional elements now looks as follows:

```
<property>
<name>the.property.name</name>
<value>The default property value</value>
<description>A textual description of the property</description>
<final>Boolean</final>
</property>
```

The description element is self-explanatory and provides the location for the descriptive text we saw for each property in the preceding HTML files.

The final property has a similar meaning as in Java: any property marked final cannot be overridden by values in any other files or by other means; we will see this shortly. Use this for those properties where for performance, integrity, security, or other reasons, you wish to enforce cluster-wide values.

Default storage location

You will see properties that modify where Hadoop stores its data on both the local disk and HDFS. There's one property used as the basis for many others hadoop.tmp.dir, which is the root location for all Hadoop files, and its default value is /tmp.

Unfortunately, many Linux distributions—including Ubuntu—are configured to remove the contents of this directory on each reboot. This means that if you do not override this property, you will lose all your HDFS data on the next host reboot. Therefore, it is worthwhile to set something like the following in core-site.xml:

```
<property>
<name>hadoop.tmp.dir</name>
<value>/var/lib/hadoop</value>
</property>
```

Remember to ensure the location is writable by the user who will start Hadoop, and that the disk the directory is located on has enough space. As you will see later, there are a number of other properties that allow more granular control of where particular types of data are stored.

Where to set properties

We have previously used the configuration files to specify new values for Hadoop properties. This is fine, but does have an overhead if we are trying to find the best value for a property or are executing a job that requires special handling.

It is possible to use the JobConf class to programmatically set configuration properties on the executing job. There are two types of methods supported, the first being those that are dedicated to setting a specific property, such as the ones we've seen for setting the job name, input, and output formats, among others. There are also methods to set properties such as the preferred number of map and reduce tasks for the job.

In addition, there are a set of generic methods, such as the following:

◆ Void set(String key, String value);

◆ Void setIfUnset(String key, String value);

◆ Void setBoolean(String key, Boolean value);

◆ Void setInt(String key, int value);

These are more flexible and do not require specific methods to be created for each property we wish to modify. However, they also lose compile time checking meaning you can use an invalid property name or assign the wrong type to a property and will only find out at runtime.

> This ability to set property values both programmatically and in the configuration files is an important reason for the ability to mark a property as final. For properties for which you do not want any submitted job to have the ability to override them, set them as final within the master configuration files.

Setting up a cluster

Before we look at how to keep a cluster running, let's explore some aspects of setting it up in the first place.

How many hosts?

When considering a new Hadoop cluster, one of the first questions is how much capacity to start with. We know that we can add additional nodes as our needs grow, but we also want to start off in a way that eases that growth.

There really is no clear-cut answer here, as it will depend largely on the size of the data sets you will be processing and the complexity of the jobs to be executed. The only near-absolute is to say that if you want a replication factor of *n*, you should have at least that many nodes. Remember though that nodes will fail, and if you have the same number of nodes as the default replication factor then any single failure will push blocks into an under-replicated state. In most clusters with tens or hundreds of nodes, this is not a concern; but for very small clusters with a replication factor of 3, the safest approach would be a five-node cluster.

Calculating usable space on a node

An obvious starting point for the required number of nodes is to look at the size of the data set to be processed on the cluster. If you have hosts with 2 TB of disk space and a 10 TB data set, the temptation would be to assume that five nodes is the minimum number needed.

This is incorrect, as it omits consideration of the replication factor and the need for temporary space. Recall that the output of mappers is written to the local disk to be retrieved by the reducers. We need to account for this non-trivial disk usage.

A good rule of thumb would be to assume a replication factor of 3, and that 25 percent of what remains should be accounted for as temporary space. Using these assumptions, the calculation of the needed cluster for our 10 TB data set on 2 TB nodes would be as follows:

◆ Divide the total storage space on a node by the replication factor:

2 TB/3 = 666 GB

◆ Reduce this figure by 25 percent to account for temp space:

666 GB * 0.75 = 500 GB

◆ Each 2 TB node therefore has approximately 500 GB (0.5 TB) of usable space
◆ Divide the data set size by this figure:

10 TB / 500 GB = 20

So our 10 TB data set will likely need a 20 node cluster as a minimum, four times our naïve estimate.

This pattern of needing more nodes than expected is not unusual and should be remembered when considering how high-spec you want the hosts to be; see the *Sizing hardware* section later in this chapter.

Location of the master nodes

The next question is where the NameNode, JobTracker, and SecondaryNameNode will live. We have seen that a DataNode can run on the same host as the NameNode and the TaskTracker can co-exist with the JobTracker, but this is unlikely to be a great setup for a production cluster.

As we will see, the NameNode and SecondaryNameNode have some specific resource requirements, and anything that affects their performance is likely to slow down the entire cluster operation.

The ideal situation would be to have the NameNode, JobTracker, and SecondaryNameNode on their own dedicated hosts. However, for very small clusters, this would result in a significant increase in the hardware footprint without necessarily reaping the full benefit.

If at all possible, the first step should be to separate the NameNode, JobTracker, and SecondaryNameNode onto a single dedicated host that does not have any DataNode or TaskTracker processes running. As the cluster continues to grow, you can add an additional server host and then move the NameNode onto its own host, keeping the JobTracker and SecondaryNameNode co-located. Finally, as the cluster grows yet further, it will make sense to move to full separation.

> As discussed in *Chapter 6, Keeping Things Running*, Hadoop 2.0 will split the Secondary NameNode into Backup NameNodes and Checkpoint NameNodes. Best practice is still evolving, but aiming towards having a dedicated host each for the NameNode and at least one Backup NameNode looks sensible.

Sizing hardware

The amount of data to be stored is not the only consideration regarding the specification of the hardware to be used for the nodes. Instead, you have to consider the amount of processing power, memory, storage types, and networking available.

Much has been written about selecting hardware for a Hadoop cluster, and once again there is no single answer that will work for all cases. The big variable is the types of MapReduce tasks that will be executed on the data and, in particular, if they are bounded by CPU, memory, I/O, or something else.

Processor / memory / storage ratio

A good way of thinking of this is to look at potential hardware in terms of the CPU / memory / storage ratio. So, for example, a quad-core host with 8 GB memory and 2 TB storage could be thought of as having two cores and 4 GB memory per 1 TB of storage.

Then look at the types of MapReduce jobs you will be running, does that ratio seem appropriate? In other words, does your workload require proportionally more of one of these resources or will a more balanced configuration be sufficient?

This is, of course, best assessed by prototyping and gathering metrics, but that isn't always possible. If not, consider what part of the job is the most expensive. For example, some of the jobs we have seen are I/O bound and read data from the disk, perform simple transformations, and then write results back to the disk. If this was typical of our workload, we could likely use hardware with more storage—especially if it was delivered by multiple disks to increase I/O—and use less CPU and memory.

Conversely, jobs that perform very heavy number crunching would need more CPU, and those that create or use large data structures would benefit from memory.

Think of it in terms of limiting factors. If your job was running, would it be CPU-bound (processors at full capacity; memory and I/O to spare), memory-bound (physical memory full and swapping to disk; CPU and I/O to spare), or I/O-bound (CPU and memory to spare, but data being read/written to/from disk at maximum possible speed)? Can you get hardware that eases that bound?

This is of course a limitless process, as once you ease one bound another will manifest itself. So always remember that the idea is to get a performance profile that makes sense in the context of your likely usage scenario.

What if you really don't know the performance characteristics of your jobs? Ideally, try to find out, do some prototyping on any hardware you have and use that to inform your decision. However, if even that is not possible, you will have to go for a configuration and try it out. Remember that Hadoop supports heterogeneous hardware—though having uniform specifications makes your life easier in the end—so build the cluster to the minimum possible size and assess the hardware. Use this knowledge to inform future decisions regarding additional host purchases or upgrades of the existing fleet.

EMR as a prototyping platform

Recall that when we configured a job on Elastic MapReduce we chose the type of hardware for both the master and data/task nodes. If you plan to run your jobs on EMR, you have a built-in capability to tweak this configuration to find the best combination of hardware specifications to price and execution speed.

However, even if you do not plan to use EMR full-time, it can be a valuable prototyping platform. If you are sizing a cluster but do not know the performance characteristics of your jobs, consider some prototyping on EMR to gain better insight. Though you may end up spending money on the EMR service that you had not planned, this will likely be a lot less than the cost of finding out you have bought completely unsuitable hardware for your cluster.

Special node requirements

Not all hosts have the same hardware requirements. In particular, the host for the NameNode may look radically different to those hosting the DataNodes and TaskTrackers.

Recall that the NameNode holds an in-memory representation of the HDFS filesystem and the relationship between files, directories, blocks, nodes, and various metadata concerning all of this. This means that the NameNode will tend to be memory bound and may require larger memory than any other host, particularly for very large clusters or those with a huge number of files. Though 16 GB may be a common memory size for DataNodes/TaskTrackers, it's not unusual for the NameNode host to have 64 GB or more of memory. If the NameNode ever ran out of physical memory and started to use swap space, the impact on cluster performance would likely be severe.

However, though 64 GB is large for physical memory, it's tiny for modern storage, and given that the filesystem image is the only data stored by the NameNode, we don't need the massive storage common on the DataNode hosts. We care much more about NameNode reliability so are likely to have several disks in a redundant configuration. Consequently, the NameNode host will benefit from multiple small drives (for redundancy) rather than large drives.

Overall, therefore, the NameNode host is likely to look quite different from the other hosts in the cluster; this is why we made the earlier recommendations regarding moving the NameNode to its own host as soon as budget/space allows, as its unique hardware requirements are more easily satisfied this way.

> The SecondaryNameNode (or CheckpointNameNode and BackupNameNode in Hadoop 2.0) share the same hardware requirements as the NameNode. You can run it on a more generic host while in its secondary capacity, but if you do ever need to switch and make it the NameNode due to failure of the primary hardware, you may be in trouble.

Storage types

Though you will find strong opinions on some of the previous points regarding the relative importance of processor, memory, and storage capacity, or I/O, such arguments are usually based around application requirements and hardware characteristics and metrics. Once we start discussing the type of storage to be used, however, it is very easy to get into flame war situations, where you will find extremely entrenched opinions.

Commodity versus enterprise class storage

The first argument will be over whether it makes most sense to use hard drives aimed at the commodity/consumer segments or those aimed at enterprise customers. The former (primarily SATA disks) are larger, cheaper, and slower, and have lower quoted figures for **mean time between failures (MTBF)**. Enterprise disks will use technologies such as SAS or Fiber Channel, and will on the whole be smaller, more expensive, faster, and have higher quoted MTBF figures.

Single disk versus RAID

The next question will be on how the disks are configured. The enterprise-class approach would be to use **Redundant Arrays of Inexpensive Disks (RAID)** to group multiple disks into a single logical storage device that can quietly survive one or more disk failures. This comes with the cost of a loss in overall capacity and an impact on the read/write rates achieved.

The other position is to treat each disk independently to maximize total storage and aggregate I/O, at the cost of a single disk failure causing host downtime.

Finding the balance

The Hadoop architecture is, in many ways, predicated on the assumption that hardware will fail. From this perspective, it is possible to argue that there is no need to use any traditional enterprise-focused storage features. Instead, use many large, cheap disks to maximize the total storage and read and write from them in parallel to do likewise for I/O throughput. A single disk failure may cause the host to fail, but the cluster will, as we have seen, work around this failure.

This is a completely valid argument and in many cases makes perfect sense. What the argument ignores, however, is the cost of bringing a host back into service. If your cluster is in the next room and you have a shelf of spare disks, host recovery will likely be a quick, painless, and inexpensive task. However, if you have your cluster hosted by a commercial collocation facility, any hands-on maintenance may cost a lot more. This is even more the case if you are using fully-managed servers where you have to pay the provider for maintenance tasks. In such a situation, the extra cost and reduced capacity and I/O from using RAID may make sense.

Network storage

One thing that will almost never make sense is to use networked storage for your primary cluster storage. Be it block storage via a **Storage Area Network (SAN)** or file-based via **Network File System (NFS)** or similar protocols, these approaches constrain Hadoop by introducing unnecessary bottlenecks and additional shared devices that would have a critical impact on failure.

Sometimes, however, you may be forced for non-technical reasons to use something like this. It's not that it won't work, just that it changes how Hadoop will perform in regards to speed and tolerance to failures, so be sure you understand the consequences if this happens.

Hadoop networking configuration

Hadoop's support of networking devices is not as sophisticated as it is for storage, and consequently you have fewer hardware choices to make compared to CPU, memory, and storage setup. The bottom line is that Hadoop can currently support only one network device and cannot, for example, use all 4-gigabit Ethernet connections on a host for an aggregate of 4-gigabit throughput. If you need network throughput greater than that provided by a single-gigabit port then, unless your hardware or operating system can present multiple ports as a single device to Hadoop, the only option is to use a 10-gigabit Ethernet device.

How blocks are placed

We have talked a lot about HDFS using replication for redundancy, but have not explored how Hadoop chooses where to place the replicas for a block.

In most traditional server farms, the various hosts (as well as networking and other devices) are housed in standard-sized racks that stack the equipment vertically. Each rack will usually have a common power distribution unit that feeds it and will often have a network switch that acts as the interface between the broader network and all the hosts in the rack.

Given this setup, we can identify three broad types of failure:

♦ Those that affect a single host (for example, CPU/memory/disk/motherboard failure)

♦ Those that affect a single rack (for example, power unit or switch failure)

♦ Those that affect the entire cluster (for example, larger power/network failures, cooling/environmental outages)

 Remember that Hadoop currently does not support a cluster that is spread across multiple data centers, so instances of the third type of failure will quite likely bring down your cluster.

By default, Hadoop will treat each node as if it is in the same physical rack. This implies that the bandwidth and latency between any pair of hosts is approximately equal and that each node is equally likely to suffer a related failure as any other.

Rack awareness

If, however, you do have a multi-rack setup, or another configuration that otherwise invalidates the previous assumptions, you can add the ability for each node to report its rack ID to Hadoop, which will then take this into account when placing replicas.

In such a setup, Hadoop tries to place the first replica of a node on a given host, the second on another within the same rack, and the third on a host in a different rack.

This strategy provides a good balance between performance and availability. When racks contain their own network switches, communication between hosts inside the rack often has lower latency than that with external hosts. This strategy places two replicas within a rack to ensure maximum speed of writing for these replicas, but keeps one outside the rack to provide redundancy in the event of a rack failure.

The rack-awareness script

If the `topology.script.file.name` property is set and points to an executable script on the filesystem, it will be used by the NameNode to determine the rack for each host.

Note that the property needs to be set and the script needs to exist only on the NameNode host.

The NameNode will pass to the script the IP address of each node it discovers, so the script is responsible for a mapping from node IP address to rack name.

If no script is specified, each node will be reported as a member of a single default rack.

Time for action – examining the default rack configuration

Let's take a look at how the default rack configuration is set up in our cluster.

1. Execute the following command:

   ```
   $ Hadoop fsck -rack
   ```

2. The result should include output similar to the following:

   ```
   Default replication factor:    3
   Average block replication:     3.3045976
   Corrupt blocks:                0
   Missing replicas:              18 (0.5217391 %)
   Number of data-nodes:          4
   Number of racks:               1


   The filesystem under path '/' is HEALTHY
   ```

What just happened?

Both the tool used and its output are of interest here. The tool is **hadoop fsck**, which can be used to examine and fix filesystem problems. As can be seen, this includes some information not dissimilar to our old friend `hadoop dfsadmin`, though that tool is focused more on the state of each node in detail while `hadoop fsck` reports on the internals of the filesystem as a whole.

One of the things it reports is the total number of racks in the cluster, which, as seen in the preceding output, has the value 1, as expected.

> This command was executed on a cluster that had recently been used for some HDFS resilience testing. This explains the figures for average block replication and under-replicated blocks.
>
> If a block ends up with more than the required number of replicas due to a host temporarily failing, the host coming back into service will put the block above the minimum replication factor. Along with ensuring that blocks have replicas added to meet the replication factor, Hadoop will also delete excess replicas to return blocks to the replication factor.

Time for action – adding a rack awareness script

We can enhance the default flat rack configuration by creating a script that derives the rack location for each host.

1. Create a script in the Hadoop user's home directory on the NameNode host called `rack-script.sh`, containing the following text. Remember to change the IP address to one of your HDFS nodes.

```
#!/bin/bash

if [ $1 = "10.0.0.101" ]; then
    echo -n "/rack1 "
else
    echo -n "/default-rack "
fi
```

2. Make this script executable.

```
$ chmod +x rack-script.sh
```

3. Add the following property to `core-site.xml` on the NameNode host:

```
<property>
<name>topology.script.file.name</name>
<value>/home/Hadoop/rack-script.sh</value>
</property>
```

4. Restart HDFS.

```
$ start-dfs.sh
```

5. Check the filesystem via `fsck`.

```
$ Hadoop fsck -rack
```

The output of the preceding command can be shown in the following screenshot:

```
hadoop@headnode: ~
File  Edit  View  Terminal  Help
hadoop@headnode:~$ hadoop fsck -rack
FSCK started by hadoop from /127.0.0.1 for path / at Wed Jan 02 15:02:13 PST 201
3
.Status: HEALTHY
 Total size:     75342464 B
 Total dirs:     3
 Total files:    1
 Total blocks (validated):       18 (avg. block size 4185692 B)
 Minimally replicated blocks:    18 (100.0 %)
 Over-replicated blocks:         0 (0.0 %)
 Under-replicated blocks:        0 (0.0 %)
 Mis-replicated blocks:          0 (0.0 %)
 Default replication factor:     3
 Average block replication:      3.0
 Corrupt blocks:                 0
 Missing replicas:               0 (0.0 %)
 Number of data-nodes:           3
 Number of racks:                2
FSCK ended at Wed Jan 02 15:02:13 PST 2013 in 1 milliseconds


The filesystem under path '/' is HEALTHY
hadoop@headnode:~$
```

What just happened?

We first created a simple script that returns one value for a named node and a default value for all others. We placed this on the NameNode host and added the needed configuration property to the NameNode `core-site.xml` file.

After starting HDFS, we used `hadoop fsck` to report on the filesystem and saw that we now have a two-rack cluster. With this knowledge, Hadoop will now employ more sophisticated block placement strategies, as described previously.

Using an external host file

A common approach is to keep a separate data file akin to the `/etc/hosts` file on Unix and use this to specify the IP/rack mapping, one per line. This file can then be updated independently and read by the rack-awareness script.

What is commodity hardware anyway?

Let's revisit the question of the general characteristics of the hosts used for your cluster, and whether they should look more like a commodity white box server or something built for a high-end enterprise environment.

Part of the problem is that "commodity" is an ambiguous term. What looks cheap and cheerful for one business may seem luxuriously high-end for another. We suggest considering the following points to keep in mind when selecting hardware and then remaining happy with your decision:

- With your hardware, are you paying a premium for reliability features that duplicate some of Hadoop's fault-tolerance capabilities?

- Are the higher-end hardware features you are paying for addressing the need or risk that you have confirmed is realistic in your environment?

- Have you validated the cost of the higher-end hardware to be higher than dealing with cheaper / less reliable hardware?

Pop quiz – setting up a cluster

Q1. Which of the following is most important when selecting hardware for your new Hadoop cluster?

1. The number of CPU cores and their speed.
2. The amount of physical memory.
3. The amount of storage.
4. The speed of the storage.
5. It depends on the most likely workload.

Q2. Why would you likely not want to use network storage in your cluster?

1. Because it may introduce a new single point of failure.
2. Because it most likely has approaches to redundancy and fault-tolerance that may be unnecessary given Hadoop's fault tolerance.
3. Because such a single device may have inferior performance to Hadoop's use of multiple local disks simultaneously.
4. All of the above.

Q3. You will be processing 10 TB of data on your cluster. Your main MapReduce job processes financial transactions, using them to produce statistical models of behavior and future forecasts. Which of the following hardware choices would be your first choice for the cluster?

1. 20 hosts each with fast dual-core processors, 4 GB memory, and one 500 GB disk drive.

2. 30 hosts each with fast dual-core processors, 8 GB memory, and two 500 GB disk drives.

3. 30 hosts each with fast quad-core processors, 8 GB memory, and one 1 TB disk drive.

4. 40 hosts each with 16 GB memory, fast quad-core processors, and four 1 TB disk drives.

Cluster access control

Once you have the shiny new cluster up and running, you need to consider questions of access and security. Who can access the data on the cluster—is there sensitive data that you really don't want the whole user base to see?

The Hadoop security model

Until very recently, Hadoop had a security model that could, at best, be described as "marking only". It associated an owner and group with each file but, as we'll see, did very little validation of a given client connection. Strong security would manage not only the markings given to a file but also the identities of all connecting users.

Time for action – demonstrating the default security

When we have previously shown listings of files, we have seen user and group names for them. However, we have not really explored what that means. Let's do so.

1. Create a test text file in the Hadoop user's home directory.

```
$ echo "I can read this!" > security-test.txt
$ hadoop fs -put security-test.txt  security-test.txt
```

2. Change the permissions on the file to be accessible only by the owner.

```
$ hadoop fs -chmod 700 security-test.txt
$ hadoop fs -ls
```

The output of the preceding command can be shown in the following screenshot:

3. Confirm you can still read the file.

```
$ hadoop fs -cat security-test.txt
```

You'll see the following line on the screen:

```
I can read this!
```

4. Connect to another node in the cluster and try to read the file from there.

```
$ ssh node2
```

```
$ hadoop fs -cat security-test.txt
```

You'll see the following line on the screen:

```
I can read this!
```

5. Log out from the other node.

```
$ exit
```

6. Create a home directory for another user and give them ownership.

```
$ hadoop m[Kfs -mkdir /user/garry
```

```
$ hadoop fs -chown garry /user/garry
```

```
$ hadoop fs -ls /user
```

The output of the preceding command can be shown in the following screenshot:

7. Switch to that user.

```
$ su garry
```

8. Try to read the test file in the Hadoop user's home directory.

```
$ hadoop/bin/hadoop fs -cat /user/hadoop/security-test.txt

cat: org.apache.hadoop.security.AccessControlException: Permission
denied: user=garry, access=READ, inode="security-test.txt":hadoop:
supergroup:rw-------
```

9. Place a copy of the file in this user's home directory and again make it accessible only by the owner.

```
$ Hadoop/bin/Hadoop fs -put security-test.txt security-test.txt
$ Hadoop/bin/Hadoop fs -chmod 700 security-test.txt
$ hadoop/bin/hadoop fs -ls
```

The output of the preceding command can be shown in following screenshot:

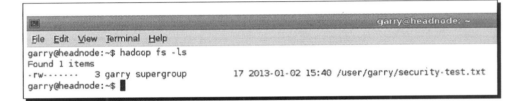

10. Confirm this user can access the file.

```
$ hadoop/bin/hadoop fs -cat security-test.txt
```

You'll see the following line on the screen:

```
I can read this!
```

11. Return to the Hadoop user.

```
$ exit
```

12. Try and read the file in the other user's home directory.

```
$ hadoop fs -cat /user/garry/security-test.txt
```

You'll see the following line on the screen:

```
I can read this!
```

What just happened?

We firstly used our Hadoop user to create a test file in its home directory on HDFS. We used the -chmod option to hadoop fs, which we have not seen before. This is very similar to the standard Unix **chmod** tool that gives various levels of read/write/execute access to the file owner, group members, and all users.

We then went to another host and tried to access the file, again as the Hadoop user. Not surprisingly, this worked. But why? What did Hadoop know about the Hadoop user that allowed it to give access to the file?

To explore this, we then created another home directory on HDFS (you can use any other account on the host you have access to), and gave it ownership by using the -chown option to hadoop fs. This should once again look similar to standard Unix -chown. Then we switched to this user and attempted to read the file stored in the Hadoop user's home directory. This failed with the security exception shown before, which is again what we expected. Once again, we copied a test file into this user's home directory and made it only accessible by the owner.

But we then muddied the waters by switching back to the Hadoop user and tried to access the file in the other account's home directory, which, surprisingly, worked.

User identity

The answer to the first part of the puzzle is that Hadoop uses the Unix ID of the user executing the HDFS command as the user identity on HDFS. So any commands executed by a user called alice will create files with an owner named alice and will only be able to read or write files to which this user has the correct access.

The security-minded will realize that to access a Hadoop cluster all one needs to do is create a user with the same name as an already existing HDFS user on any host that can connect to the cluster. So, for instance, in the previous example, any user named hadoop created on any host that can access the NameNode can read all files accessible by the user hadoop, which is actually even worse than it seems.

The super user

The previous step saw the Hadoop user access another user's files. Hadoop treats the user ID that started the cluster as the super user, and gives it various privileges, such as the ability to read, write, and modify any file on HDFS. The security-minded will realize even more the risk of having users called hadoop randomly created on hosts outside the Hadoop administrator's control.

More granular access control

The preceding situation has caused security to be a major weakness in Hadoop since its inception. The community has, however, not been standing still, and after much work the very latest versions of Hadoop support a more granular and stronger security model.

To avoid reliance on simple user IDs, the developers need to learn the user identity from somewhere, and the Kerberos system was chosen with which to integrate. This does require the establishment and maintenance of services outside the scope of this book, but if such security is important to you, consult the Hadoop documentation. Note that this support does allow integration with third-party identity systems such as Microsoft Active Directory, so it is quite powerful.

Working around the security model via physical access control

If the burden of Kerberos is too great, or security is a nice-to-have rather than an absolute, there are ways of mitigating the risk. One favored by me is to place the entire cluster behind a firewall with tight access control. In particular, only allow access to the NameNode and JobTracker services from a single host that will be treated as the cluster head node and to which all users connect.

Accessing Hadoop from non-cluster hosts

Hadoop does not need to be running on a host for it to use the command-line tools to access HDFS and run MapReduce jobs. As long as Hadoop is installed on the host and its configuration files have the correct locations of the NameNode and JobTracker, these will be found when invoking commands such as Hadoop fs and Hadoop jar.

This model works because only one host is used to interact with Hadoop; and since this host is controlled by the cluster administrator, normal users should be unable to create or access other user accounts.

Remember that this approach is not providing security. It is putting a hard shell around a soft system that reduces the ways in which the Hadoop security model can be subverted.

Managing the NameNode

Let's do some more risk reduction. In *Chapter 6, When Things Break*, I probably scared you when talking about the potential consequences of a failure of the host running the NameNode. If that section did not scare you, go back and re-read it—it should have. The summary is that the loss of the NameNode could see you losing every single piece of data on the cluster. This is because the NameNode writes a file called fsimage that contains all the metadata for the filesystem and records which blocks comprise which files. If the loss of the NameNode host makes the fsimage unrecoverable, all the HDFS data is likewise lost.

Configuring multiple locations for the fsimage class

The NameNode can be configured to simultaneously write `fsimage` to multiple locations. This is purely a redundancy mechanism, the same data is written to each location and there is no attempt to use multiple storage devices for increased performance. Instead, the policy is that multiple copies of `fsimage` will be harder to lose.

Time for action – adding an additional fsimage location

Let's now configure our NameNode to simultaneously write multiple copies of `fsimage` to give us our desired data resilience. To do this, we require an NFS-exported directory.

1. Ensure the cluster is stopped.

   ```
   $ stopall.sh
   ```

2. Add the following property to `Hadoop/conf/core-site.xml`, modifying the second path to point to an NFS-mounted location to which the additional copy of NameNode data can be written.

   ```
   <property>
   <name>dfs.name.dir</name>
   <value>${hadoop.tmp.dir}/dfs/name,/share/backup/namenode</value>
   </property>
   ```

3. Delete any existing contents of the newly added directory.

   ```
   $ rm -f /share/backup/namenode
   ```

4. Start the cluster.

   ```
   $ start-all.sh
   ```

5. Verify that `fsimage` is being written to both the specified locations by running the `md5sum` command against the two files specified before (change the following code depending on your configured locations):

   ```
   $ md5sum /var/hadoop/dfs/name/image/fsimage
   a25432981b0ecd6b70da647e9b94304a   /var/hadoop/dfs/name/image/
   fsimage
   $ md5sum /share/backup/namenode/image/fsimage
   a25432981b0ecd6b70da647e9b94304a   /share/backup/namenode/image/
   fsimage
   ```

What just happened?

Firstly, we ensured the cluster was stopped; though changes to the core configuration files are not reread by a running cluster, it's a good habit to get into in case that capability is ever added to Hadoop.

We then added a new property to our cluster configuration, specifying a value for the `data.name.dir` property. This property takes a list of comma-separated values and writes `fsimage` to each of these locations. Note how the `hadoop.tmp.dir` property discussed earlier is de-referenced, as would be seen when using Unix variables. This syntax allows us to base property values on others and inherit changes when the parent properties are updated.

Do not forget all required locations

The default value for this property is `${Hadoop.tmp.dir}/dfs/name`. When adding an additional value, remember to explicitly add the default one also, as shown before. Otherwise, only the single new value will be used for the property.

Before starting the cluster, we ensure the new directory exists and is empty. If the directory doesn't exist, the NameNode will fail to start as should be expected. If, however, the directory was previously used to store NameNode data, Hadoop will also fail to start as it will identify that both directories contain different NameNode data and it does not know which one is correct.

Be careful here! Especially if you are experimenting with various NameNode data locations or swapping back and forth between nodes; you really do not want to accidentally delete the contents from the wrong directory.

After starting the HDFS cluster, we wait for a moment and then use MD5 cryptographic checksums to verify that both locations contain the identical `fsimage`.

Where to write the fsimage copies

The recommendation is to write `fsimage` to at least two locations, one of which should be the remote (such as a NFS) filesystem, as in the previous example. `fsimage` is only updated periodically, so the filesystem does not need high performance.

In our earlier discussion regarding the choice of hardware, we alluded to other considerations for the NameNode host. Because of `fsimage` criticality, it may be useful to ensure it is written to more than one disk and to perhaps invest in disks with higher reliability, or even to write `fsimage` to a RAID array. If the host fails, using the copy written to the remote filesystem will be the easiest option; but just in case that has also experienced problems, it's good to have the choice of pulling another disk from the dead host and using it on another to recover the data.

Swapping to another NameNode host

We have ensured that `fsimage` is written to multiple locations and this is the single most important prerequisite for managing a swap to a different NameNode host. Now we need to actually do it.

This is something you really should not do on a production cluster. Absolutely not when trying for the first time, but even beyond that it's not a risk-free process. But do practice on other clusters and get an idea of what you'll do when disaster strikes.

Having things ready before disaster strikes

You don't want to be exploring this topic for the first time when you need to recover the production cluster. There are several things to do in advance that will make disaster recovery much less painful, not to mention possible:

◆ Ensure the NameNode is writing the `fsimage` to multiple locations, as done before.

◆ Decide which host will be the new NameNode location. If this is a host currently being used for a DataNode and TaskTracker, ensure it has the right hardware needed to host the NameNode and that the reduction in cluster performance due to the loss of these workers won't be too great.

◆ Make a copy of the `core-site.xml` and `hdfs-site.xml` files, place them (ideally) on an NFS location, and update them to point to the new host. Any time you modify the current configuration files, remember to make the same changes to these copies.

◆ Copy the `slaves` file from the NameNode onto either the new host or the NFS share. Also, make sure you keep it updated.

◆ Know how you will handle a subsequent failure in the new host. How quickly can you likely repair or replace the original failed host? Which host will be the location of the NameNode (and SecondaryNameNode) in the interim?

Ready? Let's do it!

Time for action – swapping to a new NameNode host

In the following steps we keep the new configuration files on an NFS share mounted to `/share/backup` and change the paths to match where you have the new files. Also use a different string to grep; we use a portion of the IP address we know isn't shared with any other host in the cluster.

1. Log on to the current NameNode host and shut down the cluster.

    ```
    $ stop-all.sh
    ```

2. Halt the host that runs the NameNode.

    ```
    $ sudo poweroff
    ```

3. Log on to the new NameNode host and confirm the new configuration files have the correct NameNode location.

    ```
    $ grep 110 /share/backup/*.xml
    ```

4. On the new host, first copy across the `slaves` file.

    ```
    $ cp /share/backup/slaves Hadoop/conf
    ```

5. Now copy across the updated configuration files.

    ```
    $ cp /share/backup/*site.xml Hadoop/conf
    ```

6. Remove any old NameNode data from the local filesystem.

    ```
    $ rm -f /var/Hadoop/dfs/name/*
    ```

7. Copy the updated configuration files to every node in the cluster.

    ```
    $ slaves.sh cp /share/backup/*site.xml Hadoop/conf
    ```

8. Ensure each node now has the configuration files pointing to the new NameNode.

    ```
    $ slaves.sh grep 110 hadoop/conf/*site.xml
    ```

9. Start the cluster.

    ```
    $ start-all.sh
    ```

10. Check HDFS is healthy, from the command line.

    ```
    $ Hadoop fs ls /
    ```

11. Verify whether HDFS is accessible from the web UI.

What just happened?

First, we shut down the cluster. This is a little un-representative as most failures see the NameNode die in a much less friendly way, but we do not want to talk about issues of filesystem corruption until later in the chapter.

We then shut down the old NameNode host. Though not strictly necessary, it is a good way of ensuring that nothing accesses the old host and gives you an incorrect view on how well the migration has occurred.

Before copying across files, we take a quick look at `core-site.xml` and `hdfs-site.xml` to ensure the correct values are specified for the `fs.default.dir` property in `core-site.xml`.

We then prepare the new host by firstly copying across the `slaves` configuration file and the cluster configuration files and then removing any old NameNode data from the local directory. Refer to the preceding steps about being very careful in this step.

Next, we use the `slaves.sh` script to get each host in the cluster to copy across the new configuration files. We know our new NameNode host is the only one with 110 in its IP address, so we grep for that in the files to ensure all are up-to-date (obviously, you will need to use a different pattern for your system).

At this stage, all should be well; we start the cluster and access via both the command-line tools and UI to confirm it is running as expected.

Don't celebrate quite yet!

Remember that even with a successful migration to a new NameNode, you aren't done quite yet. You decided in advance how to handle the SecondaryNameNode and which host would be the new designated NameNode host should the newly migrated one fail. To be ready for that, you will need to run through the "Be prepared" checklist mentioned before once more and act appropriately.

 Do not forget to consider the chance of correlated failures. Investigate the cause of the NameNode host failure in case it is the start of a bigger problem.

What about MapReduce?

We did not mention moving the JobTracker as that is a much less painful process as shown in *Chapter 6, When Things Break*. If your NameNode and JobTracker are running on the same host, you will need to modify the preceding approach by also keeping a new copy of `mapred-site.xml`, which has the location of the new host in the `mapred.job.tracker` property.

Have a go hero – swapping to a new NameNode host

Perform a migration of both the NameNode and JobTracker from one host to another.

Managing HDFS

As we saw when killing and restarting nodes in *Chapter 6, When Things Break*, Hadoop automatically manages many of the availability concerns that would consume a lot of effort on a more traditional filesystem. There are some things, however, that we still need to be aware of.

Where to write data

Just as the NameNode can have multiple locations for storage of `fsimage` specified via the `dfs.name.dir` property, we explored earlier that there is a similar-appearing property called `dfs.data.dir` that allows HDFS to use multiple data locations on a host, which we will look at now.

This is a useful mechanism that works very differently from the NameNode property. If multiple directories are specified in `dfs.data.dir`, Hadoop will view these as a series of independent locations that it can use in parallel. This is useful if you have multiple physical disks or other storage devices mounted at distinct points on the filesystem. Hadoop will use these multiple devices intelligently, maximizing not only the total storage capacity but also by balancing reads and writes across the locations to gain maximum throughput. As mentioned in the *Storage types* section, this is the approach that maximizes these factors at the cost of a single disk failure causing the whole host to fail.

Using balancer

Hadoop works hard to place data blocks on HDFS in a way that maximizes both performance and redundancy. However, in certain situations, the cluster can become unbalanced, with a large discrepancy between the data held on the various nodes. The classic situation that causes this is when a new node is added to the cluster. By default, Hadoop will consider the new node as a candidate for block placement alongside all other nodes, meaning that it will remain lightly utilized for a significant period of time. Nodes that have been out of service or have otherwise suffered issues may also have collected a smaller number of blocks than their peers.

Hadoop includes a tool called the balancer, started and stopped by the `start-balancer.sh` and `stop-balancer.sh` scripts respectively, to handle this situation.

When to rebalance

Hadoop does not have any automatic alarms that will alert you to an unbalanced filesystem. Instead, you need to keep an eye on the data reported by both `hadoop fsck` and `hadoop fsadmin` and watch for imbalances across the nodes.

In reality, this is not something you usually need to worry about, as Hadoop is very good at managing block placement and you likely only need to consider running the balancer to remove major imbalances when adding new hardware or when returning faulty nodes to service. To maintain maximum cluster health, however, it is not uncommon to have the balancer run on a scheduled basis (for example, nightly) to keep the block balancing within a specified threshold.

MapReduce management

As we saw in the previous chapter, the MapReduce framework is generally more tolerant of problems and failures than HDFS. The JobTracker and TaskTrackers have no persistent data to manage and, consequently, the management of MapReduce is more about the handling of running jobs and tasks than servicing the framework itself.

Command line job management

The `hadoop job` command-line tool is the primary interface for this job management. As usual, type the following to get a usage summary:

```
$ hadoop job --help
```

The options to the command are generally self-explanatory; it allows you to start, stop, list, and modify running jobs in addition to retrieving some elements of job history. Instead of examining each individually, we will explore the use of several of these subcommands together in the next section.

Have a go hero – command line job management

The MapReduce UI also provides access to a subset of these capabilities. Explore the UI and see what you can and cannot do from the web interface.

Job priorities and scheduling

So far, we have generally run a single job against our cluster and waited for it to complete. This has hidden the fact that, by default, Hadoop places subsequent job submissions into a **First In, First Out (FIFO)** queue. When a job finishes, Hadoop simply starts executing the next job in the queue. Unless we use one of the alternative schedulers that we will discuss in later sections, the FIFO scheduler dedicates the full cluster to the sole currently running job.

For small clusters with a pattern of job submission that rarely sees jobs waiting in the queue, this is completely fine. However, if jobs are often waiting in the queue, issues can arise. In particular, the FIFO model takes no account of job priority or resources needed. A long-running but low-priority job will execute before faster high-priority jobs that were submitted later.

To address this situation, Hadoop defines five levels of job priority: VERY_HIGH, HIGH, NORMAL, LOW, and VERY_LOW. A job defaults to NORMAL priority, but this can be changed with the `hadoop job -set-priority` command.

Time for action – changing job priorities and killing a job

Let's explore job priorities by changing them dynamically and watching the result of killing a job.

1. Start a relatively long-running job on the cluster.

   ```
   $ hadoop jar hadoop-examples-1.0.4.jar pi 100 1000
   ```

2. Open another window and submit a second job.

   ```
   $ hadoop jar hadoop-examples-1.0.4.jar wordcount test.txt out1
   ```

3. Open another window and submit a third.

   ```
   $ hadoop jar hadoop-examples-1.0.4.jar wordcount test.txt out2
   ```

4. List the running jobs.

   ```
   $ Hadoop job -list
   ```

   You'll see the following lines on the screen:

   ```
   3 jobs currently running
   JobId   State   StartTime   UserName   Priority   SchedulingInfo
   job_201201111540_0005   1   1326325810671   hadoop   NORMAL   NA
   job_201201111540_0006   1   1326325938781   hadoop   NORMAL   NA
   job_201201111540_0007   1   1326325961700   hadoop   NORMAL   NA
   ```

5. Check the status of the running job.

   ```
   $ Hadoop job -status job_201201111540_0005
   ```

   You'll see the following lines on the screen:

   ```
   Job: job_201201111540_0005
   file: hdfs://head:9000/var/hadoop/mapred/system/
   job_201201111540_0005/job.xml
   tracking URL: http://head:50030/jobdetails.
   jsp?jobid=job_201201111540_000
   map() completion: 1.0
   reduce() completion: 0.32666665
   Counters: 18
   ```

6. Raise the priority of the last submitted job to VERY_HIGH.

```
$ Hadoop job -set-priority job_201201111540_0007 VERY_HIGH
```

7. Kill the currently running job.

```
$ Hadoop job -kill job_201201111540_0005
```

8. Watch the other jobs to see which begins processing.

What just happened?

We started a job on the cluster and then queued up another two jobs, confirming that the queued jobs were in the expected order by using hadoop job -list. The hadoop job -list all command would have listed both completed as well as the current jobs and hadoop job -history would have allowed us to examine the jobs and their tasks in much more detail. To confirm the submitted job was running, we used hadoop job -status to get the current map and reduce task completion status for the job, in addition to the job counters.

We then used hadoop job -set-priority to increase the priority of the job currently last in the queue.

After using hadoop job -kill to abort the currently running job, we confirmed the job with the increased priority that executed next, even though the job remaining in the queue was submitted beforehand.

Alternative schedulers

Manually modifying job priorities in the FIFO queue certainly does work, but it requires active monitoring and management of the job queue. If we think about the problem, the reason we are having this difficulty is the fact that Hadoop dedicates the entire cluster to each job being executed.

Hadoop offers two additional job schedulers that take a different approach and share the cluster among multiple concurrently executing jobs. There is also a plugin mechanism by which additional schedulers can be added. Note that this type of resource sharing is one of those problems that is conceptually simple but is in reality very complex and is an area of much academic research. The goal is to maximize resource allocation not only at a point in time, but also over an extended period while honoring notions of relative priority.

Capacity Scheduler

The **Capacity Scheduler** uses multiple job queues (to which access control can be applied) to which jobs are submitted, each of which is allocated a portion of the cluster resources. You could, for example, have a queue for large long-running jobs that is allocated 90 percent of the cluster and one for smaller high-priority jobs allocated the remaining 10 percent. If both queues have jobs submitted, the cluster resources will be allocated in this proportion.

If, however, one queue is empty and the other has jobs to execute, the Capacity Scheduler will temporarily allocate the capacity of the empty queue to the busy one. Once a job is submitted to the empty queue, it will regain its capacity as the currently running tasks complete execution. This approach gives a reasonable balance between the desired resource allocation and preventing long periods of unused capacity.

Though disabled by default, the Capacity Scheduler supports job priorities within each queue. If a high priority job is submitted after a low priority one, its tasks will be scheduled in preference to the other jobs as capacity becomes available.

Fair Scheduler

The **Fair Scheduler** segments the cluster into pools into which jobs are submitted; there is often a correlation between the user and the pool. Though by default each pool gets an equal share of the cluster, this can be modified.

Within each pool, the default model is to share the pool across all jobs submitted to that pool. Therefore, if the cluster is split into pools for Alice and Bob, each of whom submit three jobs, the cluster will execute all six jobs in parallel. It is possible to place total limits on the number of concurrent jobs running in a pool, as too many running at once will potentially produce a large amount of temporary data and provide overall inefficient processing.

As with the Capacity Scheduler, the Fair Scheduler will over-allocate cluster capacity to other pools if one is empty, and then reclaim it as the pool receives jobs. It also supports job priorities within a pool to preferentially schedule tasks of high priority jobs over those with a lower priority.

Enabling alternative schedulers

Each of the alternative schedulers is provided as a JAR file in `capacityScheduler` and `fairScheduler` directories within the `contrib` directory in the Hadoop installation. To enable a scheduler, either add its JAR to the `hadoop/lib` directory or explicitly place it on the classpath. Note that each scheduler requires its own set of properties to configure its usage. Refer to the documentation for each for more details.

When to use alternative schedulers

The alternative schedulers are very effective, but are not really needed on small clusters or those with no need to ensure multiple job concurrency or execution of late-arriving but high-priority jobs. Each has multiple configuration parameters and requires tuning to get optimal cluster utilization. But for any large cluster with multiple users and varying job priorities, they can be essential.

Scaling

You have data and you have a running Hadoop cluster; now you get more of the former and need more of the latter. We have said repeatedly that Hadoop is an easily scalable system. So let us add some new capacity.

Adding capacity to a local Hadoop cluster

Hopefully, at this point, you should feel pretty underwhelmed at the idea of adding another node to a running cluster. All through *Chapter 6, When Things Break*, we constantly killed and restarted nodes. Adding a new node is really no different; all you need to do is perform the following steps:

1. Install Hadoop on the host.
2. Set the environment variables shown in *Chapter 2, Getting Up and Running*.
3. Copy the configuration files into the `conf` directory on the installation.
4. Add the host's DNS name or IP address to the `slaves` file on the node from which you usually run commands such as `slaves.sh` or cluster start/stop scripts.

And that's it!

Have a go hero – adding a node and running balancer

Try out the process of adding a new node and afterwards examine the state of HDFS. If it is unbalanced, run the balancer to fix things. To help maximize the effect, ensure there is a reasonable amount of data on HDFS before adding the new node.

Adding capacity to an EMR job flow

If you are using Elastic MapReduce, for non-persistent clusters, the concept of scaling does not always apply. Since you specify the number and type of hosts required when setting up the job flow each time, you need only ensure that the cluster size is appropriate for the job to be executed.

Expanding a running job flow

However, sometimes you may have a long-running job that you want to complete more quickly. In such a case, you can add more nodes to the running job flow. Recall that EMR has three different types of node: master nodes for NameNode and JobTracker, core nodes for HDFS, and task nodes for MapReduce workers. In this case, you could add additional task nodes to help crunch the MapReduce job.

Another scenario is where you have defined a job flow comprising a series of MapReduce jobs instead of just one. EMR now allows the job flow to be modified between steps in such a series. This has the advantage of each job being given a tailored hardware configuration that gives better control of balancing performance against cost.

The canonical model for EMR is for the job flow to pull its source data from S3, process that data on a temporary EMR Hadoop cluster, and then write results back to S3. If, however, you have a very large data set that requires frequent processing, the copying back and forth of data could become too time-consuming. Another model that can be employed in such a situation is to use a persistent Hadoop cluster within a job flow that has been sized with enough core nodes to store the needed data on HDFS. When processing is performed, increase capacity as shown before by assigning more task nodes to the job flow.

 These tasks to resize running job flows are not currently available from the AWS Console and need to be performed through the API or command line tools.

Summary

This chapter covered how to build, maintain, and expand a Hadoop cluster. In particular, we learned where to find the default values for Hadoop configuration properties and how to set them programmatically on a per-job level. We learned how to choose hardware for a cluster and the value in understanding your likely workload before committing to purchases, and how Hadoop can use awareness of the physical location of hosts to optimize its block placement strategy through the use of rack awareness.

We then saw how the default Hadoop security model works, its weaknesses and how to mitigate them, how to mitigate the risks of NameNode failure we introduced in *Chapter 6, When Things Break*, and how to swap to a new NameNode host if disaster strikes. We learned more about block replica placement, how the cluster can become unbalanced, and what to do if it does.

We also saw the Hadoop model for MapReduce job scheduling and learned how job priorities can modify the behavior, how the Capacity Scheduler and Fair Scheduler give a more sophisticated way of managing cluster resources across multiple concurrent job submissions, and how to expand a cluster with a new capacity.

This completes our exploration of core Hadoop in this book. In the remaining chapters, we will look at other systems and tools that build atop Hadoop to provide more sophisticated views on data and integration with other systems. We will start with a relational view on the data in HDFS through the use of Hive.

8
A Relational View on Data with Hive

MapReduce is a powerful paradigm which enables complex data processing that can reveal valuable insights. However, it does require a different mindset and some training and experience on the model of breaking processing analytics into a series of map and reduce steps. There are several products that are built atop Hadoop to provide higher-level or more familiar views on the data held within HDFS. This chapter will introduce one of the most popular of these tools, **Hive***.*

In this chapter, we will cover:

- ◆ What Hive is and why you may want to use it
- ◆ How to install and configure Hive
- ◆ Using Hive to perform SQL-like analysis of the UFO data set
- ◆ How Hive can approximate common features of a relational database such as joins and views
- ◆ How to efficiently use Hive across very large data sets
- ◆ How Hive allows the incorporation of user-defined functions into its queries
- ◆ How Hive complements another common tool, Pig

Overview of Hive

Hive is a data warehouse that uses MapReduce to analyze data stored on HDFS. In particular, it provides a query language called **HiveQL** that closely resembles the common **Structured Query Language (SQL)** standard.

Why use Hive?

In *Chapter 4, Developing MapReduce Programs*, we introduced Hadoop Streaming and explained that one large benefit of Streaming is how it allows faster turn-around in the development of MapReduce jobs. Hive takes this a step further. Instead of providing a way of more quickly developing map and reduce tasks, it offers a query language based on the industry standard SQL. Hive takes these HiveQL statements and immediately and automatically translates the queries into one or more MapReduce jobs. It then executes the overall MapReduce program and returns the results to the user. Whereas Hadoop Streaming reduces the required code/compile/submit cycle, Hive removes it entirely and instead only requires the composition of HiveQL statements.

This interface to Hadoop not only accelerates the time required to produce results from data analysis, it significantly broadens who can use Hadoop and MapReduce. Instead of requiring software development skills, anyone with a familiarity with SQL can use Hive.

The combination of these attributes is that Hive is often used as a tool for business and data analysts to perform ad hoc queries on the data stored on HDFS. Direct use of MapReduce requires map and reduce tasks to be written before the job can be executed which means a necessary delay from the idea of a possible query to its execution. With Hive, the data analyst can work on refining HiveQL queries without the ongoing involvement of a software developer. There are of course operational and practical limitations (a badly written query will be inefficient regardless of technology) but the broad principle is compelling.

Thanks, Facebook!

Just as we earlier thanked Google, Yahoo!, and Doug Cutting for their contributions to Hadoop and the technologies that inspired it, it is to Facebook that we must now direct thanks.

Hive was developed by the Facebook Data team and, after being used internally, it was contributed to the Apache Software Foundation and made freely available as open source software. Its homepage is `http://hive.apache.org`.

Setting up Hive

In this section, we will walk through the act of downloading, installing, and configuring Hive.

Prerequisites

Unlike Hadoop, there are no Hive masters, slaves, or nodes. Hive runs as a client application that processes HiveQL queries, converts them into MapReduce jobs, and submits these to a Hadoop cluster.

Although there is a mode suitable for small jobs and development usage, the usual situation is that Hive will require an existing functioning Hadoop cluster.

Just as other Hadoop clients don't need to be executed on the actual cluster nodes, Hive can be executed on any host where the following are true:

- Hadoop is installed on the host (even if no processes are running)
- The HADOOP_HOME environment variable is set and points to the location of the Hadoop installation
- The ${HADOOP_HOME}/bin directory is added to the system or user path

Getting Hive

You should download the latest stable Hive version from http://hive.apache.org/releases.html.

The Hive getting started guide at http://cwiki.apache.org/confluence/display/Hive/GettingStarted will give recommendations on version compatibility, but as a general principle, you should expect the most recent stable versions of Hive, Hadoop, and Java to work together.

Time for action – installing Hive

Let's now set up Hive so we can start using it in action.

1. Download the latest stable version of Hive and move it to the location to which you wish to have it installed:

```
$ mv hive-0.8.1.tar.gz /usr/local
```

2. Uncompress the package:

```
$ tar -xzf hive-0.8.1.tar.gz
```

3. Set the HIVE_HOME variable to the installation directory:

```
$ export HIVE_HOME=/usr/local/hive
```

4. Add the Hive home directory to the path variable:

```
$ export PATH=${HIVE_HOME}/bin:${PATH}
```

5. Create directories required by Hive on HDFS:

```
$ hadoop fs -mkdir /tmp
$ hadoop fs -mkdir /user/hive/warehouse
```

6. Make both of these directories group writeable:

```
$ hadoop fs -chmod g+w /tmp
$ hadoop fs -chmod g+w /user/hive/warehouse
```

7. Try to start Hive:

```
$ hive
```

You will receive the following response:

```
Logging initialized using configuration in jar:file:/opt/hive-
0.8.1/lib/hive-common-0.8.1.jar!/hive-log4j.properties


Hive history file=/tmp/hadoop/hive_job_log_
hadoop_201203031500_480385673.txt

hive>
```

8. Exit the Hive interactive shell:

```
$ hive> quit;
```

What just happened?

After downloading the latest stable Hive release, we copied it to the desired location and uncompressed the archive file. This created a directory, hive-<version>.

Similarly, as we previously defined HADOOP_HOME and added the bin directory within the installation to the path variable, we then did something similar with HIVE_HOME and its bin directory.

 Remember that to avoid having to set these variables every time you log in, add them to your shell login script or to a separate configuration script that you source when you want to use Hive.

We then created two directories on HDFS that Hive requires and changed their attributes to make them group writeable. The /tmp directory is where Hive will, by default, write transient data created during query execution and will also place output data in this location. The /user/hive/warehouse directory is where Hive will store the data that is written into its tables.

After all this setup, we run the hive command and a successful installation will give output similar to the one mentioned above. Running the hive command with no arguments enters an interactive shell; the hive> prompt is analogous to the sql> or mysql> prompts familiar from relational database interactive tools.

We then exit the interactive shell by typing `quit;`. Note the trailing semicolon `;`. HiveQL is, as mentioned, very similar to SQL and follows the convention that all commands must be terminated by a semicolon. Pressing *Enter* without a semicolon will allow commands to be continued on subsequent lines.

Using Hive

With our Hive installation, we will now import and analyze the UFO data set introduced in *Chapter 4, Developing MapReduce Programs*.

When importing any new data into Hive, there is generally a three-stage process:

1. Create the specification of the table into which the data is to be imported.
2. Import the data into the created table.
3. Execute HiveQL queries against the table.

This process should look very familiar to those with experience with relational databases. Hive gives a structured query view of our data and to enable that, we must first define the specification of the table's columns and import the data into the table before we can execute any queries.

 We assume a general level of familiarity with SQL and will be focusing more on how to get things done with Hive than in explaining particular SQL constructs in detail. A SQL reference may be handy for those with little familiarity with the language, though we will make sure you know what each statement does, even if the details require deeper SQL knowledge.

Time for action – creating a table for the UFO data

Perform the following steps to create a table for the UFO data:

1. Start the Hive interactive shell:

   ```
   $ hive
   ```

2. Create a table for the UFO data set, splitting the statement across multiple lines for easy readability:

   ```
   hive> CREATE TABLE ufodata(sighted STRING, reported STRING,
   sighting_location STRING,    > shape STRING, duration STRING,
   description STRING COMMENT 'Free text description')
   COMMENT 'The UFO data set.' ;
   ```

You should see the following lines once you are done:

```
OK
Time taken: 0.238 seconds
```

3. List all existing tables:

```
hive> show tables;
```

You will receive the following output:

```
OK
ufodata
Time taken: 0.156 seconds
```

4. Show tables matching a regular expression:

```
hive> show tables '.*data';
```

You will receive the following output:

```
OK
ufodata
Time taken: 0.065 seconds
```

5. Validate the table specification:

```
hive> describe ufodata;
```

You will receive the following output:

```
OK
sighted    string
reported   string
sighting_location    string
shape    string
duration    string
description    string    Free text description
Time taken: 0.086 seconds
```

6. Display a more detailed description of the table:

```
hive> describe extended ufodata;
```

You will receive the following output:

```
OK
```

```
sighted    string
reported   string
...
Detailed Table Information   Table(tableName:ufodata,
dbName:default, owner:hadoop, createTime:1330818664,
lastAccessTime:0, retention:0,
...
...location:hdfs://head:9000/user/hive/warehouse/
ufodata, inputFormat:org.apache.hadoop.mapred.
TextInputFormat, outputFormat:org.apache.hadoop.hive.ql.io.
HiveIgnoreKeyTextOutputFormat, compressed:false, numBuckets:-1,
```

What just happened?

After starting the interactive Hive interpreter, we used the CREATE TABLE command to define the structure of the UFO data table. As with standard SQL, this requires that each column in the table has a name and datatype. HiveQL also offers optional comments on each column and on the overall table, as shown previously where we add one column and one table comment.

For the UFO data, we use STRING as the data type; HiveQL, as with SQL, supports a variety of datatypes:

- **Boolean types**: BOOLEAN
- **Integer types**: TINYINT, INT, BIGINT
- **Floating point types**: FLOAT, DOUBLE
- **Textual types**: STRING

After creating the table, we use the SHOW TABLES statement to verify that the table has been created. This command lists all tables and in this case, our new UFO table is the only one in the system.

We then use a variant on SHOW TABLES that takes an optional Java regular expression to match against the table name. In this case, the output is identical to the previous command, but in systems with a large number of tables—especially when you do not know the exact name—this variant can be very useful.

> We have seen the table exists but we have not validated whether it was created properly. We next do this by using the DESCRIBE TABLE command to display the specification of the named table. We see that all is as specified (though note the table comment is not shown by this command) and then use the DESCRIBE TABLE EXTENDED variant to get much more information about the table.

We have omitted much of this final output though a few points of interest are present. Note the input format is specified as `TextInputFormat`; by default, Hive will assume any HDFS files inserted into a table are stored as text files.

We also see that the table data will be stored in a directory under the `/user/hive/warehouse` HDFS directory we created earlier.

A note on case sensitivity:

HiveQL, as with SQL, is not case sensitive in terms of keywords, columns, or table names. By convention, SQL statements use uppercase for SQL language keywords and we will generally follow this when using HiveQL within files, as shown later. However, when typing interactive commands, we will frequently take the line of least resistance and use lowercase.

Time for action – inserting the UFO data

Now that we have created a table, let us load the UFO data into it.

1. Copy the UFO data file onto HDFS:

   ```
   $ hadoop fs -put ufo.tsv /tmp/ufo.tsv
   ```

2. Confirm that the file was copied:

   ```
   $ hadoop fs -ls /tmp
   ```

   You will receive the following response:

   ```
   Found 2 items
   drwxrwxr-x   - hadoop supergroup          0 … 14:52 /tmp/hive-
   hadoop
   -rw-r--r--   3 hadoop supergroup   75342464 2012-03-03 16:01 /tmp/
   ufo.tsv
   ```

3. Enter the Hive interactive shell:

   ```
   $ hive
   ```

4. Load the data from the previously copied file into the `ufodata` table:

   ```
   hive> LOAD DATA INPATH '/tmp/ufo.tsv' OVERWRITE INTO TABLE
   ufodata;
   ```

   You will receive the following response:

   ```
   Loading data to table default.ufodata
   Deleted hdfs://head:9000/user/hive/warehouse/ufodata
   ```

```
OK

Time taken: 5.494 seconds
```

5. Exit the Hive shell:

```
hive> quit;
```

6. Check the location from which we copied the data file:

```
$ hadoop fs -ls /tmp
```

You will receive the following response:

```
Found 1 items

drwxrwxr-x    - hadoop supergroup          0 ... 16:10 /tmp/hive-
hadoop
```

What just happened?

We first copied onto HDFS the tab-separated file of UFO sightings used previously in *Chapter 4, Developing MapReduce Programs*. After validating the file's presence on HDFS, we started the Hive interactive shell and used the LOAD DATA command to load the file into the ufodata table.

Because we are using a file already on HDFS, the path was specified by INPATH alone. We could have loaded directly from a file on the local filesystem (obviating the need for the prior explicit HDFS copy) by using LOCAL INPATH.

We specified the OVERWRITE statement which will delete any existing data in the table before loading the new data. This obviously should be used with care, as can be seen from the output of the command, the directory holding the table data is removed by use of OVERWRITE.

Note the command took only a little over five seconds to execute, significantly longer than it would have taken to copy the UFO data file onto HDFS.

 Though we specified an explicit file in this example, it is possible to load multiple files with a single statement by specifying a directory as the INPATH location; in such a case, all files within the directory will be loaded into the table.

After exiting the Hive shell, we look again at the directory into which we copied the data file and find it is no longer there. If a LOAD statement is given a path to data on HDFS, it will not simply copy this into /user/hive/datawarehouse, but will move it there instead. If you want to analyze data on HDFS that is used by other applications, then either create a copy or use the EXTERNAL mechanism that will be described later.

Validating the data

Now that we have loaded the data into our table, it is good practice to do some quick validating queries to confirm all is as expected. Sometimes our initial table definition turns out to be incorrect.

Time for action – validating the table

The easiest way to do some initial validation is to perform some summary queries to validate the import. This is similar to the types of activities for which we used Hadoop Streaming in *Chapter 4, Developing MapReduce Programs*.

1. Instead of using the Hive shell, pass the following HiveQL to the `hive` command-line tool to count the number of entries in the table:

   ```
   $ hive -e "select count(*) from ufodata;"
   ```

   You will receive the following response:

   ```
   Total MapReduce jobs = 1
   Launching Job 1 out of 1
   …
   Hadoop job information for Stage-1: number of mappers: 1; number
   of reducers: 1
   2012-03-03 16:15:15,510 Stage-1 map = 0%,   reduce = 0%
   2012-03-03 16:15:21,552 Stage-1 map = 100%,   reduce = 0%
   2012-03-03 16:15:30,622 Stage-1 map = 100%,   reduce = 100%
   Ended Job = job_201202281524_0006
   MapReduce Jobs Launched:
   Job 0: Map: 1  Reduce: 1   HDFS Read: 75416209 HDFS Write: 6
   SUCESS
   Total MapReduce CPU Time Spent: 0 msec
   OK
   61393
   Time taken: 28.218 seconds
   ```

2. Display a sample of five values for the sighted column:

   ```
   $ hive -e  "select sighted from ufodata limit 5;"
   ```

   You will receive the following response:

   ```
   Total MapReduce jobs = 1
   Launching Job 1 out of 1
   ```

```
...

OK

19951009   19951009   Iowa City, IA      Man repts. witnessing
&quot;flash, followed by a classic UFO, w/ a tailfin at
back.&quot; Red color on top half of tailfin. Became triangular.
19951010   19951011   Milwaukee, WI    2 min.  Man  on Hwy 43 SW
of Milwaukee sees large, bright blue light streak by his car,
descend, turn, cross road ahead, strobe. Bizarre!
19950101   19950103   Shelton, WA        Telephoned Report:CA
woman visiting daughter witness discs and triangular ships over
Squaxin Island in Puget Sound. Dramatic.  Written report, with
illustrations, submitted to NUFORC.
19950510   19950510   Columbia, MO    2 min.  Man repts. son&apos;s
bizarre sighting of small humanoid creature in back yard.  Reptd.
in Acteon Journal, St. Louis UFO newsletter.
19950611   19950614   Seattle, WA        Anonymous caller repts.
sighting 4 ufo&apos;s in NNE sky, 45 deg. above horizon.  (No
other facts reptd.  No return tel. #.)
Time taken: 11.693 seconds
```

What just happened?

In this example, we use the `hive -e` command to directly pass HiveQL to the Hive tool instead of using the interactive shell. The interactive shell is useful when performing a series of Hive operations. For simple statements, it is often more convenient to use this approach and pass the query string directly to the command-line tool. This also shows that Hive can be called from scripts like any other Unix tool.

 When using `hive -e`, it is not necessary to terminate the HiveQL string with a semicolon, but if you are like me, the habit is hard to break. If you want multiple commands in a single string, they must obviously be separated by semicolons.

The result of the first query is 61393, the same number of records we saw when analyzing the UFO data set previously with direct MapReduce. This tells us the entire data set was indeed loaded into the table.

We then execute a second query to select five values of the first column in the table, which should return a list of five dates. However, the output instead includes the entire record which has been loaded into the first column.

The issue is that though we relied on Hive loading our data file as a text file, we didn't take into account the separator between columns. Our file is tab separated, but Hive, by default, expects its input files to have fields separated by the ASCII code 00 (control-A).

Time for action – redefining the table with the correct column separator

Let's fix our table specification as follows:

1. Create the following file as `commands.hql`:

```
DROP TABLE ufodata ;
CREATE TABLE ufodata(sighted string, reported string, sighting_
location string,
shape string, duration string, description string)
ROW FORMAT DELIMITED
FIELDS TERMINATED BY '\t' ;
LOAD DATA INPATH '/tmp/ufo.tsv' OVERWRITE INTO TABLE ufodata ;
```

2. Copy the data file onto HDFS:

```
$ hadoop fs -put ufo.tsv /tmp/ufo.tsv
```

3. Execute the HiveQL script:

```
$ hive -f commands.hql
```

You will receive the following response:

```
OK
Time taken: 5.821 seconds
OK
Time taken: 0.248 seconds
Loading data to table default.ufodata
Deleted hdfs://head:9000/user/hive/warehouse/ufodata
OK
Time taken: 0.285 seconds
```

4. Validate the number of rows in the table:

```
$ hive -e "select count(*) from ufodata;"
```

You will receive the following response:

```
OK
61393
Time taken: 28.077 seconds
```

5. Validate the contents of the reported column:

```
$ hive -e "select reported from ufodata limit 5"
```

You will receive the following response:

```
OK
19951009
19951011
19950103
19950510
19950614
Time taken: 14.852 seconds
```

What just happened?

We introduced a third way to invoke HiveQL commands in this example. In addition to using the interactive shell or passing query strings to the Hive tool, we can have Hive read and execute the contents of a file containing a series of HiveQL statements.

We first created such a file that deletes the old table, creates a new one, and loads the data file into it.

The main differences with the table specification are the ROW FORMAT and FIELDS TERMINATED BY statements. We need both these commands as the first tells Hive that the row contains multiple delimited fields, while the second specifies the actual separator. As can be seen here, we can use both explicit ASCII codes as well as common tokens such as \t for tab.

> Be careful with the separator specification as it must be precise and is case sensitive. Do not waste a few hours by accidentally writing \T instead of \t as I did recently.

Before running the script, we copy the data file onto HDFS again—the previous copy was removed by the DELETE statement—and then use hive -f to execute the HiveQL file.

As before, we then execute two simple SELECT statements to first count the rows in the table and then extract the specific values from a named column for a small number of rows.

The overall row count is, as should be expected, the same as before, but the second statement now produces what looks like correct data, showing that the rows are now correctly being split into their constituent fields.

Hive tables – real or not?

If you look closely at the time taken by the various commands in the preceding example, you'll see a pattern which may at first seem strange. Loading data into a table takes about as long as creating the table specification, but even the simple count of all row statements takes significantly longer. The output also shows that table creation and the loading of data do not actually cause MapReduce jobs to be executed, which explains the very short execution times.

When loading data into a Hive table, the process is different from what may be expected with a traditional relational database. Although Hive copies the data file into its working directory, it does not actually process the input data into rows at that point. What it does instead is create metadata around the data which is then used by subsequent HiveQL queries.

Both the CREATE TABLE and LOAD DATA statements, therefore, do not truly create concrete table data as such, instead they produce the metadata that will be used when Hive is generating MapReduce jobs to access the data conceptually stored in the table.

Time for action – creating a table from an existing file

So far we have loaded data into Hive directly from files over which Hive effectively takes control. It is also possible, however, to create tables that model data held in files external to Hive. This can be useful when we want the ability to perform Hive processing over data written and managed by external applications or otherwise required to be held in directories outside the Hive warehouse directory. Such files are not moved into the Hive warehouse directory or deleted when the table is dropped.

1. Save the following to a file called states.hql:

```
CREATE EXTERNAL TABLE states(abbreviation string, full_name
string)
ROW FORMAT DELIMITED
FIELDS TERMINATED BY '\t'
LOCATION '/tmp/states' ;
```

2. Copy the data file onto HDFS and confirm its presence afterwards:

```
$ hadoop fs -put states.txt /tmp/states/states.txt
$ hadoop fs -ls /tmp/states
```

You will receive the following response:

```
Found 1 items
-rw-r--r--   3 hadoop supergroup        654 2012-03-03 16:54 /tmp/
states/states.txt
```

3. Execute the HiveQL script:

```
$ hive -f states.hql
```

You will receive the following response:

```
Logging initialized using configuration in jar:file:/opt/hive-
0.8.1/lib/hive-common-0.8.1.jar!/hive-log4j.properties
Hive history file=/tmp/hadoop/hive_job_log_
hadoop_201203031655_1132553792.txt
OK
Time taken: 3.954 seconds
OK
Time taken: 0.594 seconds
```

4. Check the source data file:

```
$ hadoop fs -ls /tmp/states
```

You will receive the following response:

```
Found 1 items
-rw-r--r--   3 hadoop supergroup        654 … /tmp/states/states.
txt
```

5. Execute a sample query against the table:

```
$ hive -e "select full_name from states where abbreviation like
'CA'"
```

You will receive the following response:

```
Logging initialized using configuration in jar:file:/opt/hive-
0.8.1/lib/hive-common-0.8.1.jar!/hive-log4j.properties
Hive history file=/tmp/hadoop/hive_job_log_
hadoop_201203031655_410945775.txt
Total MapReduce jobs = 1
...
OK
California
Time taken: 15.75 seconds
```

What just happened?

The HiveQL statement to create an external table only differs slightly from the forms of CREATE TABLE we used previously. The EXTERNAL keyword specifies that the table exists in resources that Hive does not control and the LOCATION clause specifies where the source file or directory are to be found.

After creating the HiveQL script, we copied the source file onto HDFS. For this table, we used the data file from *Chapter 4, Developing MapReduce Programs*, which maps U.S. states to their common two-letter abbreviation.

After confirming the file was in the expected location on HDFS, we executed the query to create the table and checked the source file again. Unlike previous table creations that moved the source file into the /user/hive/warehouse directory, the states.txt file is still in the HDFS location into which it was copied.

Finally, we executed a query against the table to confirm it was populated with the source data and the expected result confirms this. This highlights an additional difference with this form of CREATE TABLE; for our previous non-external tables, the table creation statement does not ingest any data into the table, a subsequent LOAD DATA or (as we'll see later) INSERT statement performs the actual table population. With table definitions that include the LOCATION specification, we can create the table and ingest data in a single statement.

We now have two tables in Hive; the larger table with UFO sighting data and a smaller one mapping U.S. state abbreviations to their full names. Wouldn't it be a useful combination to use data from the second table to enrich the location column in the former?

Time for action – performing a join

Joins are a very frequently used tool in SQL, though sometimes appear a little intimidating to those new to the language. Essentially a **join** allows rows in multiple tables to be logically combined together based on a conditional statement. Hive has rich support for joins which we will now examine.

1. Create the following as join.hql:

```
SELECT t1.sighted, t2.full_name
FROM ufodata t1 JOIN states t2
ON (LOWER(t2.abbreviation) = LOWER(SUBSTR( t1.sighting_location,
(LENGTH(t1.sighting_location)-1)))))
LIMIT 5 ;
```

2. Execute the query:

```
$ hive -f join.hql
```

You will receive the following response:

```
OK
20060930   Alaska
20051018   Alaska
20050707   Alaska
20100112   Alaska
20100625   Alaska
Time taken: 33.255 seconds
```

What just happened?

The actual `join` query is relatively straightforward; we want to extract the sighted date and location for a series of records but instead of the raw location field, we wish to map this into the full state name. The HiveQL file we created performs such a query. The join itself is specified by the standard JOIN keyword and the matching condition is contained in the ON clause.

Things are complicated by a restriction of Hive in that it only supports equijoins, that is, those where the ON clause contains an equality check. It is not possible to specify a join condition using operators such as >, ?, <, or as we would have preferred to use here, the LIKE keyword.

Instead, therefore, we have an opportunity to introduce several of Hive's built-in functions, in particular, those to convert a string to lowercase (LOWER), to extract a substring from a string (SUBSTR) and to return the number of characters in a string (LENGTH).

We know that most location entries are of the form "city, state_abbreviation." So we use SUBSTR to extract the third and second from last characters in the string, using length to calculate the indices. We convert both the state abbreviation and extracted string to lower case via LOWER because we cannot assume that all entries in the sighting table will correctly use uniform capitalization.

After executing the script, we get the expected sample lines of output that indeed include the sighting date and full state name instead of the abbreviation.

Note the use of the LIMIT clause that simply constrains how many output rows will be returned from the query. This is also an indication that HiveQL is most similar to SQL dialects such as those found in open source databases such as MySQL.

This example shows an inner join; Hive also supports left and right outer joins as well as left semi joins. There are a number of subtleties around the use of joins in Hive (such as the aforementioned equijoin restriction) and you should really read through the documentation on the Hive homepage if you are likely to use joins, especially when using very large tables.

This is not a criticism of Hive alone; joins are incredibly powerful tools but it is probably fair to say that badly written joins or those created in ignorance of critical constraints have brought more relational databases to a grinding halt than any other type of SQL query.

Have a go hero – improve the join to use regular expressions

As well as the string functions we used previously, Hive also has functions such as RLIKE and REGEXP_EXTRACT that provide direct support for Java-like regular expression manipulation. Rewrite the preceding join specification using regular expressions to make a more accurate and elegant join statement.

Hive and SQL views

Another powerful SQL feature supported by Hive is views. These are useful when instead of a static table the contents of a logical table are specified by a SELECT statement and subsequent queries can then be executed against this dynamic view (hence the name) of the underlying data.

Time for action – using views

We can use views to hide the underlying query complexity such as the previous join example. Let us now create a view to do just that.

1. Create the following as view.hql:

```
CREATE VIEW IF NOT EXISTS usa_sightings (sighted, reported,
shape, state)
AS select t1.sighted, t1.reported, t1.shape, t2.full_name
FROM ufodata t1 JOIN states t2
ON (LOWER(t2.abbreviation) = LOWER(substr( t1.sighting_location,
(LENGTH(t1.sighting_location)-1)))) ;
```

2. Execute the script:

```
$ hive -f view.hql
```

You will receive the following response:

```
Logging initialized using configuration in jar:file:/opt/hive-
0.8.1/lib/hive-common-0.8.1.jar!/hive-log4j.properties
```

```
Hive history file=/tmp/hadoop/hive_job_log_
hadoop_201203040557_1017700649.txt
```

```
OK
```

```
Time taken: 5.135 seconds
```

3. Execute the script again:

```
$ hive -f view.hql
```

You will receive the following response:

```
Logging initialized using configuration in jar:file:/opt/hive-
0.8.1/lib/hive-common-0.8.1.jar!/hive-log4j.properties
```

```
Hive history file=/tmp/hadoop/hive_job_log_
hadoop_201203040557_851275946.txt
```

```
OK
```

```
Time taken: 4.828 seconds
```

4. Execute a test query against the view:

```
$ hive -e "select count(state) from usa_sightings where state =
'California'"
```

You will receive the following response:

```
Logging initialized using configuration in jar:file:/opt/hive-
0.8.1/lib/hive-common-0.8.1.jar!/hive-log4j.properties
```

```
Hive history file=/tmp/hadoop/hive_job_log_
hadoop_201203040558_1729315866.txt
```

```
Total MapReduce jobs = 2
```

```
Launching Job 1 out of 2
```

```
...
```

```
2012-03-04 05:58:12,991 Stage-1 map = 0%,  reduce = 0%
2012-03-04 05:58:16,021 Stage-1 map = 50%,  reduce = 0%
2012-03-04 05:58:18,046 Stage-1 map = 100%,  reduce = 0%
2012-03-04 05:58:24,092 Stage-1 map = 100%,  reduce = 100%
```

```
Ended Job = job_201203040432_0027
```

```
Launching Job 2 out of 2
```

```
...
```

```
2012-03-04 05:58:33,650 Stage-2 map = 0%,  reduce = 0%
2012-03-04 05:58:36,673 Stage-2 map = 100%,  reduce = 0%
2012-03-04 05:58:45,730 Stage-2 map = 100%,  reduce = 100%
```

```
Ended Job = job_201203040432_0028
```

```
MapReduce Jobs Launched:
```

```
Job 0: Map: 2  Reduce: 1   HDFS Read: 75416863 HDFS Write: 116
SUCESS
```

```
Job 1: Map: 1  Reduce: 1   HDFS Read: 304 HDFS Write: 5 SUCESS
```

```
Total MapReduce CPU Time Spent: 0 msec.
```

```
OK
7599
Time taken: 47.03 seconds
```

5. Delete the view:

```
$ hive -e "drop view usa_sightings"
```

You will receive the following output on your screen:

```
OK
Time taken: 5.298 seconds
```

What just happened?

We firstly created the view using the CREATE VIEW statement. This is similar to CREATE TABLE but has two main differences:

- The column definitions include only the name as the type, which will be determined from the underlying query
- The AS clause specifies the SELECT statement that will be used to generate the view

We use the previous join statement to generate the view, so in effect we are creating a table that has the location field normalized to the full state name without directly requiring the user to deal with how that normalization is performed.

The optional IF NOT EXISTS clause (which can also be used with CREATE TABLE) means that Hive will ignore duplicate attempts to create the view. Without this clause, repeated attempts to create the view will generate errors, which isn't always the desired behavior.

We then execute this script twice to both create the view and to demonstrate that the inclusion of the IF NOT EXISTS clause is preventing errors as we intended.

With the view created, we then execute a query against it, in this case, to simply count how many of the sightings took place in California. All our previous Hive statements that generate MapReduce jobs have only produced a single one; this query against our view requires a pair of chained MapReduce jobs. Looking at the query and the view specification, this isn't necessarily surprising; it's not difficult to imagine how the view would be realized by the first MapReduce job and its output fed to the subsequent counting query performed as the second job. As a consequence, you will also see this two-stage job take much longer than any of our previous queries.

Hive is actually smarter than this. If the outer query can be folded into the view creation, then Hive will generate and execute only one MapReduce job. Given the time taken to hand-develop a series of co-operating MapReduce jobs this is a great example of the benefits Hive can offer. Though a hand-written MapReduce job (or series of jobs) is likely to be much more efficient, Hive is a great tool for determining which jobs are useful in the first place. It is better to run a slow Hive query to determine an idea isn't as useful as hoped instead of spending a day developing a MapReduce job to come to the same conclusion.

We have mentioned that views can hide underlying complexity; this does often mean that executing views is intrinsically slow. For large-scale production workloads, you will want to optimize the SQL and possibly remove the view entirely.

After running the query, we delete the view through the DROP VIEW statement, which demonstrates again the similarity between how HiveQL (and SQL) handle tables and views.

Handling dirty data in Hive

The observant among you may notice that the number of California sightings reported by this query is different from the number we generated in *Chapter 4, Developing MapReduce Programs*. Why?

Recall that before running our Hadoop Streaming or Java MapReduce jobs in *Chapter 4, Developing MapReduce Programs*, we had a mechanism to ignore input rows that were malformed. Then while processing the data, we used more precise regular expressions to extract the two-letter state abbreviation from the location field. However, in Hive, we did no such pre-processing and relied on quite crude mechanisms to extract the abbreviation.

On the latter, we could use some of Hive's previously mentioned functions that support regular expressions but for the former, we'd at best be forced to add complex validation WHERE clauses to many of our queries.

A frequent pattern is to instead preprocess data before it is imported into Hive, so for example, in this case, we could run a MapReduce job to remove all malformed records in the input file and another to do the normalization of the location field in advance.

Have a go hero – do it!

Write MapReduce jobs (it could be one or two) to do this pre-processing of the input data and generate a cleaned-up file more suited for direct importation into Hive. Then write a script to execute the jobs, create a Hive table, and import the new file into the table. This will also show how easily and powerfully scriptable Hadoop and Hive can be together.

Time for action – exporting query output

We have previously either loaded large quantities of data into Hive or extracted very small quantities as query results. We can also export large result sets; let us look at an example.

1. Recreate the previously used view:

```
$ hive -f view.hql
```

2. Create the following file as `export.hql`:

```
INSERT OVERWRITE DIRECTORY '/tmp/out'
SELECT reported, shape, state
FROM usa_sightings
WHERE state = 'California' ;
```

3. Execute the script:

```
$ hive -f export.hql
```

You will receive the following response:

```
2012-03-04 06:20:44,571 Stage-1 map = 100%,   reduce = 100%
Ended Job = job_201203040432_0029
Moving data to: /tmp/out
7599 Rows loaded to /tmp/out
MapReduce Jobs Launched:
Job 0: Map: 2  Reduce: 1   HDFS Read: 75416863 HDFS Write: 210901
SUCESS
Total MapReduce CPU Time Spent: 0 msec
OK
Time taken: 46.669 seconds
```

4. Look in the specified output directory:

```
$ hadoop fs -ls /tmp/out
```

You will receive the following response:

```
Found 1 items
-rw-r--r--    3 hadoop supergroup       210901 … /tmp/out/000000_1
```

5. Examine the output file:

```
$ hadoop fs -cat /tmp/out/000000_1 | head
```

You will receive the following output on your screen:

```
20021014_  light_California
20050224_  other_California
20021001_  egg_California
20030527_  sphere_California
20050813_  light_California
20040701_  other_California
20031007_  light_California
```

What just happened?

After reusing the previous view, we created our HiveQL script using the INSERT OVERWRITE DIRECTORY command. This, as the name suggests, places the results of the subsequent statement into the specified location. The OVERWRITE modifier is again optional and simply determines if any existing content in the location is to be firstly removed or not. The INSERT command is followed by a SELECT statement which produces the data to be written to the output location. In this example, we use a query on our previously created view which you will recall is built atop a join, demonstrating how the query here can be arbitrarily complex.

There is an additional optional LOCAL modifier for occasions when the output data is to be written to the local filesystem of the host running the Hive command instead of HDFS.

When we run the script, the MapReduce output is mostly as we have come to expect but with the addition of a line stating how many rows have been exported to the specified output location.

After running the script, we check the output directory and see if the result file is there and when we look at it, the contents are as we would expect.

 Just as Hive's default separator for text files in inputs is ASCII code 0001 ('\a'), it also uses this as the default separator for output files, as shown in the preceding example.

The INSERT command can also be used to populate one table with the results of a query on others and we will look at that next. First, we need to explain a concept we will use at the same time.

Partitioning the table

We mentioned earlier that badly written joins have a long and disreputable history of causing relational databases to spend huge amounts of time grinding through unnecessary work. A similar sad tale can be told of queries that perform full table scans (visiting every row in the table) instead of using indices that allow direct access to rows of interest.

For data stored on HDFS and mapped into a Hive table, the default situation almost demands full table scans. With no way of segmenting data into a more organized structure that allows processing to apply only to the data subset of interest, Hive is forced to process the entire data set. For our UFO file of approximately 70 MB, this really is not a problem as we see the file processed in tens of seconds. However, what if it was a thousand times larger?

As with traditional relational databases, Hive allows tables to be partitioned based on the values of virtual columns and for these values to then be used in query predicates later.

In particular, when a table is created, it can have one or more partition columns and when loading data into the table, the specified values for these columns will determine the partition into which the data is written.

The most common partitioning strategy for tables that see lots of data ingested on a daily basis is for the partition column to be the date. Future queries can then be constrained to process only that data contained within a particular partition. Under the covers, Hive stores each partition in its own directory and files, which is how it can then apply MapReduce jobs only on the data of interest. Through the use of multiple partition columns, it is possible to create a rich hierarchical structure and for large tables with queries that require only small subsets of data it is worthwhile spending some time deciding on the optimal partitioning strategy.

For our UFO data set, we will use the year of the sighting as the partition value but we have to use a few less common features to make it happen. Hence, after this introduction, let us now make some partitions!

Time for action – making a partitioned UFO sighting table

We will create a new table for the UFO data to demonstrate the usefulness of partitioning.

1. Save the following query as `createpartition.hql`:

```
CREATE TABLE partufo(sighted string, reported string, sighting_
location string,shape string, duration string, description string)
PARTITIONED BY (year string)
ROW FORMAT DELIMITED
FIELDS TERMINATED BY '\t' ;
```

2. Save the following query as `insertpartition.hql`:

```
SET hive.exec.dynamic.partition=true ;
SET hive.exec.dynamic.partition.mode=nonstrict ;

INSERT OVERWRITE TABLE partufo partition (year)
SELECT sighted, reported, sighting_location, shape, duration,
description,
SUBSTR(TRIM(sighted), 1,4)   FROM ufodata ;
```

3. Create the partitioned table:

```
$ hive -f createpartition.hql
```

You will receive the following response:

```
Logging initialized using configuration in jar:file:/opt/hive-
0.8.1/lib/hive-common-0.8.1.jar!/hive-log4j.properties
Hive history file=/tmp/hadoop/hive_job_log_
hadoop_201203101838_17331656.txt
OK
Time taken: 4.754 seconds
```

4. Examine the created table:

```
OK
sighted   string
reported   string
sighting_location   string
shape   string
duration   string
description   string
year   string
Time taken: 4.704 seconds
```

5. Populate the table:

```
$ hive -f insertpartition.hql
```

You will see the following lines on the screen:

```
Total MapReduce jobs = 2
...
...
```

```
Ended Job = job_201203040432_0041

Ended Job = 994255701, job is filtered out (removed at runtime).

Moving data to: hdfs://head:9000/tmp/hive-hadoop/hive_2012-03-
10_18-38-36_380_1188564613139061024/-ext-10000

Loading data to table default.partufo partition (year=null)

        Loading partition {year=1977}

        Loading partition {year=1880}

        Loading partition {year=1975}

        Loading partition {year=2007}

        Loading partition {year=1957}

...

Table default.partufo stats: [num_partitions: 100, num_files: 100,
num_rows: 0, total_size: 74751215, raw_data_size: 0]

61393 Rows loaded to partufo

...

OK

Time taken: 46.285 seconds
```

6. Execute a count command against a partition:

   ```
   $ hive -e "select count(*) from partufo where year  = '1989'"
   ```

   You will receive the following response:

   ```
   OK
   249
   Time taken: 26.56 seconds
   ```

7. Execute a similar query on the non-partitioned table:

   ```
   $ hive -e "select count(*) from ufodata where sighted like
   '1989%'"
   ```

   You will receive the following response:

   ```
   OK
   249
   Time taken: 28.61 seconds
   ```

8. List the contents of the Hive directory housing the partitioned table:

   ```
   $ Hadoop fs -ls /user/hive/warehouse/partufo
   ```

You will receive the following response:

```
Found 100 items
drwxr-xr-x   - hadoop supergroup              0 2012-03-10 18:38 /
user/hive/warehouse/partufo/year=0000

drwxr-xr-x   - hadoop supergroup              0 2012-03-10 18:38 /
user/hive/warehouse/partufo/year=1400

drwxr-xr-x   - hadoop supergroup              0 2012-03-10 18:38 /
user/hive/warehouse/partufo/year=1762

drwxr-xr-x   - hadoop supergroup              0 2012-03-10 18:38 /
user/hive/warehouse/partufo/year=1790

drwxr-xr-x   - hadoop supergroup              0 2012-03-10 18:38 /
user/hive/warehouse/partufo/year=1860

drwxr-xr-x   - hadoop supergroup              0 2012-03-10 18:38 /
user/hive/warehouse/partufo/year=1864

drwxr-xr-x   - hadoop supergroup              0 2012-03-10 18:38 /
user/hive/warehouse/partufo/year=1865
```

What just happened?

We created two HiveQL scripts for this example. The first of these creates the new partitioned table. As we can see, it looks very much like the previous CREATE TABLE statements; the difference is in the additional PARTITIONED BY clause.

After we execute this script, we describe the table and see that from a HiveQL perspective the table appears just like the previous ufodata table but with the addition of an extra column for the year. This allows the column to be treated as any other when it comes to specifying conditions in WHERE clauses, even though the column data does not actually exist in the on-disk data files.

We next execute the second script which performs the actual loading of data into the partitioned table. There are several things of note here.

Firstly, we see that the INSERT command can be used with tables just as we previously did for directories. The INSERT statement has a specification of where the data is to go and a subsequent SELECT statement gathers the required data from existing tables or views.

The partitioning mechanism used here is taking advantage of a relatively new feature in Hive, dynamic partitions. In most cases, the partition clause in this statement would include an explicit value for the year column. But though that would work if we were uploading a day's data into a daily partition, it isn't suitable for our type of data file where the various rows should be inserted into a variety of partitions. By simply specifying the column name with no value, the partition name will be automatically generated by the value of the year column returned from the SELECT statement.

This hopefully explains the strange final clause in the `SELECT` statement; after specifying all the standard columns from `ufodata`, we add a specification that extracts a string containing the first four characters of the sighting column. Remember that because the partitioned table sees the year partition column as the seventh column, this means we are assigning the year component of the sighted string to the year column in each row. Consequently, each row is inserted into the partition associated with its sighting year.

To prove this is working as expected, we then perform two queries; one counts all records in the partition for 1989 in the partitioned table, the other counts the records in `ufodata` that begin with the string "1989", that is, the component used to dynamically create the partitions previously.

As can be seen, both queries return the same result, verifying that our partitioning strategy is working as expected. We also note that the partitioned query is a little faster than the other, though not by very much. This is likely due to the MapReduce start up times dominating the processing of our relatively modest data set.

Finally, we take a look inside the directory where Hive stores the data for the partitioned table and see that there is indeed a directory for each of the 100 dynamically-generated partitions. Any time we now express HiveQL statements that refer to specific partitions, Hive can perform a significant optimization by processing only the data found in the appropriate partitions' directories.

Bucketing, clustering, and sorting... oh my!

We will not explore it in detail here, but hierarchical partition columns are not the full extent of how Hive can optimize data access patterns within subsets of data. Within a partition, Hive provides a mechanism to further gather rows into buckets using a hash function on specified `CLUSTER BY` columns. Within a bucket, the rows can be kept in sorted order using specified `SORT BY` columns. We could, for example, have bucketed our data based on the UFO shape and within each bucket sorted on the sighting date.

These aren't necessarily features you'll need to use on day 1 with Hive, but if you find yourself using larger and larger data sets, then considering this type of optimization may help query processing time significantly.

User-Defined Function

Hive provides mechanisms for you to hook custom code directly into the HiveQL execution. This can be in the form of adding new library functions or by specifying **Hive transforms**, which work quite similarly to Hadoop Streaming. We will look at user-defined functions in this section as they are where you are most likely to have an early need to add custom code. Hive transforms are a somewhat more involved mechanism by which you can add custom map and reduce classes that are invoked by the Hive runtime. If transforms are of interest, they are well documented on the Hive wiki.

Time for action – adding a new User Defined Function (UDF)

Let us show how to create and invoke some custom Java code via a new UDF.

1. Save the following code as `City.java`:

```
package com.kycorsystems ;

import java.util.regex.Matcher ;
import java.util.regex.Pattern ;
import org.apache.hadoop.hive.ql.exec.UDF ;
import org.apache.hadoop.io.Text ;

public class City extends UDF
{
    private static Pattern pattern = Pattern.compile(
        "[a-zA-z]+?[\\. ]*[a-zA-z]+?[\\, ][^a-zA-Z]") ;

    public Text evaluate( final Text str)
    {
        Text result ;
        String location = str.toString().trim() ;
        Matcher matcher = pattern.matcher(location) ;

        if (matcher.find())
        {
            result = new Text(                    location.
substring(matcher.start(), matcher.end()-2)) ;
        }
        else
        {
            result = new Text("Unknown") ;
        }
        return result ;
    }
}
```

2. Compile this file:

```
$ javac -cp hive/lib/hive-exec-0.8.1.jar:hadoop/hadoop-1.0.4-core.
jar  -d . City.java
```

3. Package the generated class file into a JAR file:

```
$ jar cvf city.jar com
```

You will receive the following response:

```
added manifest
adding: com/(in = 0) (out= 0)(stored 0%)
adding: com/kycorsystems/(in = 0) (out= 0)(stored 0%)
adding: com/kycorsystems/City.class(in = 1101) (out= 647)(deflated
41%)
```

4. Start the interactive Hive shell:

```
$ hive
```

5. Add the new JAR file to the Hive classpath:

```
hive> add jar city.jar;
```

You will receive the following response:

```
Added city.jar to class path
Added resource: city.jar
```

6. Confirm that the JAR file was added:

```
hive> list jars;
```

You will receive the following response:

```
file:/opt/hive-0.8.1/lib/hive-builtins-0.8.1.jar
city.jar
```

7. Register the new code with a function name:

```
hive> create temporary function city as 'com.kycorsystems.City' ;
```

You will receive the following response:

```
OK
Time taken: 0.277 seconds
```

8. Execute a query using the new function:

```
hive> select city(sighting_location), count(*) as total
    > from partufo
    > where year = '1999'
    > group by city(sighting_location)
    > having  total > 15 ;
```

You will receive the following response:

```
Total MapReduce jobs = 1
Launching Job 1 out of 1
...
OK
Chicago   19
Las Vegas  19
Phoenix   19
Portland  17
San Diego  18
Seattle   26
Unknown   34
Time taken: 29.055 seconds
```

What just happened?

The Java class we wrote extends the base `org.apache.hadoop.hive.exec.ql.UDF` (User Defined Function) class. Into this class, we define a method for returning a city name given a location string that follows the general pattern we have seen previously.

UDF does not actually define a series of **evaluate** methods based on type; instead, you are free to add your own with arbitrary arguments and return types. Hive uses Java Reflection to select the correct evaluation method, and if you require a finer-grained selection, you can develop your own utility class that implements the `UDFMethodResolver` interface.

The regular expression used here is a little unwieldy; we wish to extract the name of the city, assuming it will be followed by a state abbreviation. However, inconsistency in how the names are delineated and handling of multi-word names gives us the regular expression seen before. Apart from this, the class is pretty straightforward.

We compile the `City.java` file, adding the necessary JARs from both Hive and Hadoop as we do so.

 Remember, of course, that the specific JAR filenames may be different if you are not using the same versions of both Hadoop and Hive.

We then bundle the generated class file into a JAR and start the Hive interactive shell.

After creating the JAR, we need to configure Hive to use it. This is a two-step process. Firstly, we use the `add jar` command to add the new JAR file to the classpath used by Hive. After doing so, we use the `list jars` command to confirm that our new JAR has been registered in the system.

Adding the JAR only tells Hive that some code exists, it does not say how we wish to refer to the function within our HiveQL statements. The `CREATE FUNCTION` command does this—associating a function name (in this case, `city`) with the fully qualified Java class that provides the implementation (in this case, `com.kycorsystems.City`).

With both the JAR file added to the classpath and the function created, we can now refer to our `city()` function within our HiveQL statements.

We next ran an example query that demonstrates the new function in action. Going back to the partitioned UFO sightings table, we thought it would be interesting to see where the most UFO sightings were occurring as everyone prepared for the end-of-millennium apocalypse.

As can be seen from the HiveQL statement, we can use our new function just like any other and indeed the only way to know which functions are built-in and which are UDFs is through familiarity with the standard Hive function library.

The result shows a significant concentration of sightings in the north-west and south-west of the USA, Chicago being the only exception. We did get quite a few `Unknown` results however, and it would require further analysis to determine if that was due to locations outside of the U.S. or if we need to further refine our regular expression.

To preprocess or not to preprocess...

Let us re-visit an earlier topic; the potential need to pre-process data into a cleaner form before it is imported into Hive. As can be seen from the preceding example, we could perform similar processing on the fly through a series of UDFs. We could, for example, add functions called `state` and `country` that extract or infer the further region and nation components from the location sighting string. There are rarely concrete rules for which approach is best, but a few guidelines may help.

If, as is the case here, we are unlikely to actually process the full location string for reasons other than to extract the distinct components, then preprocessing likely makes more sense. Instead of performing expensive text processing every time the column is accessed, we could either normalize it into a more predictable format or even break it out into separate city/region/country columns.

If, however, a column is usually used in HiveQL in its original form and additional processing is the exceptional case, then there is likely little benefit to an expensive processing step across the entire data set.

Use the strategy that makes the most sense for your data and workloads. Remember that UDFs are for much more than this sort of text processing, they can be used to encapsulate any type of logic that you wish to apply to data in your tables.

Hive versus Pig

Search the Internet for articles about Hive and it won't be long before you find many comparing Hive to another Apache project called **Pig**. Some of the most common questions around this comparison are why both exist, when to use one over the other, which is better, and which makes you look cooler when wearing the project t-shirt in a bar.

The overlap between the projects is that whereas Hive looks to present a familiar SQL-like interface to data, Pig uses a language called **Pig Latin** that specifies dataflow pipelines. Just as Hive translates HiveQL into MapReduce which it then executes, Pig performs similar MapReduce code generation from the Pig Latin scripts.

The biggest difference between HiveQL and Pig Latin is the amount of control expressed over how the job will be executed. HiveQL, just like SQL, specifies what is to be done but says almost nothing about how to actually structure the implementation. The HiveQL query planner is responsible for determining in which order to perform particular parts of the HiveQL command, in which order to evaluate functions, and so on. These decisions are made by Hive at runtime, analogous to a traditional relational database query planner, and this is also the level at which Pig Latin operates.

Both approaches obviate the need to write raw MapReduce code; they differ in the abstractions they provide.

The choice of Hive versus Pig will depend on your needs. If having a familiar SQL interface to the data is important as a means of making the data in Hadoop available to a wider audience, then Hive is the obvious choice. If instead you have personnel who think in terms of data pipelines and need finer-grained control over how the jobs are executed, then Pig may be a better fit. The Hive and Pig projects are looking for closer integration so hopefully the false sense of competition will decrease and instead both will be seen as complementary ways of decreasing the Hadoop knowledge required to execute MapReduce jobs.

What we didn't cover

In this overview of Hive, we have covered its installation and setup, the creation and manipulation of tables, views, and joins. We have looked at how to move data into and out of Hive, how to optimize data processing, and explored several of Hive's built-in functions.

In reality, we have barely scratched the surface. In addition to more depth on the previous topics and a variety of related concepts, we didn't even touch on topics such as the **MetaStore** where Hive stores its configuration and metadata or **SerDe (serialize/deserialize)** objects, which can be used to read data from more complex file formats such as JSON.

Hive is an incredibly rich tool with many powerful and complex features. If Hive is something that you feel may be of value to you, then it is recommended that after running through the examples in this chapter that you spend some quality time with the documentation on the Hive website. There you will also find links to the user mailing list, which is a great source of information and help.

Hive on Amazon Web Services

Elastic MapReduce has significant support for Hive with some specific mechanisms to help its integration with other AWS services.

Time for action – running UFO analysis on EMR

Let us explore the use of EMR with Hive by doing some UFO analysis on the platform.

1. Log in to the AWS management console at `http://aws.amazon.com/console`.

2. Every Hive job flow on EMR runs from an S3 bucket and we need to select the bucket we wish to use for this purpose. Select **S3** to see the list of the buckets associated with your account and then choose the bucket from which to run the example, in the example below, we select the bucket called garryt1use.

3. Use the web interface to create three directories called `ufodata`, `ufoout`, and `ufologs` within that bucket. The resulting list of the bucket's contents should look like the following screenshot:

4. Double-click on the ufodata directory to open it and within it create two subdirectories called ufo and states.

5. Create the following as s3test.hql, click on the **Upload** link within the ufodata directory, and follow the prompts to upload the file:

```
CREATE EXTERNAL TABLE IF NOT EXISTS ufodata(sighted string,
reported string, sighting_location string,
shape string, duration string, description string)
ROW FORMAT DELIMITED
FIELDS TERMINATED BY '\t'
LOCATION '${INPUT}/ufo' ;

CREATE EXTERNAL TABLE IF NOT EXISTS states(abbreviation string,
full_name string)
ROW FORMAT DELIMITED
FIELDS TERMINATED BY '\t'
LOCATION '${INPUT}/states' ;

CREATE VIEW IF NOT EXISTS usa_sightings (sighted, reported, shape,
state)
AS SELECT t1.sighted, t1.reported, t1.shape, t2.full_name
FROM ufodata t1 JOIN states t2
ON (LOWER(t2.abbreviation) = LOWER(SUBSTR( t1.sighting_location,
(LENGTH(t1.sighting_location)-1)))) ;

CREATE EXTERNAL TABLE IF NOT EXISTS state_results ( reported
string, shape string, state string)
ROW FORMAT DELIMITED
FFIELDS TERMINATED BY '\t' LINES TERMINATED BY '\n'
STORED AS TEXTFILE
LOCATION '${OUTPUT}/states' ;

INSERT OVERWRITE TABLE state_results
SELECT reported, shape, state
FROM usa_sightings
WHERE state = 'California' ;
```

The contents of `ufodata` should now look like the following screenshot:

6. Double-click the `states` directory to open it and into this, upload the `states.txt` file used earlier. The directory should now look like the following screenshot:

7. Click on the `ufodata` component at the top of the file list to return to this directory.

8. Double-click on the `ufo` directory to open it and into this, upload the `ufo.tsv` file used earlier. The directory should now look like the following screenshot:

9. Now select **Elastic MapReduce** and click on **Create a New Job Flow**. Then select the option **Run your own application** and select a Hive application, as shown in the following screenshot:

10. Click on **Continue** and then fill in the required details for the Hive job flow. Use the following screenshot as a guide, but remember to change the bucket name (the first component in the s3 :// URLs) to the bucket you set up before:

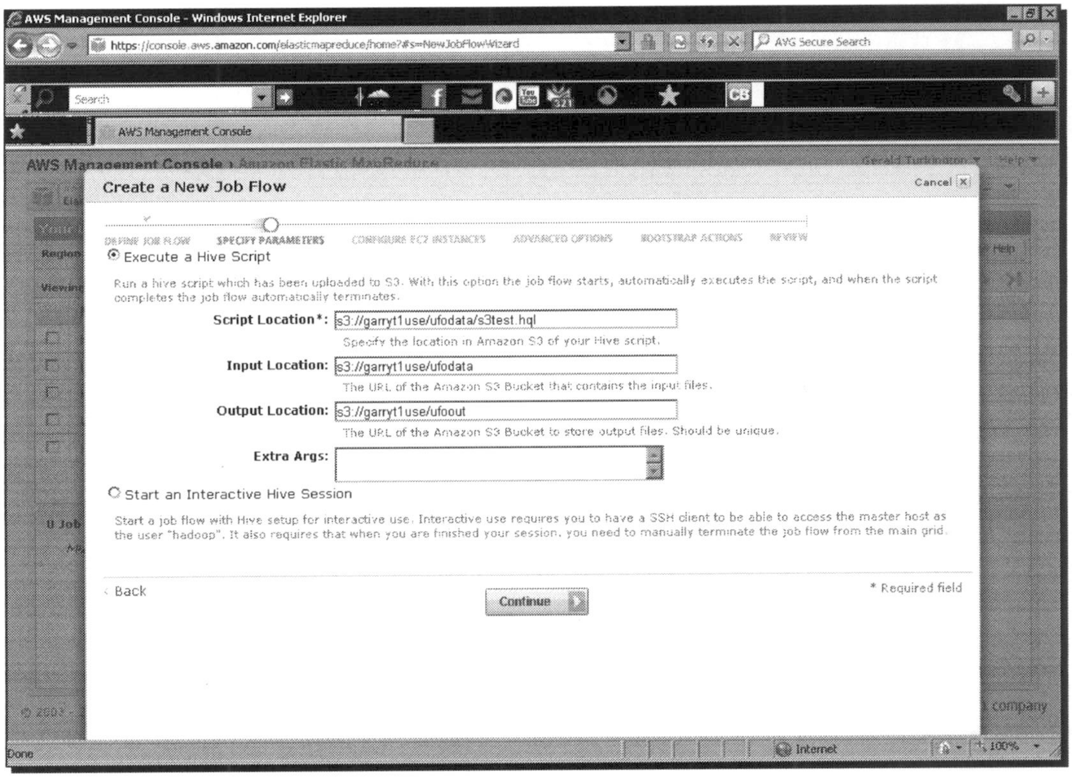

11. Click on **Continue**, review the number and the type of hosts to be used, and then click on **Continue** once again. Then fill in the name of the directory for the logs, as shown in the following screenshot:

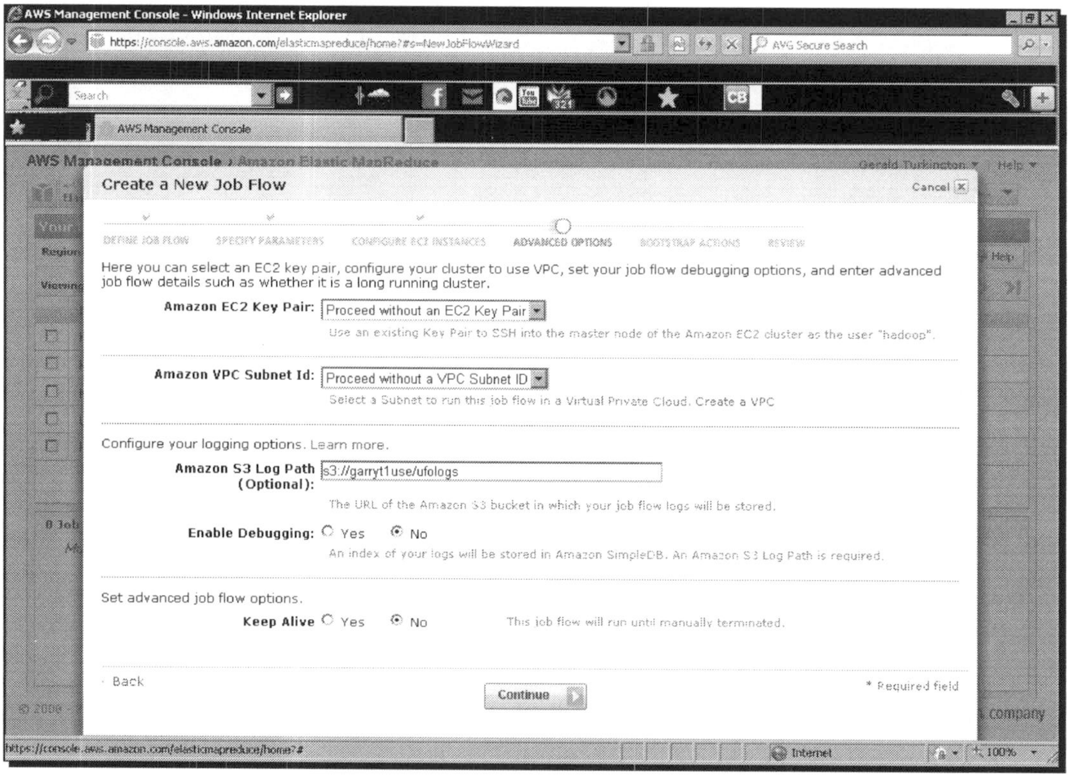

12. Click on **Continue**. Then do the same through the rest of the job creation process as there are no other default options that need to be changed for this example. Finally start the job flow and monitor its progress from the management console.

13. Once the job has completed successfully, go back to **S3** and double-click on the `ufoout` directory. Within that should be a directory called `states` and within that, a file named something like `0000000`. Double-click to download the file and verify that its contents look something like the following:

```
20021014    light    California
20050224    other    California
20021001    egg      California
20030527    sphere   California
```

What just happened?

Before we actually execute our EMR job flow, we needed to do a bit of setup in the preceding example. Firstly, we used the S3 web interface to prepare the directory structure for our job. We created three main directories to hold the input data, into which to write results and one for EMR to place logs of the job flow execution.

The HiveQL script is a modification of several of the Hive commands used earlier in this chapter. It creates the tables for the UFO sighting data and state names as well as the view joining them. Then it creates a new table with no source data and uses an `INSERT OVERWRITE TABLE` to populate the table with the results of a query.

The unique feature in this script is the way we specify the `LOCATION` clauses for each of the tables. For the input tables, we use a path relative to a variable called `INPUT` and do likewise with the `OUTPUT` variable for the result table.

Note that Hive in EMR expects the location of table data to be a directory and not a file. This is the reason for us previously creating subdirectories for each table into which we uploaded the specific source file instead of specifying the table with the direct path to the data files themselves.

After setting up the required file and directory structure within our S3 bucket, we went to the EMR web console and started the job flow creation process.

After specifying that we wish to use our own program and that it would be a Hive application, we filled in a screen with the key data required for our job flow:

- The location of the HiveQL script itself
- The directory containing input data
- The directory to be used for output data

The path to the HiveQL script is an explicit path and does not require any explanation. However, it is important to realize how the other values are mapped into the variables used within our Hive script.

The value for the input path is available to the Hive script as the INPUT variable and this is how we then specify the directory containing the UFO sighting data as ${INPUT}/ufo. Similarly, the output value specified in this form will be used as the OUTPUT variable within our Hive script.

We did not make any changes to the default host setup, which will be one small master and two small core nodes. On the next screen, we added the location into which we wanted EMR to write the logs produced by the job flow execution.

Though optional, it is useful to capture these logs, particularly in the early stages of running a new script, though obviously S3 storage does have a cost. EMR can also write indexed log data into **SimpleDB** (another AWS service), but we did not show that in action here.

After completing the job flow definition, we started it and on successful execution, went to the S3 interface to browse to the output location, which happily contained the data we were expecting.

Using interactive job flows for development

When developing a new Hive script to be executed on EMR, the previous batch job execution is not a good fit. There is usually a several minute latency between job flow creation and execution and if the job fails, then the cost of several hours of EC2 instance time will have been incurred (partial hours are rounded up).

Instead of selecting the option to create an EMR job flow to run a Hive script, as in the previous example, we can start a Hive job flow in interactive mode. This effectively spins up a Hadoop cluster without requiring a named script. You can then SSH into the master node as the Hadoop user where you will find Hive installed and configured. It is much more efficient to do the script development in this environment and then, if required, set up the batch script job flows to automatically execute the script in production.

Have a go hero – using an interactive EMR cluster

Start up an interactive Hive job flow in EMR. You will need to have SSH credentials already registered with EC2 so that you can connect to the master node. Run the previous script directly from the master node, remembering to pass the appropriate variables to the script.

Integration with other AWS products

With a local Hadoop/Hive installation, the question of where data lives usually comes down to HDFS or local filesystems. As we have seen previously, Hive within EMR gives another option with its support for external tables whose data resides in S3.

Another AWS service with similar support is **DynamoDB** (at `http://aws.amazon.com/dynamodb`), a hosted NoSQL database solution in the cloud. Hive job flows within EMR can declare external tables that either read data from DynamoDB or use it as the destination for query output.

This is a very powerful model as it allows Hive to be used to process and combine data from multiple sources while the mechanics of mapping data from one system into Hive tables happens transparently. It also allows Hive to be used as a mechanism for moving data from one system to another. The act of getting data frequently into such hosted services from existing stores is a major adoption hurdle.

Summary

We have looked at Hive in this chapter and learned how it provides many tools and features that will be familiar to anyone who uses relational databases. Instead of requiring development of MapReduce applications, Hive makes the power of Hadoop available to a much broader community.

In particular, we downloaded and installed Hive, learning that it is a client application that translates its HiveQL language into MapReduce code, which it submits to a Hadoop cluster. We explored Hive's mechanism for creating tables and running queries against these tables. We saw how Hive can support various underlying data file formats and structures and how to modify those options.

We also appreciated that Hive tables are largely a logical construct and that behind the scenes, all the SQL-like operations on tables are in fact executed by MapReduce jobs on HDFS files. We then saw how Hive supports powerful features such as joins and views and how to partition our tables to aid in efficient query execution.

We used Hive to output the results of a query to files on HDFS and saw how Hive is supported by Elastic MapReduce, where interactive job flows can be used to develop new Hive applications, and then ran automatically in batch mode.

As we have mentioned several times in this book, Hive looks like a relational database but is not really one. However, in many cases you will find existing relational databases are part of the broader infrastructure into which you need integrate. Performing that integration and how to move data across these different types of data sources will be the topic of the next chapter.

9
Working with Relational Databases

As we saw in the previous chapter, Hive is a great tool that provides a relational database-like view of the data stored in Hadoop. However, at the end of the day, it is not truly a relational database. It does not fully implement the SQL standard, and its performance and scale characteristics are vastly different (not better or worse, just different) from a traditional relational database.

In many cases, you will find a Hadoop cluster sitting alongside and used with (not instead of) relational databases. Often the business flows will require data to be moved from one store to the other; we will now explore such integration.

In this chapter, we will:

- ◆ Identify some common Hadoop/RDBMS use cases
- ◆ Explore how we can move data from RDBMS into HDFS and Hive
- ◆ Use Sqoop as a better solution for such problems
- ◆ Move data with exports from Hadoop into an RDBMS
- ◆ Wrap up with a discussion of how this can be applied to AWS

Common data paths

Back in *Chapter 1, What It's All About*, we touched on what we believe to be an artificial choice that causes a lot of controversy; to use Hadoop or a traditional relational database. As explained there, it is our contention that the thing to focus on is identifying the right tool for the task at hand and that this is likely to lead to a situation where more than one technology is employed. It is worth looking at a few concrete examples to illustrate this idea.

Hadoop as an archive store

When an RDBMS is used as the main data repository, there often arises issues of scale and data retention. As volumes of new data increase, what is to be done with the older and less valuable data?

Traditionally, there are two main approaches to this situation:

◆ Partition the RDBMS to allow higher performance of more recent data; sometimes the technology allows older data to be stored on slower and less expensive storage systems

◆ Archive the data onto tape or another offline store

Both approaches are valid, and the decision between the two often rests on just whether or not the older data is required for timely access. These are two extreme cases as the former maximizes for access at the cost of complexity and infrastructure expense, while the latter reduces costs but makes data less accessible.

The model being seen recently is for the most current data to be kept in the relational database and the older data to be pushed into Hadoop. This can either be onto HDFS as structured files or into Hive to retain the RDBMS interface. This gives the best of both worlds, allowing the lower-volume, more recent data to be accessible by high-speed, low-latency SQL queries, while the much larger volume of archived data will be accessed from Hadoop. The data therefore remains available for use cases requiring either types of access; this would be needed on a platform that does require additional integration for any queries that need to span both the recent and archive data.

Because of Hadoop's scalability, this model gives great future growth potential; we know we can continue to increase the amount of archive data being stored while retaining the ability to run analytics against it.

Hadoop as a preprocessing step

Several times in our Hive discussion, we highlighted opportunities where some preprocessing jobs to massage or otherwise clean up the data would be hugely useful. The unfortunate fact is that, in many (most?) big data situations, the large volumes of data coming from multiple sources mean that dirty data is simply a given. Although most MapReduce jobs only require a subset of the overall data to be processed, we should still expect to find incomplete or corrupt data across the data set. Just as Hive can benefit from preprocessing data, a traditional relational database can as well.

Hadoop can be a great tool here; it can pull data from multiple sources, combine them for necessary transformations, and clean up prior to the data being inserted into the relational database.

Hadoop as a data input tool

Hadoop is not just valuable in that it makes data better and is well suited to being ingested into a relational database. In addition to such tasks, Hadoop can also be used to generate additional data sets or data views that are then served from the relational database. Common patterns here are situations such as when we wish to display not only the primary data for an account but to also display alongside it secondary data generated from account history. Such views could be summaries of transactions against types of expenditure for the previous months. This data is held within Hadoop, from which can be generated the actual summaries that may be pushed back into the database for quicker display.

The serpent eats its own tail

Reality is often more complex than these well-defined situations, and it's not uncommon for the data flow between Hadoop and the relational database to be described by circles and arcs instead of a single straight line. The Hadoop cluster may, for example, do the preprocessing step on data that is then ingested into the RDBMS and then receive frequent transaction dumps that are used to build aggregates, which are sent back to the database. Then, once the data gets older than a certain threshold, it is deleted from the database but kept in Hadoop for archival purposes.

Regardless of the situation, the ability to get data from Hadoop to a relational database and back again is a critical aspect of integrating Hadoop into your IT infrastructure. So, let's see how to do it.

Setting up MySQL

Before reading and writing data from a relational database, we need a running relational database. We will use MySQL in this chapter because it is freely and widely available and many developers have used it at some point in their career. You can of course use any RDBMS for which a JDBC driver is available, but if you do so, you'll need to modify the aspects of this chapter that require direct interaction with the database server.

Time for action – installing and setting up MySQL

Let's get MySQL installed and configured with the basic databases and access rights.

1. On an Ubuntu host, install MySQL using `apt-get`:

```
$ apt-get update
$ apt-get install mysql-server
```

2. Follow the prompts, and when asked, choose a suitable root password.

3. Once installed, connect to the MySQL server:

```
$ mysql -h localhost -u root -p
```

4. Enter the root password when prompted:

```
Welcome to the MySQL monitor.  Commands end with ; or \g.
Your MySQL connection id is 40

...

Mysql>
```

5. Create a new database to use for the examples in this chapter:

```
Mysql> create database hadooptest;
```

You will receive the following response:

```
Query OK, 1 row affected (0.00 sec)
```

6. Create a user account with full access to the database:

```
Mysql>  grant all on hadooptest.* to 'hadoopuser'@'%' identified
by 'password';
```

You will receive the following response:

```
Query OK, 0 rows affected (0.01 sec)
```

7. Reload the user privileges to have the user changes take effect:

```
Mysql> flush privileges;
```

You will receive the following response:

```
Query OK, 0 rows affected (0.01 sec)
```

8. Log out as root:

```
mysql> quit;
```

You will receive the following response:

```
Bye
```

9. Log in as the newly created user, entering the password when prompted:

```
$ mysql -u hadoopuser -p
```

10. Change to the newly created database:

```
mysql> use hadooptest;
```

11. Create a test table, drop it to confirm the user has the privileges in this database, and then log out:

```
mysql> create table tabletest(id int);
mysql> drop table tabletest;
mysql> quit;
```

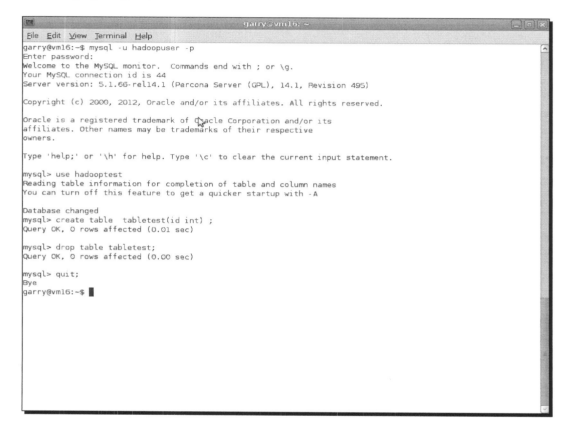

What just happened?

Due to the wonders of package managers such as `apt`, installing complex software such as MySQL is really very easy. We just use the standard process to install a package; under Ubuntu (and most other distributions in fact), requesting the main server package for MySQL will bring along all needed dependencies as well as the client packages.

During the install, you will be prompted for the root password on the database. Even if this is a test database instance that no one will use and that will have no valuable data, please give the root user a strong password. Having weak root passwords is a bad habit, and we do not want to encourage it.

After MySQL is installed, we connect to the database using the `mysql` command-line utility. This takes a range of options, but the ones we will use are as follows:

◆ `-h`: This option is used to specify the hostname of the database (the local machine is assumed if none is given)

◆ `-u`: This option is used for the username with which to connect (the default is the current Linux user)

◆ `-p`: This option is used to be prompted for the user password

MySQL has the concept of multiple databases, each of which is a collective grouping of tables. Every table needs be associated with a database. MySQL has several built-in databases, but we use the CREATE DATABASE statement to create a new one called `hadooptest` for our later work.

MySQL refuses connections/requests to perform actions unless the requesting user has explicitly been given the needed privileges to perform the action. We do not want to do everything as the root user (a bad practice and quite dangerous since the root can modify/delete everything), so we create a new user called `hadoopuser` by using the GRANT statement.

The GRANT statement we used actually does three distinct things:

◆ Creates the `hadoopuser` account

◆ Sets the `hadoopuser` password; we set it to `password`, which obviously you should never do; pick something easy to memorize

◆ Gives `hadoopuser` all privileges on the `hadooptest` database and all its tables

We issue the FLUSH PRIVILEGES command to have these changes take effect and then we log out as root and connect as the new user to check whether all is working.

The USE statement here is a little superfluous. In future, we can instead add the database name to the `mysql` command-line tool to automatically change to that database.

Connecting as the new user is a good sign, but to gain full confidence, we create a new table in the `hadooptest` database and then drop it. Success here shows that `hadoopuser` does indeed have the requested privileges to modify the database.

Did it have to be so hard?

We are perhaps being a little cautious here by checking every step of the process along the way. However, I have found in the past that subtle typos, in the GRANT statement in particular, can result in really hard-to-diagnose problems later on. And to continue our paranoia, let's make one change to the default MySQL configuration that we won't need quite yet, but which if we don't do, we'll be sorry later.

For any production database, you would of course not have security-sensitive statements, such as GRANT, present that were typed in from a book. Refer to the documentation of your database to understand user accounts and privileges.

Time for action – configuring MySQL to allow remote connections

We need to change the common default MySQL behavior, which will prevent us from accessing the database from other hosts.

1. Edit /etc/mysql/my.cnf in your favorite text editor and look for this line:

   ```
   bind-address = 127.0.0.1
   ```

2. Change it to this:

   ```
   # bind-address = 127.0.0.1
   ```

3. Restart MySQL:

   ```
   $ restart mysql
   ```

What just happened?

Most out-of-the-box MySQL configurations allow access only from the same host on which the server is running. This is absolutely the correct default from a security standpoint. However, it can also cause real confusion if, for example, you launch MapReduce jobs that try to access the database on that host. You may see the job fail with connection errors. If that happens, you fire up the mysql command-line client on the host; this will succeed. Then, perhaps, you will write a quick JDBC client to test connectivity. This will also work. Only when you try these steps from one of the Hadoop worker nodes will the problem be apparent. Yes, this has bit ten me several times in the past!

The previous change tells MySQL to bind to all available interfaces and thus be accessible from remote clients.

After making the change, we need to restart the server. In Ubuntu 11.10, many of the service scripts have been ported to the Upstart framework, and we can use the handy restart command directly.

If you are using a distribution other than Ubuntu—or potentially even a different version of Ubuntu—the global MySQL configuration file may be in a different location; /etc/my.cnf, for example, on CentOS and Red Hat Enterprise Linux.

Don't do this in production!

Or at least not without thinking about the consequences. In the earlier example, we gave a really bad password to the new user; do not do that. However, especially don't do something like that if you then make the database available across the network. Yes, it is a test database with no valuable data, but it is amazing how many test databases live for a very long time and start getting more and more critical. And will you remember to remove that user with the weak password after you are done?

Enough lecturing. Databases need data. Let's add a table to the hadooptest database that we'll use throughout this chapter.

Time for action – setting up the employee database

No discussion of databases is complete without the example of an employee table, so we will follow tradition and start there.

1. Create a tab-separated file named employees.tsv with the following entries:

```
Alice    Engineering   50000   2009-03-12
Bob      Sales    35000   2011-10-01
Camille  Marketing   40000   2003-04-20
David    Executive   75000   2001-03-20
Erica    Support    34000   2011-07-07
```

2. Connect to the MySQL server:

```
$ mysql -u hadoopuser -p hadooptest
```

3. Create the table:

```
Mysql> create table employees(
first_name varchar(10) primary key,
dept varchar(15),
salary int,
start_date date
) ;
```

4. Load the data from the file into the database:

```
mysql> load data local infile '/home/garry/employees.tsv'
    -> into table employees
    -> fields terminated by '\t' lines terminated by '\n' ;
```

```
                              garry@vm16: ~                        _ □ ✕
File  Edit  View  Terminal  Help
Server version: 5.1.66-rel14.1 (Percona Server (GPL), 14.1, Revision 495)

Copyright (c) 2000, 2012, Oracle and/or its affiliates. All rights reserved.

Oracle is a registered trademark of Oracle Corporation and/or its
affiliates. Other names may be trademarks of their respective
owners.

Type 'help;' or '\h' for help. Type  \c  to clear the current input statement.

mysql> create table employees(
    -> first_name varchar(10) primary key,
    -> dept varchar(15),
    -> salary int,
    -> start_date date);
Query OK, 0 rows affected (0.02 sec)

mysql> load data local infile '/home/garry/employees.tsv'
    -> into table employees
    -> fields terminated by '\t' lines terminated by '\n';
Query OK, 5 rows affected (0.01 sec)
Records: 5  Deleted: 0  Skipped: 0  Warnings: 0

mysql> █
```

What just happened?

This is pretty standard database stuff. We created a tab-separated data file, created the table in the database, and then used the LOAD DATA LOCAL INFILE statement to import the data into the table.

We are using a very small set of data here as it is really for illustration purposes only.

Be careful with data file access rights

Don't omit the LOCAL part from the LOAD DATA statement; doing so sees MySQL try and load the file as the MySQL user, and this usually results in access problems.

Getting data into Hadoop

Now that we have put in all that up-front effort, let us look at ways of bringing the data out of MySQL and into Hadoop.

Using MySQL tools and manual import

The simplest way to export data into Hadoop is to use existing command-line tools and statements. To export an entire table (or indeed an entire database), MySQL offers the `mysqldump` utility. To do a more precise export, we can use a `SELECT` statement of the following form:

```
SELECT col1, col2 from table
INTO OUTFILE '/tmp/out.csv'
FIELDS TERMINATED by ',', LINES TERMINATED BY '\n';
```

Once we have an export file, we can move it into HDFS using `hadoop fs -put` or into Hive through the methods discussed in the previous chapter.

Have a go hero – exporting the employee table into HDFS

We don't want this chapter to turn into a MySQL tutorial, so look up the syntax of the `mysqldump` utility, and use it or the `SELECT ... INTO OUTFILE` statement to export the employee table into a tab-separated file you then copy onto HDFS.

Accessing the database from the mapper

For our trivial example, the preceding approaches are fine, but what if you need to export a much larger set of data, especially if it then is to be processed by a MapReduce job?

The obvious approach is that of direct JDBC access within a MapReduce input job that pulls the data from the database and writes it onto HDFS, ready for additional processing.

This is a valid technique, but there are a few not-so-obvious gotchas.

You need to be careful how much load you place on the database. Throwing this sort of job onto a very large cluster could very quickly melt the database as hundreds or thousands of mappers try to simultaneously open connections and read the same table. The simplest access pattern is also likely to see one query per row, which obviates the ability to use more efficient bulk access statements. Even if the database can take the load, it is quite possible for the database network connection to quickly become the bottleneck.

To effectively parallelize the query across all the mappers, you need a strategy to partition the table into segments each mapper will retrieve. You then need to determine how each mapper is to have its segment parameters passed in.

If the retrieved segments are large, there is a chance that you will end up with long-running tasks that get terminated by the Hadoop framework unless you explicitly report progress.

That is actually quite a lot of work for a conceptually simple task. Wouldn't it be much better to use an existing tool for the purpose? There is indeed such a tool that we will use throughout the rest of this chapter, Sqoop.

A better way – introducing Sqoop

Sqoop was created by Cloudera (http://www.cloudera.com), a company that provides numerous services related to Hadoop in addition to producing its own packaging of the Hadoop distribution, something we will discuss in *Chapter 11, Where to Go Next.*

As well as providing this packaged Hadoop product, the company has also created a number of tools that have been made available to the community, and one of these is Sqoop. Its job is to do exactly what we need, to copy data between Hadoop and relational databases. Though originally developed by Cloudera, it has been contributed to the Apache Software Foundation, and its homepage is http://sqoop.apache.org.

Time for action – downloading and configuring Sqoop

Let's download and get Sqoop installed and configured.

1. Go to the Sqoop homepage, select the link for the most stable version that is no earlier than 1.4.1, and match it with the version of Hadoop you are using. Download the file.

2. Copy the retrieved file where you want it installed on your system; then uncompress it:

```
$mv sqoop-1.4.1-incubating__hadoop-1.0.0.tar.gz_ /usr/local
$ cd /usr/local
$ tar -xzf sqoop-1.4.1-incubating__hadoop-1.0.0.tar.gz_
```

3. Make a symlink:

```
$ ln -s sqoop-1.4.1-incubating__hadoop-1.0.0 sqoop
```

4. Update your environment:

```
$ export SQOOP_HOME=/usr/local/sqoop
$ export PATH=${SQOOP_HOME}/bin:${PATH}
```

5. Download the JDBC driver for your database; for MySQL, we find it at http://dev.mysql.com/downloads/connector/j/5.0.html.

6. Copy the downloaded JAR file into the Sqoop `lib` directory:

```
$ cp mysql-connector-java-5.0.8-bin.jar /opt/sqoop/lib
```

7. Test Sqoop:

```
$ sqoop help
```

You will see the following output:

```
usage: sqoop COMMAND [ARGS]

Available commands:
  codegen            Generate code to interact with database
records
...
  version            Display version information

See 'sqoop help COMMAND' for information on a specific command.
```

What just happened?

Sqoop is a pretty straightforward tool to install. After downloading the required version from the Sqoop homepage—being careful to pick the one that matches our Hadoop version—we copied and unpacked the file.

Once again, we needed to set an environment variable and added the Sqoop `bin` directory to our path so we can either set these directly in our shell, or as before, add these steps to a configuration file we can source prior to a development session.

Sqoop needs access to the JDBC driver for your database; for us, we downloaded the MySQL Connector and copied it into the Sqoop `lib` directory. For the most popular databases, this is as much configuration as Sqoop requires; if you want to use something exotic, consult the Sqoop documentation.

After this minimal install, we executed the `sqoop` command-line utility to validate that it is working properly.

 You may see warning messages from Sqoop telling you that additional variables such as `HBASE_HOME` have not been defined. As we are not talking about HBase in this book, we do not need this setting and will be omitting such warnings from our screenshots.

Sqoop and Hadoop versions

We were very specific in the version of Sqoop to be retrieved before; much more so than for previous software downloads. In Sqoop versions prior to 1.4.1, there is a dependency on an additional method on one of the core Hadoop classes that was only available in the Cloudera Hadoop distribution or versions of Hadoop after 0.21.

Unfortunately, the fact that Hadoop 1.0 is effectively a continuation of the 0.20 branch meant that Sqoop 1.3, for example, would work with Hadoop 0.21 but not 0.20 or 1.0. To avoid this version confusion, we recommend using version 1.4.1 or later, which removes the dependency.

There is no additional MySQL configuration required; we would discover if the server had not been configured to allow remote clients, as described earlier, through use of Sqoop.

Sqoop and HDFS

The simplest import we can perform is to dump data from a database table onto structured files on HDFS. Let's do that.

Time for action – exporting data from MySQL to HDFS

We'll use a straightforward example here, where we just pull all the data from a single MySQL table and write it to a single file on HDFS.

1. Run Sqoop to export data from MySQL onto HDFS:

   ```
   $ sqoop import --connect jdbc:mysql://10.0.0.100/hadooptest
   --username hadoopuser \ > --password password --table employees
   ```

2. Examine the output directory:

```
$ hadoop fs -ls employees
```

You will receive the following response:

```
Found 6 items
-rw-r--r--    3 hadoop supergroup        0 2012-05-21 04:10 /
user/hadoop/employees/_SUCCESS
drwxr-xr-x    - hadoop supergroup        0 2012-05-21 04:10 /
user/hadoop/employees/_logs
-rw-r--r--    3 … /user/hadoop/employees/part-m-00000
-rw-r--r--    3 … /user/hadoop/employees/part-m-00001
-rw-r--r--    3 … /user/hadoop/employees/part-m-00002
-rw-r--r--    3 … /user/hadoop/employees/part-m-00003
```

3. Display one of the result files:

```
$ hadoop fs -cat /user/hadoop/employees/part-m-00001
```

You will see the following output:

```
Bob,Sales,35000,2011-10-01
Camille,Marketing,40000,2003-04-20
```

What just happened?

We did not need any preamble; a single Sqoop statement is all we require here. As can be seen, the Sqoop command line takes many options; let's unpack them one at a time.

The first option in Sqoop is the type of task to be performed; in this case, we wish to import data from a relational source into Hadoop. The `--connect` option specifies the JDBC URI for the database, of the standard form `jdbc:<driver>://<host>/<database>`. Obviously, you need to change the IP or hostname to the server where your database is running.

We use the `--username` and `--password` options to specify those attributes and finally use `--table` to indicate from which table we wish to retrieve the data. That is it! Sqoop does the rest.

The Sqoop output is relatively verbose, but do read it as it gives a good idea of exactly what is happening.

 Repeated executions of Sqoop may however include a nested error about a generated file already existing. Ignore that for now.

Firstly, in the preceding steps, we see Sqoop telling us not to use the `--password` option as it is inherently insecure. Sqoop has an alternative `-P` command, which prompts for the password; we will use that in future examples.

We also get a warning about using a textual primary key column and that it's a very bad idea; more on that in a little while.

After all the setup and warnings, however, we see Sqoop execute a MapReduce job and complete it successfully.

By default, Sqoop places the output files into a directory in the home directory of the user who ran the job. The files will be in a directory of the same name as the source table. To verify this, we used `hadoop fs -ls` to check this directory and confirmed that it contained several files, likely more than we would have expected, given such a small table. Note that we slightly abbreviated the output here to allow it to fit on one line.

We then examined one of the output files and discovered the reason for the multiple files; even though the table is tiny, it was still split across multiple mappers, and hence, output files. Sqoop uses four map tasks by default. It may look a little strange in this case, but the usual situation will be a much larger data import. Given the desire to copy data onto HDFS, this data is likely to be the source of a future MapReduce job, so multiple files makes perfect sense.

Mappers and primary key columns

We intentionally set up this situation by somewhat artificially using a textual primary key column in our employee data set. In reality, the primary key would much more likely be an auto-incrementing, numeric employee ID. However, this choice highlighted the nature of how Sqoop processes tables and its use of primary keys.

Sqoop uses the primary key column to determine how to divide the source data across its mappers. But, as the warnings before state, this means we are reliant on string-based comparisons, and in an environment with imperfect case significance, the results may be incorrect. The ideal situation is to use a numeric column as suggested.

Alternatively, it is possible to control the number of mappers using the `-m` option. If we use `-m 1`, there will be a single mapper and no attempt will be made to partition the primary key column. For small data sets such as ours, we can also do this to ensure a single output file.

This is not just an option; if you try to import from a table with no primary key, Sqoop will fail with an error stating that the only way to import from such a table is to explicitly set a single mapper.

Other options

Don't assume that Sqoop is all or nothing when it comes to importing data. Sqoop has several other options to specify, restrict, and alter the data extracted from the database. We will illustrate these in the following sections, where we discuss Hive, but bear in mind that most can also be used when exporting into HDFS.

Sqoop's architecture

Now that we have seen Sqoop in action, it is worthwhile taking a few moments to clarify its architecture and see how it works. In several ways, Sqoop interacts with Hadoop in much the same way that Hive does; both are single client programs that create one or more MapReduce jobs to perform their tasks.

Sqoop does not have any server processes; the command-line client we run is all there is to it. However, because it can tailor its generated MapReduce code to the specific tasks at hand, it tends to utilize Hadoop quite efficiently.

The preceding example of splitting a source RDBMS table on a primary key is a good example of this. Sqoop knows the number of mappers that will be configured in the MapReduce job—the default is four, as previously mentioned—and from this, it can do smart partitioning of the source table.

If we assume a table with 1 million records and four mappers, then each will process 2,50,000 records. With its knowledge of the primary key column, Sqoop can create four SQL statements to retrieve the data that each use the desired primary key column range as caveats. In the simplest case, this could be as straightforward as adding something like `WHERE id BETWEEN 1 and 250000` to the first statement and using different `id` ranges for the others.

We will see the reverse behavior when exporting data from Hadoop as Sqoop again parallelizes data retrieval across multiple mappers and works to optimize the insertion of this data into the relational database. However, all these smarts are pushed into the MapReduce jobs executed on Hadoop; the Sqoop command-line client's job is to generate this code as efficiently as possible and then get out of the way as the processing occurs.

Importing data into Hive using Sqoop

Sqoop has significant integration with Hive, allowing it to import data from a relational source into either new or existing Hive tables. There are multiple ways in which this process can be tailored, but again, let's start with the simple case.

Time for action – exporting data from MySQL into Hive

For this example, we'll export all the data from a single MySQL table into a correspondingly named table in Hive. You will need Hive installed and configured as detailed in the previous chapter.

1. Delete the output directory created in the previous section:

```
$ hadoop fs -rmr employees
```

You will receive the following response:

```
Deleted hdfs://head:9000/user/hadoop/employees
```

2. Confirm Hive doesn't already contain an employees table:

```
$ hive -e "show tables like 'employees'"
```

You will receive the following response:

```
OK
Time taken: 2.318 seconds
```

3. Perform the Sqoop import:

```
$ sqoop import --connect jdbc:mysql://10.0.0.100/hadooptest
--username hadoopuser -P
--table employees --hive-import --hive-table employees
```

4. Check the contents in Hive:

```
$ hive -e "select * from employees"
```

You will receive the following response:

```
OK
Alice    Engineering   50000   2009-03-12
Camille  Marketing     40000   2003-04-20
David    Executive     75000   2001-03-20
Erica    Support       34000   2011-07-07
Time taken: 2.739 seconds
```

5. Examine the created table in Hive:

```
$ hive -e "describe employees"
```

You will receive the following response:

```
OK
first_name   string
dept    string
salary    int
start_date   string
Time taken: 2.553 seconds
```

What just happened?

Again, we use the Sqoop command with two new options, `--hive-import` to tell Sqoop the final destination is Hive and not HDFS, and `--hive-table` to specify the name of the table in Hive where we want the data imported.

In actuality, we don't need to specify the name of the Hive table if it is the same as the source table specified by the `--table` option. However, it does make things more explicit, so we will typically include it.

As before, do read the full Sqoop output as it provides great insight into what's going on, but the last few lines highlight the successful import into the new Hive table.

We see Sqoop retrieving five rows from MySQL and then going through the stages of copying them to HDFS and importing into Hive. We will talk about the warning re type conversions next.

After Sqoop completes the process, we use Hive to retrieve the data from the new Hive table and confirm that it is what we expected. Then, we examine the definition of the created table.

At this point, we do see one strange thing; the `start_date` column has been given a type string even though it was originally a SQL DATE type in MySQL.

The warning we saw during the Sqoop execution explains this situation:

```
12/05/23 13:06:33 WARN hive.TableDefWriter: Column start_date had to be
cast to a less precise type in Hive
```

The cause of this is that Hive does not support any temporal datatype other than TIMESTAMP. In those cases where imported data is of another type, relating to dates or times, Sqoop converts it to a string. We will look at a way of dealing with this situation a little later.

This example is a pretty common situation, but we do not always want to import an entire table into Hive. Sometimes, we want to only include particular columns or to apply a predicate to reduce the number of selected items. Sqoop allows us to do both.

Time for action – a more selective import

Let's see how this works by performing an import that is limited by a conditional expression.

1. Delete any existing employee import directory:

    ```
    $ hadoop fs -rmr employees
    ```

    You will receive the following response:

    ```
    Deleted hdfs://head:9000/user/hadoop/employees
    ```

2. Import selected columns with a predicate:

    ```
    sqoop import --connect jdbc:mysql://10.0.0.100/hadooptest
    --username hadoopuser -P
    --table employees --columns first_name,salary
     --where "salary > 45000"
    --hive-import --hive-table salary
    ```

    You will receive the following response:

    ```
    12/05/23 15:02:03 INFO hive.HiveImport: Hive import complete.
    ```

3. Examine the created table:

    ```
    $ hive -e "describe salary"
    ```

    You will receive the following response:

    ```
    OK
    first_name  string
    ```

```
salary    int
Time taken: 2.57 seconds
```

4. Examine the imported data:

```
$ hive -e "select * from salary"
```

You will see the following output:

```
OK
Alice    50000
David    75000
Time taken: 2.754 seconds
```

What just happened?

This time, our Sqoop command first added the --columns option that specifies which columns to include in the import. This is a comma-separated list.

We also used the --where option that allows the free text specification of a WHERE clause that is applied to the SQL used to extract data from the database.

The combination of these options is that our Sqoop command should import only the names and salaries of those with a salary greater than the threshold specified in the WHERE clause.

We execute the command, see it complete successfully, and then examine the table created in Hive. We see that it indeed only contains the specified columns, and we then display the table contents to verify that the where predicate was also applied correctly.

Datatype issues

In *Chapter 8, A Relational View on Data with Hive*, we mentioned that Hive does not support all the common SQL datatypes. The DATE and DATETIME types in particular are not currently implemented though they do exist as identified Hive issues; so hopefully, they will be added in the future. We saw this impact our first Hive import earlier in this chapter. Though the start_date column was of type DATE in MySQL, the Sqoop import flagged a conversion warning, and the resultant column in Hive was of type STRING.

Sqoop has an option that is of use here, that is, we can use --map-column-hive to explicitly tell Sqoop how to create the column in the generated Hive table.

Time for action – using a type mapping

Let's use a type mapping to improve our data import.

1. Delete any existing output directory:

   ```
   $ hadoop fs -rmr employees
   ```

2. Execute Sqoop with an explicit type mapping:

   ```
   sqoop import --connect jdbc:mysql://10.0.0.100/hadooptest
   --username hadoopuser
   -P --table employees
   --hive-import --hive-table employees
   --map-column-hive start_date=timestamp
   ```

   You will receive the following response:

   ```
   12/05/23 14:53:38 INFO hive.HiveImport: Hive import complete.
   ```

3. Examine the created table definition:

   ```
   $ hive -e "describe employees"
   ```

   You will receive the following response:

   ```
   OK
   first_name  string
   dept  string
   salary  int
   start_date  timestamp
   Time taken: 2.547 seconds
   ```

4. Examine the imported data:

   ```
   $ hive -e "select * from employees";
   ```

   You will receive the following response:

   ```
   OK
   Failed with exception java.io.IOException:java.lang.
   IllegalArgumentException: Timestamp format must be yyyy-mm-dd
   hh:mm:ss[.fffffffff]
   Time taken: 2.73 seconds
   ```

What just happened?

Our Sqoop command line here is similar to our original Hive import, except for the addition of the column mapping specification. We specified that the start_date column should be of type TIMESTAMP, and we could have added other specifications. The option takes a comma-separated list of such mappings.

After confirming Sqoop executed successfully, we examined the created Hive table and verified that the mapping was indeed applied and that the start_date column has type TIMESTAMP.

We then tried to retrieve the data from the table and could not do so, receiving an error about type format mismatch.

On reflection, this should not be a surprise. Though we specified the desired column type was to be TIMESTAMP, the actual data being imported from MySQL was of type DATE, which does not contain the time component required in a timestamp. This is an important lesson. Ensuring that the type mappings are correct is only one part of the puzzle; we must also ensure the data is valid for the specified column type.

Time for action – importing data from a raw query

Let's see an example of an import where a raw SQL statement is used to select the data to be imported.

1. Delete any existing output directory:

   ```
   $ hadoop fs -rmr employees
   ```

2. Drop any existing Hive employee table:

   ```
   $ hive -e 'drop table employees'
   ```

3. Import data using an explicit query:

   ```
   sqoop import --connect jdbc:mysql://10.0.0.100/hadooptest
   --username hadoopuser -P
   --target-dir employees
   --query 'select first_name, dept, salary,
   timestamp(start_date) as start_date from employees where
   $CONDITIONS'
   --hive-import --hive-table employees
   --map-column-hive start_date=timestamp -m 1
   ```

4. Examine the created table:

   ```
   $ hive -e "describe employees"
   ```

You will receive the following response:

```
OK
first_name   string
dept    string
salary   int
start_date   timestamp
Time taken: 2.591 seconds
```

5. Examine the data:

```
$ hive -e "select * from employees"
```

You will receive the following response:

```
OK
Alice   Engineering   50000   2009-03-12 00:00:00
Bob     Sales   35000   2011-10-01 00:00:00
Camille   Marketing   40000   2003-04-20 00:00:00
David   Executive   75000   2001-03-20 00:00:00
Erica   Support   34000   2011-07-07 00:00:00
Time taken: 2.709 seconds
```

What just happened?

To achieve our goal, we used a very different form of the Sqoop import. Instead of specifying the desired table and then either letting Sqoop import all columns or a specified subset, here we use the `--query` option to define an explicit SQL statement.

In the statement, we select all the columns from the source table but apply the `timestamp()` function to convert the `start_date` column to the correct type. (Note that this function simply adds a `00:00` time element to the date). We alias the result of this function, which allows us to name it in the type mapping option.

Because we have no `--table` option, we have to add `--target-dir` to tell Sqoop the name of the directory it should create on HDFS.

The WHERE clause in the SQL is required by Sqoop even though we are not actually using it. Having no `--table` option does not just remove Sqoop's ability to auto-generate the name of the export directory, it also means that Sqoop does not know from where data is being retrieved, and hence, how to partition the data across multiple mappers. The `$CONDITIONS` variable is used in conjunction with a `--where` option; specifying the latter provides Sqoop with the information it needs to partition the table appropriately.

We take a different route here and instead explicitly set the number of mappers to 1, which obviates the need for an explicit partitioning clause.

After executing Sqoop, we examine the table definition in Hive, which as before, has the correct datatypes for all columns. We then look at the data, and this is now successful, with the start_date column data being appropriately converted into the TIMESTAMP values.

 When we mentioned in the *Sqoop and HDFS* section that Sqoop provided mechanisms to restrict the data extracted from the database, we were referring to the query, where, and columns options. Note that these can be used by any Sqoop import regardless of the destination.

Have a go hero

Though it truly is not needed for such a small data set, the $CONDITIONS variable is an important tool. Modify the preceding Sqoop statement to use multiple mappers with an explicit partitioning statement.

Sqoop and Hive partitions

In *Chapter 8, A Relational View on Data with Hive*, we talked a lot about Hive partitions and highlighted how important they are in allowing query optimization for very large tables. The good news is that Sqoop can support Hive partitions; the bad news is that the support is not complete.

To import data from a relational database into a partitioned Hive table, we use the --hive-partition-key option to specify the partition column and the --hive-partition-value option to specify the value for the partition into which this Sqoop command will import data.

This is excellent but does require each Sqoop statement to be imported into a single Hive partition; there is currently no support for Hive auto-partitioning. Instead, if a data set is to be imported into multiple partitions in a table, we need use a separate Sqoop statement for insertion into each partition.

Field and line terminators

Until now, we have been implicitly relying on some defaults but should discuss them at this point. Our original text file was tab separated, but you may have noticed that the data we exported onto HDFS was comma-separated. If you go look in the files under /user/hive/warehouse/employees (remember this is the default location on HDFS where Hive keeps its source files), the records use ASCII code 001 as the separator. What is going on?

In the first instance, we let Sqoop use its defaults, which in this case, means using a comma to separate fields and using \n for records. However, when Sqoop is importing into Hive, it instead employs the Hive defaults, which include using the 001 code (^A) to separate fields.

We can explicitly set separators using the following Sqoop options:

- ◆ fields-terminated-by: This is the separator between fields
- ◆ lines-terminated-by: The line terminator
- ◆ escaped-by: Used to escape characters (for example, \)
- ◆ enclosed-by: The character enclosing fields (for example, ")
- ◆ optionally-enclosed-by: Similar to the preceding option but not mandatory
- ◆ mysql-delimiters: A shortcut to use the MySQL defaults

This may look a little intimidating, but it's not as obscure as the terminology may suggest, and the concepts and syntax should be familiar to those with SQL experience. The first few options are pretty self-explanatory; where it gets less clear is when talking of enclosing and optionally enclosing characters.

This is really about (usually free-form) data where a given field may include characters that have special meanings. For example, a string column in a comma-separated file that includes commas. In such a case, we could enclose the string columns within quotes to allow the commas within the field. If all fields need such enclosing characters, we would use the first form; if it was only required for a subset of the fields, it could be specified as optional.

Getting data out of Hadoop

We said that the data flow between Hadoop and a relational database is rarely a linear single direction process. Indeed the situation where data is processed within Hadoop and then inserted into a relational database is arguably the more common case. We will explore this now.

Writing data from within the reducer

Thinking about how to copy the output of a MapReduce job into a relational database, we find similar considerations as when looking at the question of data import into Hadoop.

The obvious approach is to modify a reducer to generate the output for each key and its associated values and then to directly insert them into a database via JDBC. We do not have to worry about source column partitioning, as with the import case, but do still need to think about how much load we are placing on the database and whether we need to consider timeouts for long-running tasks. In addition, just as with the mapper situation, this approach tends to perform many single queries against the database, which is typically much less efficient than bulk operations.

Writing SQL import files from the reducer

Often, a superior approach is not to work around the usual MapReduce case of generating output files, as with the preceding example, but instead to exploit it.

All relational databases have the ability to ingest data from source files, either through custom tools or through the use of the LOAD DATA statement. Within the reducer, therefore, we can modify the data output to make it more easily ingested into our relational destination. This obviates the need to consider issues such as reducers placing load on the database or how to handle long-running tasks, but it does require a second step external to our MapReduce job.

A better way – Sqoop again

It probably won't come as a surprise—certainly not if you've looked at the output of Sqoop's inbuilt help or its online documentation—to learn that Sqoop can also be our tool of choice for data export from Hadoop.

Time for action – importing data from Hadoop into MySQL

Let's demonstrate this by importing data into a MySQL table from an HDFS file.

1. Create a tab-separated file named newemployees.tsv with the following entries:

   ```
   Frances  Operations  34000  2012-03-01
   Greg  Engineering  60000  2003-11-18
   Harry  Intern  22000  2012-05-15
   Iris  Executive  80000  2001-04-08
   Jan  Support  28500  2009-03-30
   ```

2. Create a new directory on HDFS and copy the file into it:

   ```
   $hadoop fs -mkdir edata
   $ hadoop fs -put newemployees.tsv edata/newemployees.tsv
   ```

3. Confirm the current number of records in the employee table:

   ```
   $ echo "select count(*) from employees" |
   ```

```
mysql -u hadoopuser -p hadooptest
```

You will receive the following response:

```
Enter password:
count(*)
5
```

4. Run a Sqoop export:

```
$ sqoop export --connect jdbc:mysql://10.0.0.100/hadooptest
--username hadoopuser  -P --table employees
--export-dir edata --input-fields-terminated-by '\t'
```

You will receive the following response:

```
12/05/27 07:52:22 INFO mapreduce.ExportJobBase: Exported 5
records.
```

5. Check the number of records in the table after the export:

```
Echo "select count(*) from employees"
| mysql -u hadoopuser -p hadooptest
```

You will receive the following response:

```
Enter password:
count(*)
10
```

6. Check the data:

```
$ echo "select * from employees"
| mysql -u hadoopuser -p hadooptest
```

You will receive the following response:

```
Enter password:
first_name  dept  salary  start_date
Alice  Engineering  50000  2009-03-12
...
Frances  Operations  34000  2012-03-01
Greg  Engineering  60000  2003-11-18
Harry  Intern  22000  2012-05-15
Iris  Executive  80000  2001-04-08
Jan  Support  28500  2009-03-30
```

What just happened?

We first created a data file containing information on five more employees. We created a directory for our data on HDFS into which we copied the new file.

Before running the export, we confirmed that the table in MySQL contained the original five employees only.

The Sqoop command has a similar structure as before with the biggest change being the use of the `export` command. As the name suggests, Sqoop exported export data from Hadoop into a relational database.

We used several similar options as before, mainly to specify the database connection, the username and password needed to connect, and the table into which to insert the data.

Because we are exporting data from HDFS, we needed to specify the location containing any files to be exported which we do via the `--export-dir` option. All files contained within the directory will be exported; they do not need be in a single file; Sqoop will include all files within its MapReduce job. By default, Sqoop uses four mappers; if you have a large number of files it may be more effective to increase this number; do test, though, to ensure that load on the database remains under control.

The final option passed to Sqoop specified the field terminator used in the source files, in this case, the tab character. It is your responsibility to ensure the data files are properly formatted; Sqoop will assume there is the same number of elements in each record as columns in the table (though null is acceptable), separated by the specified field separator character.

After watching the Sqoop command complete successfully, we saw it reports that it exported five records. We check, using the `mysql` tool, the number of rows now in the database and then view the data to confirm that our old friends are now joined by the new employees.

Differences between Sqoop imports and exports

Though similar conceptually and in the command-line invocations, there are a number of important differences between Sqoop imports and exports that are worth exploring.

Firstly, Sqoop imports can assume much more about the data being processed; through either explicitly named tables or added predicates, there is much information about both the structure and type of the data. Sqoop exports, however, are given only a location of source files and the characters used to separate and enclose fields and records. While Sqoop imports into Hive can automatically create a new table based on the provided table name and structure, a Sqoop export must be into an existing table in the relational database.

Even though our earlier demonstration with dates and timestamps showed there are some sharp edges, Sqoop imports are also able to determine whether the source data complies with the defined column types; the data would not have been possible to insert into the database otherwise. Sqoop exports again only have access effectively to fields of characters with no understanding of the real datatype. If you have the luxury of very clean and well-formatted data, this may never matter, but for the rest of us, there will be a need to consider data exports and type conversions, particularly in terms of null and default values. The Sqoop documentation goes into these options in some detail and is worth a read.

Inserts versus updates

Our preceding example was very straightforward; we added an entire new set of data that can happily coexist with the existing contents of the table. Sqoop exports by default do a series of appends, adding each record as a new row in the table.

However, what if we later want to update data when, for example, our employees get increased salaries at the end of the year? With the database table defining `first_name` as a primary key, any attempt to insert a new row with the same name as an existing employee will fail with a failed primary key constraint.

In such cases, we can set the Sqoop `--update-key` option to specify the primary key, and Sqoop will generate UPDATE statements based on this key (it can be a comma-separated list of keys), as opposed to INSERT statements adding new rows.

> In this mode, any record that does not match an existing key value will silently be ignored, and Sqoop will not flag errors if a statement updates more than one row.

If we also want the option of an update that adds new rows for non-existing data, we can set the `--update-mode` option to `allowinsert`.

Have a go hero

Create another data file that contains three new employees as well as updated salaries for two of the existing employees. Use Sqoop in import mode to both add the new employees as well as apply the needed updates.

Sqoop and Hive exports

Given the preceding example, it may not be surprising to learn that Sqoop does not currently have any direct support to export a Hive table into a relational database. More precisely, there are no explicit equivalents to the `--hive-import` option we used earlier.

However, in some cases, we can work around this. If a Hive table is storing its data in text format, we could point Sqoop at the location of the table data files on HDFS. In case of tables referring to external data, this may be straightforward, but once we start seeing Hive tables with complex partitioning, the directory structure becomes more involved.

Hive can also store tables as binary SequenceFiles, and a current limitation is that Sqoop cannot transparently export from tables stored in this format.

Time for action – importing Hive data into MySQL

Regardless of these limitations, let's demonstrate that, in the right situations, we can use Sqoop to directly export data stored in Hive.

1. Remove any existing data in the employee table:

```
$ echo "truncate employees" | mysql -u hadoopuser -p hadooptest
```

You will receive the following response:

```
Query OK, 0 rows affected (0.01 sec)
```

2. Check the contents of the Hive warehouse for the employee table:

```
$ hadoop fs -ls /user/hive/warehouse/employees
```

You will receive the following response:

```
Found 1 items
… /user/hive/warehouse/employees/part-m-00000
```

3. Perform the Sqoop export:

```
sqoop export --connect jdbc:mysql://10.0.0.100/hadooptest
--username hadoopuser -P --table employees \
--export-dir /user/hive/warehouse/employees
--input-fields-terminated-by '\001'
--input-lines-terminated-by '\n'
```

```
              at javax.security.auth.Subject.doAs(Subject.java:415)
              at org.apache.hadoop.security.UserGroupInformation.doAs(UserGroupInformation.java:1121)
              at org.apache.hadoop.mapred.Child.main(Child.java:249)

13/01/05 23:32:16 INFO mapred.JobClient: Task Id : attempt_201301052139_0007_m_000000_1, Status : FAILED
java.lang.IllegalArgumentException
              at java.sql.Date.valueOf(Date.java:140)
              at employees.__loadFromFields(employees.java:260)
              at employees.parse(employees.java:197)
              at org.apache.sqoop.mapreduce.TextExportMapper.map(TextExportMapper.java:77)
              at org.apache.sqoop.mapreduce.TextExportMapper.map(TextExportMapper.java:36)
              at org.apache.hadoop.mapreduce.Mapper.run(Mapper.java:144)
              at org.apache.sqoop.mapreduce.AutoProgressMapper.run(AutoProgressMapper.java:182)
              at org.apache.hadoop.mapred.MapTask.runNewMapper(MapTask.java:764)
              at org.apache.hadoop.mapred.MapTask.run(MapTask.java:370)
              at org.apache.hadoop.mapred.Child$4.run(Child.java:255)
              at java.security.AccessController.doPrivileged(Native Method)
              at javax.security.auth.Subject.doAs(Subject.java:415)
              at org.apache.hadoop.security.UserGroupInformation.doAs(UserGroupInformation.java:1121)
              at org.apache.hadoop.mapred.Child.main(Child.java:249)

13/01/05 23:32:22 INFO mapred.JobClient: Task Id : attempt_201301052139_0007_m_000000_2, Status : FAILED
java.lang.IllegalArgumentException
              at java.sql.Date.valueOf(Date.java:140)
              at employees.__loadFromFields(employees.java:260)
              at employees.parse(employees.java:197)
              at org.apache.sqoop.mapreduce.TextExportMapper.map(TextExportMapper.java:77)
              at org.apache.sqoop.mapreduce.TextExportMapper.map(TextExportMapper.java:36)
              at org.apache.hadoop.mapreduce.Mapper.run(Mapper.java:144)
              at org.apache.sqoop.mapreduce.AutoProgressMapper.run(AutoProgressMapper.java:182)
              at org.apache.hadoop.mapred.MapTask.runNewMapper(MapTask.java:764)
              at org.apache.hadoop.mapred.MapTask.run(MapTask.java:370)
              at org.apache.hadoop.mapred.Child$4.run(Child.java:255)
              at java.security.AccessController.doPrivileged(Native Method)
              at javax.security.auth.Subject.doAs(Subject.java:415)
              at org.apache.hadoop.security.UserGroupInformation.doAs(UserGroupInformation.java:1121)
              at org.apache.hadoop.mapred.Child.main(Child.java:249)


13/01/05 23:32:34 INFO mapred.JobClient: Job complete: job_201301052139_0007
13/01/05 23:32:34 INFO mapred.JobClient: Counters: 7
13/01/05 23:32:34 INFO mapred.JobClient:   Job Counters
13/01/05 23:32:34 INFO mapred.JobClient:     SLOTS_MILLIS_MAPS=27906
13/01/05 23:32:34 INFO mapred.JobClient:     Total time spent by all reduces waiting after reserving slots (ms)=0
13/01/05 23:32:34 INFO mapred.JobClient:     Total time spent by all maps waiting after reserving slots (ms)=0
13/01/05 23:32:34 INFO mapred.JobClient:     Launched map tasks=4
13/01/05 23:32:34 INFO mapred.JobClient:     Data-local map tasks=4
13/01/05 23:32:34 INFO mapred.JobClient:     SLOTS_MILLIS_REDUCES=0
13/01/05 23:32:34 INFO mapred.JobClient:     Failed map tasks=1
13/01/05 23:32:34 INFO mapreduce.ExportJobBase: Transferred 0 bytes in 38.1447 seconds (0 bytes/sec)
13/01/05 23:32:34 INFO mapreduce.ExportJobBase: Exported 0 records.
13/01/05 23:32:34 ERROR tool.ExportTool: Error during export: Export job failed!
hadoop@vml6:/home/garry$
hadoop@vml6:/home/garry$
```

What just happened?

Firstly, we truncated the `employees` table in MySQL to remove any existing data and then confirmed the employee table data was where we expected it to be.

> Note that Sqoop may also create an empty file in this directory with the suffix `_SUCCESS`; if this is present it should be deleted before running the Sqoop export.

The Sqoop `export` command is like before; the only changes are the different source location for the data and the addition of explicit field and line terminators. Recall that Hive, by default, uses ASCII code 001 and \n for its field and line terminators, respectively (also recall, though, that we have previously imported files into Hive with other separators, so this is something that always needs to be checked).

We execute the Sqoop command and watch it fail due to `Java IllegalArgumentExceptions` when trying to create instances of `java.sql.Date`.

We are now hitting the reverse of the problem we encountered earlier; the original type in the source MySQL table had a datatype not supported by Hive, and we converted the data to match the available type of `TIMESTAMP`. When exporting data back again, however, we are now trying to create a `DATE` using a `TIMESTAMP` value, which is not possible without some conversion.

The lesson here is that our earlier approach of doing a one-way conversion only worked for as long as we only had data flowing in one direction. As soon as we need bi-directional data transfer, mismatched types between Hive and the relational store add complexity and require the insertion of conversion routines.

Time for action – fixing the mapping and re-running the export

In this case, however, let us do what probably makes more sense—modifying the definition of the employee table to make it consistent in both data sources.

1. Start the `mysql` utility:

   ```
   $ mysql -u hadoopuser -p hadooptest
   Enter password:
   ```

2. Change the type of the `start_date` column:

   ```
   mysql> alter table employees modify column start_date timestamp;
   ```

   You will receive the following response:

   ```
   Query OK, 0 rows affected (0.02 sec)
   Records: 0  Duplicates: 0  Warnings: 0
   ```

3. Display the table definition:

```
mysql> describe employees;
```

```
hadoop@vm16: ~
File Edit View Terminal Help
hadoop@vm16:~$ fg
mysql -u hadoopuser -p -h 10.0.0.100 hadooptest
describe employees;
+------------+-------------+------+-----+-------------------+-----------------------------+
| Field      | Type        | Null | Key | Default           | Extra                       |
+------------+-------------+------+-----+-------------------+-----------------------------+
| first_name | varchar(10) | NO   | PRI | NULL              |                             |
| dept       | varchar(15) | YES  |     | NULL              |                             |
| salary     | int(11)     | YES  |     | NULL              |                             |
| start_date | timestamp   | NO   |     | CURRENT_TIMESTAMP | on update CURRENT_TIMESTAMP |
+------------+-------------+------+-----+-------------------+-----------------------------+
4 rows in set (0.00 sec)

mysql>
```

4. Quit the `mysql` tool:

```
mysql> quit;
```

5. Perform the Sqoop export:

```
sqoop export --connect jdbc:mysql://10.0.0.100/hadooptest
--username hadoopuser -P -table employees

--export-dir /user/hive/warehouse/employees

--input-fields-terminated-by '\001'

--input-lines-terminated-by '\n'
```

You will receive the following response:

```
12/05/27 09:17:39 INFO mapreduce.ExportJobBase: Exported 10
records.
```

6. Check the number of records in the MySQL database:

```
$ echo "select count(*) from employees"
| mysql -u hadoopuser -p hadooptest
```

You will receive the following output:

```
Enter password:
count(*)
10
```

What just happened?

Before trying the same Sqoop export as last time, we used the `mysql` tool to connect to the database and modify the type of the `start_date` column. Note, of course, that such changes should never be made casually on a production system, but given that we have a currently empty test table, there are no issues here.

After making the change, we re-ran the Sqoop export and this time it succeeded.

Other Sqoop features

Sqoop has a number of other features that we won't discuss in detail, but we'll highlight them so the interested reader can look them up in the Sqoop documentation.

Incremental merge

The examples we've used have been all-or-nothing processing that, in most cases, make the most sense when importing data into empty tables. There are mechanisms to handle additions, but if we foresee Sqoop performing ongoing imports, some additional support is available.

Sqoop supports the concept of incremental imports where an import task is additionally qualified by a date and only records more recent than that date are processed by the task. This allows the construction of long-running workflows that include Sqoop.

Avoiding partial exports

We've already seen how errors can occur when exporting data from Hadoop into a relational database. For us, it wasn't a significant problem as the issue caused all exported records to fail. But it isn't uncommon for only part of an export to fail and result in partially committed data in the database.

To mitigate this risk, Sqoop allows the use of a staging table; it loads all the data into this secondary table, and only after all data is successfully inserted, performs the move into the main table in a single transaction. This can be very useful for failure-prone workloads but does come with some important restrictions, such as the inability to support update mode. For very large imports, there are also performance and load impacts on the RDBMS of a single very long-running transaction.

Sqoop as a code generator

We've been ignoring an error during Sqoop processing that we casually brushed off a while ago—the exception thrown because the generated code required by Sqoop already exists.

When performing an import, Sqoop generates Java class files that provide a programmatic means of accessing the fields and records in the created files. Sqoop uses these classes internally, but they can also be used outside of a Sqoop invocation, and indeed, the Sqoop codegen command can regenerate the classes outside of an export task.

AWS considerations

We've not mentioned AWS so far in this chapter as there's been nothing in Sqoop that either supports or prevents its use on AWS. We can run Sqoop on an EC2 host as easily as on a local one, and it can access either a manually or EMR-created Hadoop cluster optionally running Hive. The only possible quirk when considering use in AWS is security group access as many default EC2 configurations will not allow traffic on the ports used by most relational databases (3306 by default for MySQL). But, that's no more of an issue than if our Hadoop cluster and MySQL database were to be located on different sides of a firewall or any other network security boundary.

Considering RDS

There is another AWS service that we've not mentioned before that does deserve an introduction now. Amazon **Relational Database Service (RDS)** offers hosted relational databases in the cloud and provides MySQL, Oracle, and Microsoft SQL Server options. Instead of having to worry about the installation, configuration, and management of a database engine, RDS allows an instance to be started from either the console or command-line tools. You then just point your database client tool at the database and start creating tables and manipulating data.

RDS and EMR are a powerful combination, providing hosted services that take much of the pain out of manually managing such services. If you need a relational database but don't want to worry about its management, RDS may be for you.

The RDS and EMR combination can be particularly powerful if you use EC2 hosts to generate data or store data in S3. Amazon has a general policy that there is no cost for data transfer from one service to another within a single region. Consequently, it's possible to have a fleet of EC2 hosts generating large data volumes that get pushed into a relational database in RDS for query access and are stored in EMR for archival and long-term analytics. Getting data into the storage and processing systems is often a technically challenging activity that can easily consume significant expense if the data needs be moved across commercial network links. Architectures built atop collaborating AWS services such as EC2, RDS, and EMR can minimize both these concerns.

Summary

In this chapter, we have looked at the integration of Hadoop and relational databases. In particular, we explored the most common use cases and saw that Hadoop and relational databases can be highly complimentary technologies. We considered ways of exporting data from a relational database onto HDFS files and realized that issues such as primary key column partitioning and long-running tasks make it harder than it first seems.

We then introduced Sqoop, a Cloudera tool now donated to the Apache Software Foundation and that provides a framework for such data migration. We used Sqoop to import data from MySQL into HDFS and then Hive, highlighting how we must consider aspects of datatype compatibility in such tasks. We also used Sqoop to do the reverse—copying data from HDFS into a MySQL database—and found out that this path has more subtle considerations than the other direction, briefly discussed issues of file formats and update versus insert tasks, and introduced additional Sqoop capabilities, such as code generation and incremental merging.

Relational databases are an important—often critical—part of most IT infrastructures. But, they aren't the only such component. One that has been growing in importance—often with little fanfare—is the vast quantities of log files generated by web servers and other applications. The next chapter will show how Hadoop is ideally suited to process and store such data.

10
Data Collection with Flume

In the previous two chapters, we've seen how Hive and Sqoop give a relational database interface to Hadoop and allow it to exchange data with "real" databases. Although this is a very common use case, there are, of course, many different types of data sources that we may want to get into Hadoop.

In this chapter, we will cover:

- An overview of data commonly processed in Hadoop
- Simple approaches to pull this data into Hadoop
- How Apache Flume can make this task a lot easier
- Common patterns for simple through sophisticated, Flume setups
- Common issues, such as the data lifecycle, that need to be considered regardless of technology

A note about AWS

This chapter will discuss AWS less than any other in the book. In fact, we won't even mention it after this section. There are no Amazon services akin to Flume so there is no AWS-specific product that we could explore. On the other hand, when using Flume, it works exactly the same, be it on a local host or EC2 virtual instance. The rest of this chapter, therefore, assumes nothing about the environment on which the examples are executed; they will perform identically on each.

Data data everywhere...

In discussions concerning integration of Hadoop with other systems, it is easy to think of it as a one-to-one pattern. Data comes out of one system, gets processed in Hadoop, and then is passed onto a third.

Things may be like that on day one, but the reality is more often a series of collaborating components with data flows passing back and forth between them. How we build this complex network in a maintainable fashion is the focus of this chapter.

Types of data

For the sake of the discussion, we will categorize data into two broad categories:

- **Network traffic**, where data is generated by a system and sent across a network connection
- **File data**, where data is generated by a system and written to files on a filesystem somewhere

We don't assume these data categories are different in any way other than how the data is retrieved.

Getting network traffic into Hadoop

When we say network data, we mean things like information retrieved from a web server via an HTTP connection, database contents pulled by a client application, or messages sent across a data bus. In each case, the data is retrieved by a client application that either pulls the data across the network or listens for its arrival.

 In several of the following examples, we will use the `curl` utility to either retrieve or send network data. Ensure that it is installed on your system and install it if not.

Time for action – getting web server data into Hadoop

Let's take a look at how we can simplistically copy data from a web server onto HDFS.

1. Retrieve the text of the NameNode web interface to a local file:

   ```
   $ curl localhost:50070 > web.txt
   ```

2. Check the file size:

   ```
   $ ls -ldh web.txt
   ```

You will receive the following response:

```
-rw-r--r-- 1 hadoop hadoop 246 Aug 19 08:53 web.txt
```

3. Copy the file to HDFS:

```
$ hadoop fs -put web.txt web.txt
```

4. Check the file on HDFS:

```
$ hadoop fs -ls
```

You will receive the following response:

```
Found 1 items

-rw-r--r--   1 hadoop supergroup          246 2012-08-19 08:53 /
user/hadoop/web.txt
```

What just happened?

There shouldn't be anything that is surprising here. We use the `curl` utility to retrieve a web page from the embedded web server hosting the NameNode web interface and save it to a local file. We check the file size, copy it to HDFS, and verify the file has been transferred successfully.

The point of note here is not the series of actions—it is after all just another use of the `hadoop fs` command we have used since *Chapter 2, Getting Up and Running*—rather the pattern used is what we should discuss.

Though the data we wanted was in a web server and accessible via the HTTP protocol, the out of the box Hadoop tools are very file-based and do not have any intrinsic support for such remote information sources. This is why we need to copy our network data into a file before transferring it to HDFS.

We can, of course, write data directly to HDFS through the programmatic interface mentioned back in *Chapter 3, Writing MapReduce Jobs*, and this would work well. This would, however, require us to start writing custom clients for every different network source from which we need to retrieve data.

Have a go hero

Programmatically retrieving data and writing it to HDFS is a very powerful capability and worth some exploration. A very popular Java library for HTTP is the **Apache HTTPClient**, within the **HTTP Components** project found at `http://hc.apache.org/ httpcomponents-client-ga/index.html`.

Use the HTTPClient and the Java HDFS interface to retrieve a web page as before and write it to HDFS.

Getting files into Hadoop

Our previous example showed the simplest method for getting file-based data into Hadoop and the use of the standard command-line tools or programmatic APIs. There is little else to discuss here, as it is a topic we have dealt with throughout the book.

Hidden issues

Though the preceding approaches are good as far as they go, there are several reasons why they may be unsuitable for production use.

Keeping network data on the network

Our model of copying network-accessed data to a file before placing it on HDFS will have an impact on performance. There is added latency due to the round-trip to disk, the slowest part of a system. This may not be an issue for large amounts of data retrieved in one call—though disk space potentially becomes a concern—but for small amounts of data retrieved at high speed, it may become a real problem.

Hadoop dependencies

For the file-based approach, it is implicit in the model mentioned before that the point at which we can access the file must have access to the Hadoop installation and be configured to know the location of the cluster. This potentially adds additional dependencies in the system; this could force us to add Hadoop to hosts that really need to know nothing about it. We can mitigate this by using tools like SFTP to retrieve the files to a Hadoop-aware machine and from there, copy onto HDFS.

Reliability

Notice the complete lack of error handling in the previous approaches. The tools we are using do not have built-in retry mechanisms which means we would need to wrap a degree of error detection and retry logic around each data retrieval.

Re-creating the wheel

This last point touches on perhaps the biggest issue with these ad hoc approaches; it is very easy to end up with a dozen different strings of command-line tools and scripts, each of which is doing very similar tasks. The potential costs in terms of duplicate effort and more difficult error tracking can be significant over time.

A common framework approach

Anyone with experience in enterprise computing will, at this point, be thinking that this sounds like a problem best solved with some type of common integration framework. This is exactly correct and is indeed a general type of product well known in fields such as **Enterprise Application Integration (EAI)**.

What we need though is a framework that is Hadoop-aware and can easily integrate with Hadoop (and related projects) without requiring massive effort in writing custom adaptors. We could create our own, but instead let's look at **Apache Flume** which provides much of what we need.

Introducing Apache Flume

Flume, found at `http://flume.apache.org`, is another Apache project with tight Hadoop integration and we will explore it for the remainder of this chapter.

Before we explain what Flume can do, let's make it clear what it is not. Flume is described as a system for the retrieval and distribution of logs, meaning line-oriented textual data. It is not a generic data-distribution platform; in particular, don't look to use it for the retrieval or movement of binary data.

However, since the vast majority of the data processed in Hadoop matches this description, it is likely that Flume will meet many of your data retrieval needs.

> Flume is also not a generic data serialization framework like **Avro** that we used in *Chapter 5, Advanced MapReduce Techniques*, or similar technologies such as **Thrift** and **Protocol Buffers**. As we'll see, Flume makes assumptions about the data format and provides no ways of serializing data outside of these.

Flume provides mechanisms for retrieving data from multiple sources, passing it to remote locations (potentially multiple locations in either a fan-out or pipeline model), and then delivering it to a variety of destinations. Though it does have a programmatic API that allows the development of custom sources and destinations, the base product has built-in support for many of the most common scenarios. Let's install it and take a look.

A note on versioning

Flume has gone through some major changes in recent times. The original Flume (now renamed **Flume OG** for Original Generation) is being superseded by **Flume NG (Next Generation)**. Though the general principles and capabilities are very similar, the implementation is quite different.

Because Flume NG is the future, we will cover it in this book. For some time though, it will lack several of the features of the more mature Flume OG, so if you find a specific requirement that Flume NG doesn't meet then it may be worth looking at Flume OG.

Time for action – installing and configuring Flume

Let's get Flume downloaded and installed.

1. Retrieve the most recent Flume NG binary from `http://flume.apache.org/` and download and save it to the local filesystem.

2. Move the file to the desired location and uncompress it:
   ```
   $ mv apache-flume-1.2.0-bin.tar.gz /opt
   $ tar -xzf /opt/apache-flume-1.2.0-bin.tar.gz
   ```

3. Create a symlink to the installation:
   ```
   $ ln -s /opt/apache-flume-1.2.0 /opt/flume
   ```

4. Define the FLUME_HOME environment variable:
   ```
   Export FLUME_HOME=/opt/flume
   ```

5. Add the Flume bin directory to your path:
   ```
   Export PATH=${FLUME_HOME}/bin:${PATH}
   ```

6. Verify that JAVA_HOME is set:
   ```
   Echo ${JAVA_HOME}
   ```

7. Verify that the Hadoop libraries are in the classpath:
   ```
   $ echo ${CLASSPATH}
   ```

8. Create the directory that will act as the Flume conf directory:
   ```
   $ mkdir /home/hadoop/flume/conf
   ```

9. Copy the needed files into the conf directory:
   ```
   $ cp /opt/flume/conf/log4j.properties /home/hadoop/flume/conf
   $ cp /opt/flume/conf/flume-env.sh.sample /home/hadoop/flume/conf/
   flume-env.sh
   ```

10. Edit flume-env.sh and set JAVA_HOME.

What just happened?

The Flume installation is straightforward and has similar prerequisites to previous tools we have installed.

Firstly, we retrieved the latest version of Flume NG (any version of 1.2.x or later will do) and saved it to the local filesystem. We moved it to the desired location, uncompressed it, and created a convenience symlink to the location.

We needed to define the FLUME_HOME environment variable and add the bin directory within the installation directory to our classpath. As before, this can be done directly on the command line or within convenience scripts.

Flume requires JAVA_HOME to be defined and we confirmed this is the case. It also requires Hadoop libraries, so we checked that the Hadoop classes are in the classpath.

The last steps are not strictly necessary for demonstration though will be used in production. Flume looks for a configuration directory within which are files defining the default logging properties and environment setup variables (such as JAVA_HOME). We find Flume performs most predictably when this directory is properly set up, so we did this now and don't need to change it much later.

We assumed /home/hadoop/flume is the working directory within which the Flume configuration and other files will be stored; change this based on what's appropriate for your system.

Using Flume to capture network data

Now that we have Flume installed, let's use it to capture some network data.

Time for action – capturing network traffic in a log file

In the first instance, let's use a simple Flume configuration that will capture the network data to the main Flume log file.

1. Create the following file as agent1.conf within your Flume working directory:

```
agent1.sources = netsource
agent1.sinks = logsink
agent1.channels = memorychannel

agent1.sources.netsource.type = netcat
agent1.sources.netsource.bind = localhost
agent1.sources.netsource.port = 3000
```

```
agent1.sinks.logsink.type = logger

agent1.channels.memorychannel.type = memory
agent1.channels.memorychannel.capacity = 1000
agent1.channels.memorychannel.transactionCapacity = 100

agent1.sources.netsource.channels = memorychannel
agent1.sinks.logsink.channel = memorychannel
```

2. Start a Flume agent:

```
$ flume-ng agent --conf conf --conf-file 10a.conf  --name agent1
```

The output of the preceding command can be shown in the following screenshot:

3. In another window, open a telnet connection to port 3000 on the local host and then type some text:

```
$ curl telnet://localhost:3000
Hello
OK
Flume!
OK
```

4. Close the curl connection with *Ctrl + C*.

5. Look at the Flume log file:

```
$ tail flume.log
```

You will receive the following response:

```
2012-08-19 00:37:32,702 INFO sink.LoggerSink: Event: { headers:{}
body: 68 65 6C 6C 6F                                Hello }
2012-08-19 00:37:32,702 INFO sink.LoggerSink: Event: { headers:{}
body: 6D 65                                         Flume }
```

What just happened?

Firstly, we created a Flume configuration file within our Flume working directory. We'll go into this in more detail later, but for now, think of Flume receiving data through a component called a **source** and writing it to a destination called a **sink**.

In this case, we create a **Netcat** source which listens on a port for network connections. You can see we configure it to bind to port 3000 on the local machine.

The configured sink is of the type `logger` which, not surprisingly, writes its output to a log file. The rest of the configuration file defines an **agent** called `agent1`, which uses this source and sink.

We then start a Flume agent by using the `flume-ng` binary. This is the tool we'll use to launch all Flume processes. Note that we give a few options to this command:

◆ The `agent` argument tells Flume to start an agent, which is the generic name for a running Flume process involved in data movement

◆ The `conf` directory, as mentioned earlier

◆ The particular configuration file for the process we are going to launch

◆ The name of the agent within the configuration file

The agent will start and no further output will appear on that screen. (Obviously, we would run the process in the background in a production setting.)

In another window, we open a telnet connection to port 3000 on the local machine using the `curl` utility. The traditional way of opening such sessions is of course the telnet program itself, but many Linux distributions have curl installed by default; almost none use the older `telnet` utility.

We type a word on each line and hit *Enter* then kill the session with a *Ctrl + C* command. Finally, we look at the `flume.log` file that is being written into the Flume working directory and see an entry for each of the words we typed in.

Time for action – logging to the console

It's not always convenient to have to look at log files, particularly when we already have the agent screen open. Let's modify the agent to also log events to the screen.

1. Restart the Flume agent with an additional argument:

```
$ flume-ng agent --conf conf --conf-file 10a.conf --name agent1
-Dflume.root.logger=INFO,console
```

You will receive the following response:

```
Info: Sourcing environment configuration script /home/hadoop/
flume/conf/flume-env.sh

...

org.apache.flume.node.Application --conf-file 10a.conf --name
agent1

2012-08-19 00:41:45,462 (main) [INFO - org.apache.flume.lifecycle.
LifecycleSupervisor.start(LifecycleSupervisor.java:67)] Starting
lifecycle supervisor 1
```

2. In another window, connect to the server via curl:

```
$ curl telnet://localhost:3000
```

3. Type in `Hello` and `Flume` on separate lines, hit *Ctrl + C*, and then check the agent window:

What just happened?

We added this example as it becomes very useful when debugging or creating new flows.

As seen in the previous example, Flume will, by default, write its logs to a file on the filesystem. More precisely, this is the default behavior as specified within the log4j property file within our `conf` directory. Sometimes we want more immediate feedback without constantly looking at log files or having to change the property file.

By explicitly setting the `flume.root.logger` variable on the command line, we can override the default logger configuration and have the output sent directly to the agent window. The logger is standard log4j, so the usual log levels such as `DEBUG` and `INFO` are supported.

Writing network data to log files

The default log sink behavior of Flume writing its received data into log files has some
limitations, particularly if we want to use the captured data in other applications.
By configuring a different type of sink, we can instead write the data into more
consumable data files.

Time for action – capturing the output of a command to a flat file

Let's show this in action, along the way demonstrating a new kind of source as well.

1. Create the following file as `agent2.conf` within the Flume working directory:

    ```
    agent2.sources = execsource
    agent2.sinks = filesink
    agent2.channels = filechannel

    agent2.sources.execsource.type = exec
    agent2.sources.execsource.command = cat /home/hadoop/message

    agent2.sinks.filesink.type = FILE_ROLL
    agent2.sinks.filesink.sink.directory = /home/hadoop/flume/files
    agent2.sinks.filesink.sink.rollInterval = 0

    agent2.channels.filechannel.type = file
    agent2.channels.filechannel.checkpointDir = /home/hadoop/flume/fc/
    checkpoint
    agent2.channels.filechannel.dataDirs = /home/hadoop/flume/fc/data

    agent2.sources.execsource.channels = filechannel
    agent2.sinks.filesink.channel = filechannel
    ```

2. Create a simple test file in the home directory:

    ```
    $ echo "Hello again Flume!" > /home/hadoop/message
    ```

3. Start the agent:

    ```
    $ flume-ng agent --conf conf --conf-file agent2.conf --name agent2
    ```

4. In another window, check file sink output directory:

    ```
    $ ls files
    $ cat files/*
    ```

The output of the preceding command can be shown in the following screenshot:

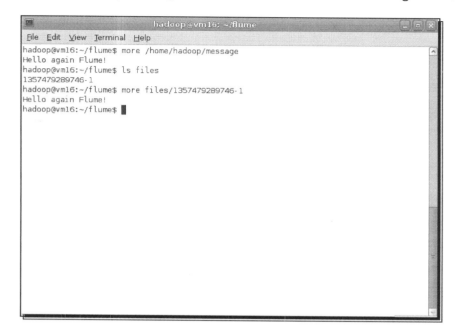

What just happened?

The previous example follows a similar pattern as before. We created the configuration file for a Flume agent, ran the agent, and then confirmed it had captured the data we expected.

This time we used an exec source and a `file_roll` sink. The former, as the name suggests, executes a command on the host and captures its output as the input to the Flume agent. Although, in the previous case, the command is executed only once, this was for illustration purposes only. More common uses will use commands that produce an ongoing stream of data. Note that the exec sink can be configured to restart the command if it does terminate.

The output of the agent is written to a file as specified in the configuration file. By default, Flume rotates (rolls) to a new file every 30 seconds; we disable this capability to make it easier to track what's going on in a single file.

We see the file does indeed contain the output of the specified `exec` command.

Logs versus files

It may not be immediately obvious why Flume has both log and file sinks. Conceptually both do the same thing, so what's the difference?

The logger sink in reality is more of a debug tool than anything else. It doesn't just record the information captured by the source, but adds a lot of additional metadata and events. The file sink however records the input data exactly as it was received with no alteration—though such is possible if required as we will see later.

In most cases, you'll want the file sink to capture the input data but the log may also be of use in non-production situations depending on your needs.

Time for action – capturing a remote file in a local flat file

Let's show another example of capturing data to a file sink. This time we will use another Flume capability that allows it to receive data from a remote client.

1. Create the following file as `agent3.conf` in the Flume working directory:

```
agent3.sources = avrosource
agent3.sinks = filesink
agent3.channels = jdbcchannel

agent3.sources.avrosource.type = avro
agent3.sources.avrosource.bind = localhost
agent3.sources.avrosource.port = 4000
agent3.sources.avrosource.threads = 5

agent3.sinks.filesink.type = FILE_ROLL
agent3.sinks.filesink.sink.directory = /home/hadoop/flume/files
agent3.sinks.filesink.sink.rollInterval = 0

agent3.channels.jdbcchannel.type = jdbc

agent3.sources.avrosource.channels = jdbcchannel
agent3.sinks.filesink.channel = jdbcchannel
```

2. Create a new test file as /home/hadoop/message2:

```
Hello from Avro!
```

3. Start the Flume agent:

```
$ flume-ng agent –conf conf –conf-file agent3.conf –name agent3
```

4. In another window, use the Flume Avro client to send a file to the agent:

```
$ flume-ng avro-client -H localhost -p 4000 -F /home/hadoop/
message
```

5. As before, check the file in the configured output directory:

```
$ cat files/*
```

The output of the preceding command can be shown in following screenshot:

```
hadoop@vm16:~/flume$ more /home/hadoop/message2
Hello from Avro!
hadoop@vm16:~/flume$ more files/1357480840402-1
hadoop@vm16:~/flume$ flume-ng avro-client -H localhost -p 4000 -F /home/hadoop/message2
Warning: No configuration directory set! Use --conf <dir> to override.
Info: Including Hadoop libraries found via (/opt/hadoop/bin/hadoop) for HDFS access
Info: Excluding /opt/hadoop-1.0.3/libexec/../lib/slf4j-api-1.4.3.jar from classpath
Info: Excluding /opt/hadoop-1.0.3/libexec/../lib/slf4j-log4j12-1.4.3.jar from classpath
+ exec /opt/jdk/bin/java -Xmx20m -cp '/opt/flume/lib/*:/opt/hadoop-1.0.3/libexec/../conf:/opt/jdk/lib/tools.jar:/opt/hadoop-1.0.3/libexec/..:/opt/hadoop-1.0.
3/libexec/../hadoop-core-1.0.3.jar:/opt/hadoop-1.0.3/libexec/../lib/asm-3.2.jar:/opt/hadoop-1.0.3/libexec/../lib/aspectjrt-1.6.5.jar:/opt/hadoop-1.0.3/libexe
c/../lib/aspectjtools-1.6.5.jar:/opt/hadoop-1.0.3/libexec/../lib/avro-1.7.2.jar:/opt/hadoop-1.0.3/libexec/../lib/avro-mapred-1.7.2.jar:/opt/hadoop-1.0.3/libe
xec/../lib/commons-beanutils-1.7.0.jar:/opt/hadoop-1.0.3/libexec/../lib/commons-beanutils-core-1.8.0.jar:/opt/hadoop-1.0.3/libexec/../lib/commons-cli-1.2.jar
:/opt/hadoop-1.0.3/libexec/../lib/commons-codec-1.4.jar:/opt/hadoop-1.0.3/libexec/../lib/commons-collections-3.2.1.jar:/opt/hadoop-1.0.3/libexec/../lib/commo
ns-configuration-1.6.jar:/opt/hadoop-1.0.3/libexec/../lib/commons-daemon-1.0.1.jar:/opt/hadoop-1.0.3/libexec/../lib/commons-digester-1.8.jar:/opt/hadoop-1.0.
3/libexec/../lib/commons-el-1.0.jar:/opt/hadoop-1.0.3/libexec/../lib/commons-httpclient-3.0.1.jar:/opt/hadoop-1.0.3/libexec/../lib/commons-io-2.1.jar:/opt/ha
doop-1.0.3/libexec/../lib/commons-lang-2.4.jar:/opt/hadoop-1.0.3/libexec/../lib/commons-logging-1.1.1.jar:/opt/hadoop-1.0.3/libexec/../lib/commons-logging-ap
i-1.0.4.jar:/opt/hadoop-1.0.3/libexec/../lib/commons-math-2.1.jar:/opt/hadoop-1.0.3/libexec/../lib/commons-net-1.4.1.jar:/opt/hadoop-1.0.3/libexec/../lib/cor
e-3.1.1.jar:/opt/hadoop-1.0.3/libexec/../lib/hadoop-capacity-scheduler-1.0.3.jar:/opt/hadoop-1.0.3/libexec/../lib/hadoop-fairscheduler-1.0.3.jar:/opt/hadoop-
1.0.3/libexec/../lib/hadoop-thriftfs-1.0.3.jar:/opt/hadoop-1.0.3/libexec/../lib/hsqldb-1.8.0.10.jar:/opt/hadoop-1.0.3/libexec/../lib/jackson-core-asl-1.8.8.j
ar:/opt/hadoop-1.0.3/libexec/../lib/jackson-mapper-asl-1.8.8.jar:/opt/hadoop-1.0.3/libexec/../lib/jasper-compiler-5.5.12.jar:/opt/hadoop-1.0.3/libexec/../lib
/jasper-runtime-5.5.12.jar:/opt/hadoop-1.0.3/libexec/../lib/jdeb-0.8.jar:/opt/hadoop-1.0.3/libexec/../lib/jersey-core-1.8.jar:/opt/hadoop-1.0.3/libexec/../li
b/jersey-json-1.8.jar:/opt/hadoop-1.0.3/libexec/../lib/jersey-server-1.8.jar:/opt/hadoop-1.0.3/libexec/../lib/jets3t-0.6.1.jar:/opt/hadoop-1.0.3/libexec/../l
ib/jetty-6.1.26.jar:/opt/hadoop-1.0.3/libexec/../lib/jetty-util-6.1.26.jar:/opt/hadoop-1.0.3/libexec/../lib/jsch-0.1.42.jar:/opt/hadoop-1.0.3/libexec/../lib/
junit-4.5.jar:/opt/hadoop-1.0.3/libexec/../lib/kfs-0.2.2.jar:/opt/hadoop-1.0.3/libexec/../lib/log4j-1.2.15.jar:/opt/hadoop-1.0.3/libexec/../lib/mockito-all-1
.8.5.jar:/opt/hadoop-1.0.3/libexec/../lib/oro-2.0.8.jar:/opt/hadoop-1.0.3/libexec/../lib/paranamer-2.5.jar:/opt/hadoop-1.0.3/libexec/../lib/servlet-api-2.5-2
0081211.jar:/opt/hadoop-1.0.3/libexec/../lib/xmlenc-0.52.jar:/opt/hadoop-1.0.3/libexec/../lib/jsp-2.1/jsp-2.1.jar:/opt/hadoop-1.0.3/libexec/../lib/jsp-2.1/js
p-api-2.1.jar' -Djava.library.path=:/opt/hadoop-1.0.3/libexec/../lib/native/Linux-i386-32 org.apache.flume.client.avro.AvroCLIClient -H localhost -p 4000 -F
/home/hadoop/message2
hadoop@vm16:~/flume$ more files/1357480840402-1
Hello from Avro!
hadoop@vm16:~/flume$ 
```

What just happened?

As before, we created a new configuration file and this time used an Avro source for the agent. Recall from *Chapter 5, Advanced MapReduce Techniques*, that Avro is a data serialization framework; that is, it manages the packaging and transport of data from one point to another across the network. Similarly to the Netcat source, the Avro source requires configuration parameters that specify its network settings. In this case, it will listen on port 4000 on the local machine. The agent is configured to use the file sink as before and we start it up as usual.

Flume comes with both an Avro source and a standalone Avro client. The latter can be used to read a file and send it to an Avro source anywhere on the network. In our example, we just use the local machine, but note that the Avro client requires the explicit hostname and port of the Avro source to which it should send the file. So this is not a constraint; an Avro client can send files to a listening Flume Avro source anywhere on the network.

The Avro client reads the file, sends it to the agent, and this gets written to the file sink. We check this behavior by confirming that the file contents are in the file sink location as expected.

Sources, sinks, and channels

We intentionally used a variety of sources, sinks, and channels in the previous examples just to show how they can be mixed and matched. However, we have not explored them—especially channels—in much detail. Let's dig a little deeper now.

Sources

We've looked at three sources: Netcat, exec, and Avro. Flume NG also supports a sequence generator source (mostly for testing) as well as both TCP and UDP variants of a source that reads **syslogd** data. Each source is configured within an agent and after receiving enough data to produce a Flume event, it sends this newly created event to the channel to which the source is connected. Though a source may have logic relating to how it reads data, translates events, and handles failure situations, the source has no knowledge of how the event is to be stored. The source has the responsibility of delivering the event to the configured channel, and all other aspects of the event processing are invisible to the source.

Sinks

In addition to the logger and file roll sinks we used previously, Flume also supports sinks for HDFS, HBase (two types), Avro (for agent chaining), null (for testing), and IRC (for an Internet Relay Chat service). The sink is conceptually similar to the source but in reverse.

The sink waits for events to be received from the configured channel about whose inner workings it knows nothing. On receipt, the sink handles the output of the event to its particular destination, managing all issues around time outs, retries, and rotation.

Channels

So what are these mysterious channels that connect the source and sink? They are, as the name and configuration entries before suggest, the communication and retention mechanism that manages event delivery.

When we define a source and a sink, there may be significant differences in how they read and write data. An exec source may, for example, receive data much faster than a file roll sink can write it or the source may have times (such as when rolling to a new file or dealing with system I/O congestion) that writing needs be paused. The channel, therefore, needs buffer data between the source and sink to allow data to stream through the agent as efficiently as possible. This is why the channel configuration portions of our configuration files include elements such as capacity.

The **memory** channel is the easiest to understand as the events are read from the source into memory and passed to the sink as it is able to receive them. But if the agent process dies mid-way through the process (be it due to software or hardware failure), then all the events currently in the memory channel are lost forever.

The **file** and **JDBC** channels that we also used provide persistent storage of events to prevent such loss. After reading an event from a source, the file channel writes the contents to a file on the filesystem that is deleted only after successful delivery to the sink. Similarly, the JDBC channel uses an embedded Derby database to store events in a recoverable fashion.

This is a classic performance versus reliability trade-off. The memory channel is the fastest but has the risk of data loss. The file and JDBC channels are typically much slower but effectively provide guaranteed delivery to the sink. Which channel you choose depends on the nature of the application and the values of each event.

 Don't worry too much about this trade-off; in the real world, the answer is usually obvious. Also be sure to look carefully at the reliability of the source and sink being used. If those are unreliable and you drop events anyway, do you gain much from a persistent channel?

Or roll your own

Don't feel limited by the existing collection of sources, sinks, and channels. Flume offers an interface to define your own implementation of each. In addition, there are a few components present in Flume OG that have not yet been incorporated into Flume NG but may appear in the future.

Understanding the Flume configuration files

Now that we've talked through sources, sinks, and channels, let's take a look at one of the configuration files from earlier in a little more detail:

```
agent1.sources = netsource
agent1.sinks = logsink
agent1.channels = memorychannel
```

These first lines name the agent and define the sources, sinks, and channels associated with it. We can have multiple values on each line; the values are space separated:

```
agent1.sources.netsource.type = netcat
agent1.sources.netsource.bind = localhost
agent1.sources.netsource.port = 3000
```

These lines specify the configuration for the source. Since we are using the Netcat source, the configuration values specify how it should bind to the network. Each type of source has its own configuration variables.

```
agent1.sinks.logsink.type = logger
```

This specifies the sink to be used is the logger sink which is further configured via the command line or the log4j property file.

```
agent1.channels.memorychannel.type = memory
agent1.channels.memorychannel.capacity = 1000
agent1.channels.memorychannel.transactionCapacity = 100
These lines specify the channel to be used and then add the type
specific configuration values.  In this case we are using the memory
channel and we specify its capacity but - since it is non-persistent -
no external storage mechanism.
agent1.sources.netsource.channels = memorychannel
agent1.sinks.logsink.channel = memorychannel
```

These last lines configure the channel to be used for the source and sink. Though we used different configuration files for our different agents, we could just as easily place all the elements in a single configuration file as the respective agent names provide the necessary separation. This can, however, produce a pretty verbose file which can be a little intimidating when you are just learning Flume. We can also have multiple flows within a given agent, we could, for example, combine the first two preceding examples into a single configuration file and agent.

Have a go hero

Do just that! Create a configuration file that specifies the capabilities of both our previous `agent1` and `agent2` from the preceding example in a single composite agent that contains:

- A Netcat source and its associated logger sink
- An exec source and its associated file sink
- Two memory channels, one for each of the source/sink pairs mentioned before

To get you started, here's how the component definitions could look:

```
agentx.sources = netsource execsource
agentx.sinks = logsink filesink
agentx.channels = memorychannel1 memorychannel2
```

It's all about events

Let's discuss one more definition before we try another example. Just what is an event?

Remember that Flume is explicitly based around log files, so in most cases, an event equates to a line of text followed by a new line character. That is the behavior we've seen with the sources and sinks we've used.

This isn't always the case, however, the UDP syslogd source, for example, treats each packet of data received as a single event, which gets passed through the system. When using these sinks and sources, however, these definitions of events are unchangeable and when reading files, for example, we have no choice but to use line-based events.

Time for action – writing network traffic onto HDFS

This discussion of Flume in a book about Hadoop hasn't actually used Hadoop at all so far. Let's remedy that by writing data onto HDFS via Flume.

1. Create the following file as `agent4.conf` within the Flume working directory:

```
agent4.sources = netsource
agent4.sinks = hdfssink
agent4.channels = memorychannel

agent4.sources.netsource.type = netcat
agent4.sources.netsource.bind = localhost
agent4.sources.netsource.port = 3000

agent4.sinks.hdfssink.type = hdfs
agent4.sinks.hdfssink.hdfs.path = /flume
agent4.sinks.hdfssink.hdfs.filePrefix = log
agent4.sinks.hdfssink.hdfs.rollInterval = 0
agent4.sinks.hdfssink.hdfs.rollCount = 3
agent4.sinks.hdfssink.hdfs.fileType = DataStream

agent4.channels.memorychannel.type = memory
agent4.channels.memorychannel.capacity = 1000
agent4.channels.memorychannel.transactionCapacity = 100

agent4.sources.netsource.channels = memorychannel
agent4.sinks.hdfssink.channel = memorychannel
```

2. Start the agent:

```
$ flume-ng agent –conf conf –conf-file agent4.conf –name agent4
```

3. In another window, open a telnet connection and send seven events to Flume:

```
$ curl telnet://localhost:3000
```

4. Check the contents of the directory specified in the Flume configuration file and then examine the file contents:

```
$ hadoop fs -ls /flume
$ hadoop fs –cat "/flume/*"
```

The output of the preceding command can be shown in the following screenshot:

```
                              hadoop@vm16: ~
 File  Edit  View  Terminal  Help
hadoop@vm16:~$ curl   telnet://localhost:3000
Hello
OK
Hadoop
OK
how
OK
are
OK
you
OK
today?
OK
Bye!
OK
^C
hadoop@vm16:~$ hadoop fs -ls /flume
Found 3 items
-rw-r--r--   1 hadoop supergroup         17 2013-01-06 14:37 /flume/log-.1357483063181
-rw-r--r--   1 hadoop supergroup         15 2013-01-06 14:37 /flume/log-.1357483063182
-rw-r--r--   1 hadoop supergroup          0 2013-01-06 14:37 /flume/log-.1357483063183.tmp
hadoop@vm16:~$ hadoop fs -cat "/flume/*"
Hello
Hadoop
how
are
you
today?
Bye!
hadoop@vm16:~$ █
```

What just happened?

This time we paired a Netcat source with the HDFS sink. As can be seen from the configuration file, we need to specify aspects such as the location for the files, any file prefix, and the strategy for rolling from one file to another. In this case, we specified files within the /flume directory, each starting with log- and with a maximum of three entries in each file (obviously, such a low value is for testing only).

After starting the agent, we use curl once more to send seven single word events to Flume. We then used the Hadoop command-line utility to look at the directory contents and verify that our input data was being written to HDFS.

Note that the third HDFS file has a .tmp extension. Remember that we specified three entries per file but only input seven values. We, therefore, filled up two files and started on another. Flume gives the file currently being written a .tmp extension, which makes it easy to differentiate the completed files from in-progress files when specifying which files to process via MapReduce jobs.

Time for action – adding timestamps

We mentioned earlier that there were mechanisms to have file data written in slightly more sophisticated ways. Let's do something very common and write our data into a directory with a dynamically-created timestamp.

1. Create the following configuration file as `agent5.conf`:

```
agent5.sources = netsource
agent5.sinks = hdfssink
agent5.channels = memorychannel

agent5.sources.netsource.type = netcat
agent5.sources.netsource.bind = localhost
agent5.sources.netsource.port = 3000
agent5.sources.netsource.interceptors = ts

agent5.sources.netsource.interceptors.ts.type = org.apache.flume.
interceptor.TimestampInterceptor$Builder

agent5.sinks.hdfssink.type = hdfs
agent5.sinks.hdfssink.hdfs.path = /flume-%Y-%m-%d
agent5.sinks.hdfssink.hdfs.filePrefix = log-
agent5.sinks.hdfssink.hdfs.rollInterval = 0
agent5.sinks.hdfssink.hdfs.rollCount = 3
agent5.sinks.hdfssink.hdfs.fileType = DataStream

agent5.channels.memorychannel.type = memory
agent5.channels.memorychannel.capacity = 1000
agent5.channels.memorychannel.transactionCapacity = 100

agent5.sources.netsource.channels = memorychannel
agent5.sinks.hdfssink.channel = memorychannel
```

2. Start the agent:

```
$ flume-ng agent –conf conf –conf-file agent5.conf –name agent5
```

3. In another window, open up a telnet session and send seven events to Flume:

```
$ curl telnet://localhost:3000
```

4. Check the directory name on HDFS and the files within it:

```
$ hadoop fs -ls /
```

The output of the preceding code can be shown in the following screenshot:

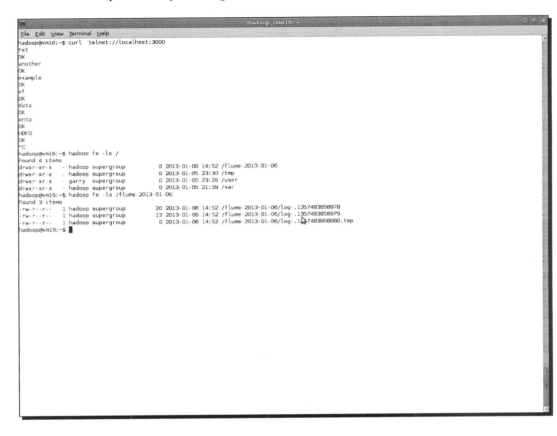

What just happened?

We made a few changes to the previous configuration file. We added an
interceptor specification to the Netcat source and gave its implementation
class as TimestampInterceptor.

Flume interceptors are plugins that can manipulate and modify events before they
pass from the source to the channel. Most interceptors either add metadata to the
event (as in this case) or drop events based on certain criteria. In addition to several
inbuilt interceptors, there is naturally a mechanism for user-defined interceptors.

We used the **timestamp** interceptor here which adds to the event metadata the Unix
timestamp at the time the event is read. This allows us to extend the definition of the
HDFS path into which events are to be written.

While previously we simply wrote all events to the /flume directory, we now specified the path as /flume-%Y-%m-%d. After running the agent and sending some data to Flume, we looked at HDFS and saw that these variables have been expanded to give the directory a year/month/date suffix.

The HDFS sink supports many other variables such as the hostname of the source and additional temporal variables that can allow precise partitioning to the level of seconds.

The utility here is plain; instead of having all events written into a single directory that becomes enormous over time, this simple mechanism can give automatic partitioning, making data management easier but also providing a simpler interface to the data for MapReduce jobs. If, for example, most of your MapReduce jobs process hourly data, then having Flume partition incoming events into hourly directories will make your life much easier.

To be precise, the event passing through Flume has had a complete Unix timestamp added, that is, accurate to the nearest second. In our example, we used only date-related variables in the directory specification, if hourly or finer-grained directory partitioning is required, then the time-related variables would be used.

> This assumes that the timestamp at the point of processing is sufficient for your needs. If files are being batched and then fed to Flume, then a file's contents may have timestamps from the previous hour than when they are being processed. In such a case, you could write a custom interceptor to set the timestamp header based on the contents of the file.

To Sqoop or to Flume...

An obvious question is whether Sqoop or Flume is most appropriate if we have data in a relational database that we want to export onto HDFS. We've seen how Sqoop can perform such an export and we could do something similar using Flume, either with a custom source or even just by wrapping a call to the mysql command within an exec source.

A good rule of thumb is to look at the type of data and ask if it is log data or something more involved.

Flume was created in large part to handle log data and it excels in this area. But in most cases, Flume networks are responsible for delivering events from sources to sinks without any real transformation on the log data itself. If you have log data in multiple relational databases, then Flume is likely a great choice, though I would question the long-term scalability of using a database for storing log records.

Non-log data may require data manipulation that only Sqoop is capable of performing. Many of the transformations we performed in the previous chapter using Sqoop, such as specifying subsets of columns to be retrieved, are really not possible using Flume. It's also quite possible that if you are dealing with structured data that requires individual field processing, then Flume alone is not the ideal tool. If you want direct Hive integration then Sqoop is your only choice.

Remember, of course, that the tools can also work together in more complex workflows. Events could be gathered together onto HDFS by Flume, processed through MapReduce, and then exported into a relational database by Sqoop.

Time for action – multi level Flume networks

Let's put together a few pieces we touched on earlier and see how one Flume agent can use another as its sink.

1. Create the following file as `agent6.conf`:

```
agent6.sources = avrosource
agent6.sinks = avrosink
agent6.channels = memorychannel

agent6.sources.avrosource.type = avro
agent6.sources.avrosource.bind = localhost
agent6.sources.avrosource.port = 2000
agent6.sources.avrosource.threads = 5

agent6.sinks.avrosink.type = avro
agent6.sinks.avrosink.hostname = localhost
agent6.sinks.avrosink.port = 4000

agent6.channels.memorychannel.type = memory
agent6.channels.memorychannel.capacity = 1000
agent6.channels.memorychannel.transactionCapacity = 100

agent6.sources.avrosource.channels = memorychannel
agent6.sinks.avrosink.channel = memorychannel
```

2. Start an agent configured as per the `agent3.conf` file created earlier, that is, with an Avro source and a file sink:

```
$ flume-ng client –conf conf –conf-file agent3.conf agent3
```

3. In a second window, start another agent; this one configured with the preceding file:

```
$ flume-ng client –conf conf –conf-file agent6.conf agent6
```

4. In a third window, use the Avro client to send a file to each of the Flume agents:

```
$ flume-ng avro-client -H localhost -p 4000 -F /home/hadoop/
message

$ flume-ng avro-client -H localhost -p 2000 -F /home/hadoop/
message2
```

5. Check the output directory for files and examine the file present:

What just happened?

Firstly, we defined a new agent with an Avro source and also an Avro sink. We've not used this sink before; instead of writing the events to a local location or HDFS, this sink sends the events to a remote source using Avro.

We start an instance of this new agent and then also start an instance of agent3 we used earlier. Recall this agent has an Avro source and a file roll sink. We configure the Avro sink in the first agent to point to the host and port of the Avro sink in the second and by doing so, build a data-routing chain.

With both agents running, we then use the Avro client to send a file to each and confirm that both appear in the file location configured as the destination for the `agent3` sink.

This isn't just technical capability for its own sake. This capability is the building block that allows Flume to build arbitrarily complex distributed event collection networks. Instead of one copy of each agent, think of multiple agents of each type feeding events into the next link in the chain, which acts as an event aggregation point.

Time for action – writing to multiple sinks

We need one final piece of capability to build such networks, namely, an agent that can write to multiple sinks. Let's create one.

1. Create the following configuration file as `agent7.conf`:

```
agent7.sources = netsource
agent7.sinks = hdfssink filesink
agent7.channels = memorychannel1 memorychannel2

agent7.sources.netsource.type = netcat
agent7.sources.netsource.bind = localhost
agent7.sources.netsource.port = 3000
agent7.sources.netsource.interceptors = ts

agent7.sources.netsource.interceptors.ts.type = org.apache.flume.
interceptor.TimestampInterceptor$Builder

agent7.sinks.hdfssink.type = hdfs
agent7.sinks.hdfssink.hdfs.path = /flume-%Y-%m-%d
agent7.sinks.hdfssink.hdfs.filePrefix = log
agent7.sinks.hdfssink.hdfs.rollInterval = 0
agent7.sinks.hdfssink.hdfs.rollCount = 3
agent7.sinks.hdfssink.hdfs.fileType = DataStream

agent7.sinks.filesink.type = FILE_ROLL
agent7.sinks.filesink.sink.directory = /home/hadoop/flume/files
agent7.sinks.filesink.sink.rollInterval = 0

agent7.channels.memorychannel1.type = memory
agent7.channels.memorychannel1.capacity = 1000
agent7.channels.memorychannel1.transactionCapacity = 100

agent7.channels.memorychannel2.type = memory
```

```
agent7.channels.memorychannel2.capacity = 1000
agent7.channels.memorychannel2.transactionCapacity = 100

agent7.sources.netsource.channels = memorychannel1 memorychannel2
agent7.sinks.hdfssink.channel = memorychannel1
agent7.sinks.filesink.channel = memorychannel2

agent7.sources.netsource.selector.type = replicating
```

2. Start the agent:

```
$ flume-ng agent –conf conf –conf-file agent7.conf –name agent7
```

3. Open a telnet session and send an event to Flume:

```
$ curl telnet://localhost:3000
```

You will receive the following response:

```
Replicating!
```

Check the contents of the HDFS and file sinks:

```
$ cat files/*
$ hdfs fs –cat "/flume-*/*"
```

The output of the preceding command can be shown in the following screenshot:

What just happened?

We created a configuration file containing a single Netcat source and both the file and HDFS sink. We configured separate memory channels connecting the source to both sinks.

We then set the source selector type to `replicating`, which means events will be sent to all configured channels.

After starting the agent as normal and sending an event to the source, we confirmed that the event was indeed written to both the filesystem and HDFS sinks.

Selectors replicating and multiplexing

The source selector has two modes, replicating as we have seen here and multiplexing. A **multiplexing** source selector will use logic to determine to which channel an event should be sent, depending on the value of a specified header field.

Handling sink failure

By their nature of being output destinations, it is to be expected that sinks may fail or become unresponsive over time. As with any input/output device, a sink may be saturated, run out of space, or go offline.

Just as Flume associates selectors with sources to allow the replication and multiplexing behavior we have just seen it also supports the concept of sink processors.

There are two defined sink processors, namely, the **failover** sink processor and the **load balancing** sink processor.

The sink processors view the sinks as being within a group and, dependent on their type, react differently when an event arrives. The load balancing sink processor sends events to sinks one at a time, using either a round-robin or random algorithm to select which sink to use next. If a sink fails, the event is retried on another sink, but the failed sink remains in the pool.

The failover sink, in contrast, views the sinks as a prioritized list and only tries a lower priority sink if the ones above it have failed. Failed sinks are removed from the list and are only retried after a cooling-off period that increases with subsequent failures.

Have a go hero - Handling sink failure

Set up a Flume configuration that has three configured HDFS sinks, each writing to different locations on HDFS. Use the load balancer sink processor to confirm events are written to each sink, and then use the failover sink processor to show the prioritization.

Can you force the agent to select a processor other than the highest priority one?

Next, the world

We have now covered most of the key features of Flume. As mentioned earlier, Flume is a framework and this should be considered carefully; Flume has much more flexibility in its deployment model than any other product we have looked at.

It achieves its flexibility through a relatively small set of capabilities; the linking of sources to sinks via channels and multiple variations that allow multi-agent or multi-channel configurations. This may not seem like much, but consider that these building blocks can be composed to create a system such as the following where multiple web server farms feed their logs into a central Hadoop cluster:

- Each node in each farm runs an agent pulling each local log file in turn.
- These log files are sent to a highly-available aggregation point, one within each farm which also performs some processing and adds additional metadata to the events, categorizing them as three types of records.
- These first level aggregators then send the events to one of the series of agents that access the Hadoop cluster. The aggregators offer multiple access points and event types 1 and 2 are sent to the first, event type 3 to the second.
- Within the final aggregator, they write event type 1 and 2 to different locations on HDFS, with type 2 also being written to a local filesystem. Event type 3 is written directly into HBase.

It is amazing how simple primitives can be composed to build complex systems like this!

Have a go hero - Next, the world

As a thought experiment, try to work through the preceding scenario and determine what sort of Flume setup would be required at each step in the flow.

The bigger picture

It's important to realize that "simply" getting data from one point to another is rarely the extent of your data considerations. Terms such as **data lifecycle management** have become widely used recently for good reason. Let's briefly look at some things to consider, ideally before you have the data flooding across the system.

Data lifecycle

The main question to be asked in terms of data lifecycle is for how long will the value you gain from data storage be greater than the storage costs. Keeping data forever may seem attractive but the costs of holding more and more data will increase over time. These costs are not just financial; many systems see their performance degrade as volumes increase.

This question isn't—or at least rarely should be—decided by technical factors. Instead, you need the value and costs to the business to be the driving factors. Sometimes data becomes worthless very quickly, other times the business cannot delete it for either competitive or legal reasons. Determine the position and act accordingly.

Remember of course that it is not a binary decision between keeping or deleting data; you can also migrate data across tiers of storage that decrease in cost and performance as they age.

Staging data

On the other side of the process, it is often worthwhile to think about how data is fed into processing platforms such as MapReduce. With multiple data sources, the last thing you often want is to have all the data arrive on a single massive volume.

As we saw earlier, Flume's ability to parameterize the location to which it writes on HDFS is a great tool to aid this problem. However, often it is useful to view this initial drop-off point as a temporary staging area to which data is written prior to processing. After it is processed, it may be moved into the long-term directory structure.

Scheduling

At many points in the flows, we have discussed that there is an implicit need for an external task to do something. As mentioned before, we want MapReduce to process files once they are written to HDFS by Flume, but how is that task scheduled? Alternatively, how do we manage the post-processing, the archival or deletion of old data, even the removal of log files on the source hosts?

Some of these tasks, such as the latter, are likely managed by existing systems such as **logrotate** on Linux but the others may be things you need to build. Obvious tools such as **cron** may be good enough, but as system complexity increases, you may need to investigate more sophisticated scheduling systems. We will briefly mention one such system with tight Hadoop integration in the next chapter.

Summary

This chapter discussed the problem of how to retrieve data from across the network and make it available for processing in Hadoop. As we saw, this is actually a more general challenge and though we may use Hadoop-specific tools, such as Flume, the principles are not unique. In particular, we covered an overview of the types of data we may want to write to Hadoop, generally categorizing it as network or file data. We explored some approaches for such retrieval using existing command-line tools. Though functional, the approaches lacked sophistication and did not suit extension into more complex scenarios.

We looked at Flume as a flexible framework for defining and managing data (particularly from log files) routing and delivery, and learned the Flume architecture which sees data arrive at sources, be processed through channels, and then written to sinks.

We then explored many of Flume's capabilities such as how to use the different types of sources, sinks, and channels. We saw how the simple building blocks could be composed into very complex systems and we closed with some more general thoughts on data management.

This concludes the main content of this book. In the next chapter, we will sketch out a number of other projects that may be of interest and highlight some ways of engaging the community and getting support.

11
Where to Go Next

This book has, as the title suggests, sought to give a beginner to Hadoop in-depth knowledge of the technology and its application. As has been seen on several occasions, there is a lot more to the Hadoop ecosystem than the core product itself. We will give a quick highlight of some potential areas of interest in this chapter.

In this chapter we will discuss:

- ◆ What we covered in this book
- ◆ What we didn't cover in this book
- ◆ Upcoming Hadoop changes
- ◆ Alternative Hadoop distributions
- ◆ Other significant Apache projects
- ◆ Alternative programming abstractions
- ◆ Sources of information and help

What we did and didn't cover in this book

With our focus on beginners, the aim of this book was to give you a strong grounding in the core Hadoop concepts and tools. In addition, we provided experiences with some other tools that help you integrate the technology into your infrastructure.

Though Hadoop started as the single core product, it's fair to say that the ecosystem surrounding Hadoop has exploded in recent years. There are alternative distributions of the technology, some providing commercial custom extensions. There are a plethora of related projects and tools that build upon Hadoop and provide specific functionality or alternative approaches to existing ideas. It's a really exciting time to get involved with Hadoop; let's take a quick tour of what is out there.

 Note, of course, that any overview of the ecosystem is both skewed by the author's interests and preferences and outdated the moment it is written. In other words, don't for a moment think this is all that's available; consider it a whetting of the appetite.

Upcoming Hadoop changes

Before discussing alternative Hadoop distributions, let's look at some changes to Hadoop itself in the near future. We've already discussed the HDFS changes coming in Hadoop 2.0, particularly the high availability of NameNode enabled by the new BackupNameNode and CheckpointNameNode services. This is a significant capability for Hadoop as it will make HDFS much more robust, greatly enhancing its enterprise credentials and streamlining cluster operations. The impact of NameNode HA is hard to exaggerate; it will almost certainly become one of those capabilities that no one will be able to remember how we lived without in a few years' time.

MapReduce is not standing still while all this is going on, and in fact, the changes being introduced may not have as much immediate impact but are actually much more fundamental.

These changes were initially developed under the name **MapReduce 2.0** or **MRV2**. However, the name now being used is **YARN (Yet Another Resource Negotiator)**, which is more accurate as the changes are much more about Hadoop as a platform than MapReduce itself. The goal of YARN is to build a framework on Hadoop that allows cluster resources to be allocated to given applications and for MapReduce to be only one of these applications.

If you consider the JobTracker today, it is responsible for two quite different tasks: managing the progress of a given MapReduce job (but also identifying which cluster resources are available at any point in time) and allocating the resources to the various stages of the job. YARN separates these out into distinct roles; a global **ResourceManager** that uses NodeManagers on each host to manage the cluster's resources and a distinct **ApplicationManager** (the first example of which is MapReduce) that communicates with the ResourceManager to get the resources it needs for its job.

The MapReduce interface in YARN will be unchanged, so from a client perspective, all existing code will still run on the new platform. But as new ApplicationManagers are developed, we will start to see Hadoop being used more as a generic task processing platform with multiple types of processing models supported. Early examples of other models being ported to YARN are stream-based processing and a port of the **Message Passing Interface (MPI)**, which is broadly used in scientific computing.

Alternative distributions

Way back in *Chapter 2*, *Getting Up and Running*, we went to the Hadoop homepage from which we downloaded the installation package. Odd as it may seem, this is far from the only way to get Hadoop. Odder still may be the fact that most production deployments don't use the Apache Hadoop distribution.

Why alternative distributions?

Hadoop is open source software. Anyone can, providing they comply with the Apache Software License that governs Hadoop, make their own release of the software. There are two main reasons alternative distributions have been created.

Bundling

Some providers seek to build a pre-bundled distribution containing not only Hadoop but also other projects, such as Hive, HBase, Pig, and many more. Though installation of most projects is rarely difficult—with the exception of HBase, which has historically been more difficult to set up by hand—there can be subtle version incompatibilities that don't arise until a particular production workload hits the system. A bundled release can provide a pre-integrated set of compatible versions that are known to work together.

The bundled release can also provide the distribution not only in a tarball file but also in packages that are easily installed through package managers such as RPM, Yum, or APT.

Free and commercial extensions

Being an open source project with a relatively liberal distribution license, creators are also free to enhance Hadoop with proprietary extensions that are made available either as free open source or commercial products.

This can be a controversial issue as some open source advocates dislike any commercialization of successful open source projects; to them it appears that the commercial entity is freeloading by taking the fruits of the open source community without having to build it for themselves. Others see this as a healthy aspect of the flexible Apache license; the base product will always be free and individuals and companies can choose to go with commercial extensions or not. We do not pass judgment either way, but be aware that this is a controversy you will almost certainly encounter.

Given the reasons for the existence of alternative distributions, let's look at a few popular examples.

Cloudera Distribution for Hadoop

The most widely used Hadoop distribution is the **Cloudera Distribution for Hadoop**, referred to as **CDH**. Recall that Cloudera is the company that first created Sqoop and contributed it back to the open source community and is where Doug Cutting now works.

The Cloudera distribution is available at `http://www.cloudera.com/hadoop` and contains a large number of Apache products, from Hadoop itself, Hive, Pig, and HBase through tools such as Sqoop and Flume, to other lesser-known products such as Mahout and Whir. We'll talk about some of these later.

CDH is available in several package formats and deploys the software in a ready-to-go fashion. The base Hadoop product, for example, is separated into different packages for the components such as NameNode, TaskTracker, and so on, and for each, there is integration with the standard Linux service infrastructure.

CDH was the first widely available alternative distribution, and its breadth of available software, proven level of quality, and free cost has made it a very popular choice.

Cloudera does also offer additional commercial-only products, such as a Hadoop management tool, in addition to training, support, and consultancy services. Details are available on the company webpage.

Hortonworks Data Platform

In 2011, the Yahoo division responsible for so much of the development of Hadoop was spun off into a new company called **Hortonworks**. They have also produced their own pre-integrated Hadoop distribution, called the **Hortonworks Data Platform** (**HDP**) and available at `http://hortonworks.com/products/hortonworksdataplatform/`.

HDP is conceptually similar to CDH, but both products have differences in their focus. Hortonworks makes much of the fact that HDP is fully open source, including the management tool. They also have positioned HDP as a key integration platform through support for tools such as Talend Open Studio. Hortonworks does not offer commercial software; its business model focuses instead on offering professional services and support for the platform.

Both Cloudera and Hortonworks are venture-backed companies with significant engineering expertise; both companies employ many of the most prolific contributors to Hadoop. The underlying technology is however the same Apache projects; the differences are how they are packaged, the versions employed, and the additional value-added offerings provided by the companies.

MapR

A different type of distribution is offered by **MapR Technologies**, though the company and distribution are usually referred to simply as **MapR**. Available at `http://www.mapr.com`, the distribution is based on Hadoop but has added a number of changes and enhancements.

One main MapR focus is on performance and availability, for example, it was the first distribution to offer a high-availability solution for the Hadoop NameNode and JobTracker, which you will remember (from *Chapter 7, Keeping Things Running*) is a significant weakness in core Hadoop. It also offers native integration with NFS file systems, which makes processing of existing data much easier; MapR replaced HDFS with a full POSIX-compliant filesystem that can easily be mounted remotely.

MapR provides both a community and enterprise edition of its distribution; not all the extensions are available in the free product. The company also offers support services as part of the enterprise product subscription, in addition to training and consultancy.

IBM InfoSphere Big Insights

The last distribution we'll mention here comes from IBM. The **IBM InfoSphere Big Insights** distribution is available at `http://www-01.ibm.com/software/data/infosphere/biginsights/` and (like MapR) offers commercial improvements and extensions to the open source Hadoop core.

Big Insights comes in two versions, the free IBM InfoSphere Big Insights Basic Edition and the commercial IBM InfoSphere Big Insights Enterprise Edition. Big Insights, big names! The basic edition is an enhanced set of Apache Hadoop products, adding some free management and deployment tools as well as integration with other IBM products.

The Enterprise Edition is actually quite different from the Basic Edition; it is more of a layer atop Hadoop, and in fact, can be used with other distributions such as CDH or HDP. The Enterprise Edition provides an array of data visualization, business analysis, and processing tools. It also has deep integration with other IBM products such as InfoSphere Streams, DB2, and GPFS.

Choosing a distribution

As can be seen, the available distributions (and we didn't cover them all) range from convenience packaging and integration of fully open source products through to entire bespoke integration and analysis layers atop them. There is no overall best distribution; think carefully about your needs and consider the alternatives. Since all the previous distributions offer a free download of at least a basic version, it's also good to simply have a try and experience the options for yourself.

Other Apache projects

Whether you use a bundled distribution or stick with the base Apache Hadoop download, you will encounter many references to other, related Apache projects. We have covered Hive, Sqoop, and Flume in this book; we'll now highlight some of the others.

Note that this coverage seeks to point out the highlights (from my perspective) as well as give a taste of the wide range of the types of projects available. As before, keep looking out; there will be new ones launching all the time.

HBase

Perhaps the most popular Apache Hadoop-related project that we didn't cover in this book is **HBase**; its homepage is at `http://hbase.apache.org`. Based on the BigTable model of data storage publicized by Google in an academic paper (sound familiar?), HBase is a non-relational data store sitting atop HDFS.

Whereas both MapReduce and Hive tasks focus on batch-like data access patterns, HBase instead seeks to provide very low latency access to data. Consequently, HBase can, unlike the already mentioned technologies, directly support user-facing services.

The HBase data model is not the relational approach we saw used in Hive and all other RDBMSs. Instead, it is a key-value, schemaless solution that takes a column-oriented view of data; columns can be added at run-time and depend on the values inserted into HBase. Each lookup operation is then very fast as it is effectively a key-value mapping from the row key to the desired column. HBase also treats timestamps as another dimension on the data, so one can directly retrieve data from a point in time.

The data model is very powerful but does not suit all use cases, just as the relational model isn't universally applicable. But if you have a need for structured low-latency views on large-scale data stored in Hadoop, HBase is absolutely something you should look at.

Oozie

We have said many times that Hadoop clusters do not live in a vacuum and need to integrate with other systems and into broader workflows. **Oozie**, available at `http://oozie.apache.org`, is a Hadoop-focused workflow scheduler that addresses this latter scenario.

In its simplest form, Oozie provides mechanisms to schedule the execution of MapReduce jobs based either on a time-based criteria (for example, do this every hour) or on data availability (for example, do this when new data arrives in this location). It allows the specification of multi-stage workflows that can describe a complete end-to-end process.

In addition to straight-forward MapReduce jobs, Oozie can also schedule jobs that run Hive or Pig commands as well as tasks entirely outside of Hadoop (such as sending emails, running shell scripts, or running commands on remote hosts).

There are many ways of building workflows; a common approach is with **Extract Transform and Load** (**ETL**) tools such as **Pentaho Kettle** (`http://kettle.pentaho.com`) and **Spring Batch** (`http://static.springsource.org/spring-batch`). These, for example, do include some Hadoop integration but the traditional dedicated workflow engines may not. Consider Oozie if you are building workflows with significant Hadoop interaction and you do not have an existing workflow tool with which you have to integrate.

Whir

When looking to use cloud services such as Amazon AWS for Hadoop deployments, it is usually a lot easier to use a higher-level service such as ElasticMapReduce as opposed to setting up your own cluster on EC2. Though there are scripts to help, the fact is that the overhead of Hadoop-based deployments on cloud infrastructures can be involved. That is where Apache **Whir** from `http://whir.apache.org` comes in.

Whir is not focused on Hadoop; it is about supplier-independent instantiation of cloud services of which Hadoop is a single example. Whir provides a programmatic way of specifying and creating Hadoop-based deployments on cloud infrastructures in a way that handles all the underlying service aspects for you. And it does this in a provider-independent fashion so that once you've launched on, say, EC2, you can use the same code to create the identical setup on another provider such as Rackspace or Eucalyptus. This makes vendor lock-in—often a concern with cloud deployments—less of an issue.

Whir is not quite there yet. Today it is limited in what services it can create and only supports a single provider, AWS. However, if you are interested in cloud deployment with less pain, it is worth watching its progress.

Mahout

The previous projects are all general-purpose in that they provide a capability that is independent of any area of application. Apache **Mahout**, located at `http://mahout.apache.org`, is instead a library of machine learning algorithms built atop Hadoop and MapReduce.

The Hadoop processing model is often well suited for machine learning applications where the goal is to extract value and meaning from a large dataset. Mahout provides implementations of such common ML techniques as clustering and recommenders.

If you have a lot of data and need help finding the key patterns, relationships, or just the needles in the haystack, Mahout may be able to help.

MRUnit

The final Apache Hadoop project we will mention also highlights the wide range of what is available. To a large extent, it does not matter how many cool technologies you use and which distribution if your MapReduce jobs frequently fail due to latent bugs. The recently promoted MRUnit from `http://mrunit.apache.org` can help here.

Developing MapReduce jobs can be difficult, especially in the early days, but testing and debugging them is almost always hard. MRUnit takes the unit test model of its namesakes such as JUnit and DBUnit and provides a framework to help write and execute tests that can help improve the quality of your code. Build up a test suite, integrate with automated test, and build tools, and suddenly, all those software engineering best practices that you wouldn't dream of not following when writing non-MapReduce code are available here also.

MRUnit may be of interest, well, if you ever write any MapReduce jobs. In my humble opinion, it's a really important project; please check it out.

Other programming abstractions

Hadoop is not just extended by additional functionality; there are tools to provide entirely different paradigms for writing the code used to process your data within Hadoop.

Pig

We mentioned **Pig** (`http://pig.apache.org`) in *Chapter 8, A Relational View on Data with Hive*, and won't say much else about it here. Just remember that it is available and may be useful if you have processes or people for whom a data flow definition of the Hadoop processes is a more intuitive or better fit than writing raw MapReduce code or HiveQL scripts. Remember that the major difference is that Pig is an imperative language (it defines how the process will be executed), while Hive is more declarative (defines the desired results but not how they will be produced).

Cascading

Cascading is not an Apache project but is open source and is available at `http://www.cascading.org`. While Hive and Pig effectively define different languages with which to express data processing, Cascading provides a set of higher-level abstractions.

Instead of thinking of how multiple MapReduce jobs may process and share data with Cascading, the model is a data flow using pipes and multiple joiners, taps, and similar constructs. These are built programmatically (the core API was originally Java, but there are numerous other language bindings), and Cascading manages the translation, deployment, and execution of the workflow on the cluster.

If you want a higher-level interface to MapReduce and the declarative style of Pig and Hive doesn't suit, the programmatic model of Cascading may be what you are looking for.

AWS resources

Many Hadoop technologies can be deployed on AWS as part of a self-managed cluster. But just as Amazon offers support for Elastic MapReduce, which handles Hadoop as a managed service, there are a few other services that are worth mentioning.

HBase on EMR

This isn't really a distinct service per se, but just as EMR has native support for Hive and Pig, it also now offers direct support for HBase clusters. This is a relatively new capability, and it will be interesting to see how well it works in practice; HBase has historically been quite sensitive to the quality of the network and system load.

SimpleDB

Amazon SimpleDB (`http://aws.amazon.com/simpledb`) is a service offering an HBase-like data model. This isn't actually implemented atop Hadoop, but we'll mention this and the following service as they do provide hosted alternatives worth considering if a HBase-like data model is of interest. The service has been around for several years and is very mature with well understood use cases.

SimpleDB does have some limitations, particularly on table size and the need to manually partition large datasets, but if you have a need for an HBase-type store at smaller volumes, it may be a good fit. It's also easy to set up and can be a nice way of having a go at the column-based data model.

DynamoDB

A more recent service from AWS is **DynamoDB**, available at `http://aws.amazon.com/dynamodb`. Though its data model is again very similar to that of SimpleDB and HBase, it is aimed at a very different type of application. Where SimpleDB has quite a rich search API but is very limited in terms of size, DynamoDB provides a more constrained API but with a service guarantee of near-unlimited scalability.

The DynamoDB pricing model is particularly interesting; instead of paying for a certain number of servers hosting the service, you allocate a certain read/write capacity and DynamoDB manages the resources required to meet this provisioned capacity. This is an interesting development as it is a purer service model, where the mechanism of delivering the desired performance is kept completely opaque to the service user. Look at DynamoDB if you need a much larger scale of data store than SimpleDB can offer, but do consider the pricing model carefully as provisioning too much capacity can become very expensive very quickly.

Sources of information

You don't just need new technologies and tools, no matter how cool they are. Sometimes, a little help from a more experienced source can pull you out of a hole. In this regard you are well covered; the Hadoop community is extremely strong in many areas.

Source code

It's sometimes easy to overlook, but Hadoop and all the other Apache projects are after all fully open source. The actual source code is the ultimate source (pardon the pun) of information about how the system works. Becoming familiar with the source and tracing through some of the functionality can be hugely informative, not to mention helpful, when you hit unexpected behavior.

Mailing lists and forums

Almost all the projects and services listed earlier have their own mailing lists and/or forums; check out the homepages for the specific links. If using AWS, make sure to check out the AWS developer forums at `https://forums.aws.amazon.com`.

Remember to always read posting guidelines carefully and understand the expected etiquette. These are tremendous sources of information, and the lists and forums are often frequently visited by the developers of the particular project. Expect to see the core Hadoop developers on the Hadoop lists, Hive developers on the Hive list, EMR developers on the EMR forums, and so on.

LinkedIn groups

There are a number of Hadoop and related groups on the professional social network, LinkedIn. Do a search for your particular areas of interest, but a good starting point may be the general Hadoop Users group at `http://www.linkedin.com/groups/Hadoop-Users-988957`.

HUGs

If you want more face-to-face interaction, look for a **Hadoop User Group (HUG)** in your area; most should be listed at `http://wiki.apache.org/hadoop/HadoopUserGroups`. These tend to arrange semi-regular get-togethers that combine things such as quality presentations, the ability to discuss technology with like-minded individuals, and often pizza and drinks.

No HUG near where you live? Consider starting one!

Conferences

Though it's a relatively new technology, Hadoop already has some significant conference action involving the open source, academic, and commercial worlds. Events such as the **Hadoop Summit** are pretty big; it and and other events are linked to via http://wiki.apache.org/hadoop/Conferences.

Summary

In this chapter, we took a quick gallop around the broader Hadoop ecosystem. We looked at the upcoming changes in Hadoop, particularly HDFS high availability and YARN, why alternative Hadoop distributions exist and some of the more popular ones, and other Apache projects that provide capabilities, extensions, or Hadoop supporting tools.

We also looked at the alternative ways of writing or creating Hadoop jobs and sources of information and how to connect with other enthusiasts.

Now go have fun and build something amazing!

Pop Quiz Answers

Chapter 3, Understanding MapReduce

Pop quiz – key/value pairs

Q1	2
Q2	3

Pop quiz – walking through a run of WordCount

Q1	1
Q2	3
Q3	2. Reducer C cannot be used because if such reduction were to occur, the final reducer could receive from the combiner a series of means with no knowledge of how many items were used to generate them, meaning the overall mean is impossible to calculate. Reducer D is subtle as the individual tasks of selecting a maximum or minimum are safe for use as combiner operations. But if the goal is to determine the overall variance between the maximum and minimum value for each key, this would not work. If the combiner that received the maximum key had values clustered around it, this would generate small results; similarly for the one receiving the minimum value. These subranges have little value in isolation and again the final reducer cannot construct the desired result.

Chapter 7, Keeping Things Running

Q1	5. Though some general guidelines are possible and you may need to generalize whether your cluster will be running a variety of jobs, the best fit depends on the anticipated workload.
Q2	4. Network storage comes in many flavors but in many cases you may find a large Hadoop cluster of hundreds of hosts reliant on a single (or usually a pair) of storage devices. This adds a new failure scenario to the cluster and one with a less uncommon likelihood than many others. Where storage technology does look to address failure mitigation it is usually through disk-level redundancy. These disk arrays can be highly performant but will usually have a penalty on either reads or writes. Giving Hadoop control of its own failure handling and allowing it full parallel access to the same number of disks is likely to give higher overall performance.
Q3	3. Probably! We would suggest avoiding the first configuration as, though it has just enough raw storage and is far from underpowered, there is a good chance the setup will provide little room for growth. An increase in data volumes would immediately require new hosts and additional complexity in the MapReduce job could require additional processor power or memory.
	Configurations B and C both look good as they have surplus storage for growth and provide similar head-room for both processor and memory. B will have the higher disk I/O and C the better CPU performance. Since the primary job is involved in financial modelling and forecasting, we expect each task to be reasonably heavyweight in terms of CPU and memory needs. Configuration B may have higher I/O but if the processors are running at 100 percent utilization it is likely the extra disk throughput will not be used. So the hosts with greater processor power are likely the better fit.
	Configuration D is more than adequate for the task and we don't choose it for that very reason; why buy more capacity than we know we need?

Index

Avro client 329
Avro code 153
Avro data
    consuming, with Java 156, 157
    creating, with Ruby 155, 156
AvroJob 158
AvroKey 158
AvroMapper 158
Avro-mapred JAR files 153
AvroReducer 158
AvroValue 158
Avro, within MapReduce
    output data, examining with Java 163, 165
    output data, examining with Ruby 163
    shape summaries, generating 158-162
AWS
    about 22, 315
    considerations 313
    Elastic Compute Cloud (EC2) 22
    Elastic MapReduce (EMR) 22
    Simple Storage Service (S3) 22
AWS account
    creating 45
    management console 46
    needed services, signing up 45
AWS credentials
    about 54
    access key 54
    account ID 54
    key pairs 54
    secret access key 54
AWS developer forums
    URL 356
AWS ecosystem
    about 55
    URL 55
AWS management console
    URL 270, 273-276
    used, for WordCount on EMR 46-51
AWS resources
    about 355
    DynamoDB 355
    HBase on EMR 355
    SimpleDB 355

B

BackupNameNode 348
base HDFS directory
    changing 34
big data processing
    about 8
    aspects 8
    different approach 11-14
    historical trends 9
Bloom filter 136
breadth-first search (BFS) 138

C

candidate technologies
    about 152
    Avro 152
    Protocol Buffers 152
    Thrift 152
capacity
    adding, to EMR job flow 235
    adding, to local Hadoop cluster 235
Capacity Scheduler 233
capacityScheduler directory 234
Cascading
    about 354
    URL 354
CDH 350
ChainMapper class
    using 108, 109
channels 330, 331
CheckpointNameNode 348
C++ interface
    using 94
city() function 268
classic data processing systems
    about 9
    scale-out approach 10
    scale-up 9, 10
Cloud computing, with AWS
    about 20
    third approach 20
    types of cost 21

timestamp() function 301
TimestampInterceptor class 336
timestamps
  adding 335-337
  used, for writing data into directory 335-337
traditional relational databases 136
type mapping
  used, for improving data import 299, 300

U

Ubuntu 283
UDFMethodResolver interface 267
UDP syslogd source 333
UFO analysis
  running, on EMR 270-273
ufodata 264
UFO dataset
  shape data, summarizing 102, 103
  shape/time analysis, performing from com-
    mand line 107
  sighting duration, correlating to UFO shape
    103-105
  Streaming scripts, using outside Hadoop 106
  UFO data, summarizing 99-101
  UFO shapes, examining 101
UFO data table, Hive
  creating 241-243
  data, loading 244, 245
  data, validating 246, 247
  redefining, with correct column
    separator 248, 249
UFO sighting dataset
  getting 98
UFO sighting records
  description 98
  duration 98
  location date 98
  recorded date 98
  shape 98
  sighting date 98
Unix chmod 223
update statement
  versus insert statement 307

user-defined functions (UDF)
  about 264
  adding 265-267
user identity, Hadoop security model
  about 223
  super user 223
USE statement 284

V

VersionedWritable wrapper class 88
versioning 319

W

web server data
  getting, into Hadoop 316, 317
WHERE clause 301
Whir
  about 353
  URL 353
WordCount example
  combiner class, using 80, 81
  executing 39-42
  fixing, to work with combiner 81, 82
  implementing, Streaming used 95, 96
  input, splitting 75
  JobTracker monitoring 76
  mapper and reducer implementations, using
    73, 74
  mapper execution 77
  mapper input 76
  mapper output 77
  optional partition function 78
  partitioning 77, 78
  reduce input 77
  reducer execution 79
  reducer input 78
  reducer output 79
  reducer, using as combiner 81
  shutdown 79
  start-up 75
  task assignment 75
  task start-up 76

Thank you for buying
Hadoop Beginner's Guide

About Packt Publishing

Packt, pronounced 'packed', published its first book "*Mastering phpMyAdmin for Effective MySQL Management*" in April 2004 and subsequently continued to specialize in publishing highly focused books on specific technologies and solutions.

Our books and publications share the experiences of your fellow IT professionals in adapting and customizing today's systems, applications, and frameworks. Our solution based books give you the knowledge and power to customize the software and technologies you're using to get the job done. Packt books are more specific and less general than the IT books you have seen in the past. Our unique business model allows us to bring you more focused information, giving you more of what you need to know, and less of what you don't.

Packt is a modern, yet unique publishing company, which focuses on producing quality, cutting-edge books for communities of developers, administrators, and newbies alike. For more information, please visit our website: www.packtpub.com.

About Packt Open Source

In 2010, Packt launched two new brands, Packt Open Source and Packt Enterprise, in order to continue its focus on specialization. This book is part of the Packt Open Source brand, home to books published on software built around Open Source licences, and offering information to anybody from advanced developers to budding web designers. The Open Source brand also runs Packt's Open Source Royalty Scheme, by which Packt gives a royalty to each Open Source project about whose software a book is sold.

Writing for Packt

We welcome all inquiries from people who are interested in authoring. Book proposals should be sent to author@packtpub.com. If your book idea is still at an early stage and you would like to discuss it first before writing a formal book proposal, contact us; one of our commissioning editors will get in touch with you.

We're not just looking for published authors; if you have strong technical skills but no writing experience, our experienced editors can help you develop a writing career, or simply get some additional reward for your expertise.

Hadoop MapReduce Cookbook

ISBN: 978-1-84951-728-7   Paperback: 308 pages

Recipes for analyzing large and complex data sets with Hadoop MapReduce

1. Learn to process large and complex data sets, starting simply, then diving in deep

2. Solve complex big data problems such as classifications, finding relationships, online marketing and recommendations

3. More than 50 Hadoop MapReduce recipes, presented in a simple and straightforward manner, with step-by-step instructions and real world examples

Hadoop Real World Solutions Cookbook

ISBN: 978-1-84951-912-0   Paperback: 325 pages

Realistic, simple code examples to solve problems at scale with Hadoop and related technologies

1. Solutions to common problems when working in the Hadoop environment

2. Recipes for (un)loading data, analytics, and troubleshooting

3. In depth code examples demonstrating various analytic models, analytic solutions, and common best practices

Please check **www.PacktPub.com** for information on our titles

Made in the USA
Lexington, KY
11 August 2014